KESSLER

THE AGE OF THE ECONOMIC REVOLUTION, 1876–1900
Second Edition

THE SCOTT, FORESMAN AMERICAN HISTORY SERIES

Carl N. Degler, Editor

John C. Miller   The Emergence of the Nation, 1783–1815

Leonard Richards   The Advent of American Democracy, 1815–1845

David M. Potter   Division and the Stresses of Reunion, 1845–1876

Carl N. Degler   The Age of the Economic Revolution, 1876–1900

Richard M. Abrams   The Burdens of Progress, 1900–1929

Thomas C. Cochran   The Great Depression and World War II, 1929–1945

Carl N. Degler   Affluence and Anxiety, America Since 1945

The
AGE
of the
ECONOMIC
REVOLUTION
1876
1900

Second Edition

Carl N. Degler
Stanford University

Carl N. Degler, Editor
American History Series

Scott, Foresman and Company   Glenview, Illinois
Dallas, Texas Oakland, N.J. Palo Alto, Cal. Tucker, Ga. Brighton, England

To David M. Potter

Cover photo: Brown Brothers

Library of Congress Cataloging in Publication Data

Degler, Carl N
The age of the economic revolution, 1876–1900.

Includes bibliographical references and index.
1. United States—Economic conditions—1865–1918.
2. United States—Politics and government—1865–1900.
3. United States—Social conditions—1865-1918.
I. Title.
HC105.D34 1976   309.1′73′08   76-16554
ISBN 0-673-07967-8 1 2 3 4 5 6 7– CPC—82 81 80 79 78 77

FOREWORD

This book is one in a series that encompasses the history of the United States from the early days of the Republic to the present. The individual volumes cover specific chronological periods and may be used either separately or in combination. Both this book and the series as a whole are intended to be different from the material covered in the usual survey text.

Customarily a textbook is largely filled with a chronological account of the "essential" facts of the past. Facts and chronology are, it is true, the building stones of historical knowledge, and familiarity with both is essential, but they do not provide the structure of the past by themselves. Rather it is the framework of an era that students must grasp if they are to retain and make sense out of the myriad facts that any book—text or other—throws in their path. By framework, however, we are not suggesting a skeleton or outline, but the unity or essential thrust of the period—in short, its meaning.

Emphasis falls throughout upon explanation of the past. Why did events turn out as they did? What significance did these developments have for subsequent American history? What importance do they have for the present? How does the American experience compare with that of other countries in similar circumstances? How and why did American attitudes and values alter during the period in question?

The organization and some of the less important facts that are to be found in more conventional textbooks are absent from these pages. It is the conviction of the author and the editor of the series that understanding the relationship among events is more important than just memorizing customarily agreed-upon facts. Therefore, some facts have been omitted simply because they do not contribute to an understanding of the structure of the period.

This book has been written for American college students; that is, readers who have some acquaintance with the history of the United States. While the usual effort has been made to clarify and define obscure or unfamiliar terms and persons, a certain basic familiarity with the subject has been taken for granted. No students who have passed successfully through an American high school need worry about their ability to comprehend what appears within these covers, but it is hoped that their understanding of the direction and the causes behind the movements of American history will be enhanced by reading this book.

Carl N. Degler

PREFACE TO THE SECOND EDITION

For some periods of American history, political developments provide an effective framework for organizing the many facts of an era, as, for example, has been done in regard to the Age of Jackson or the Era of Franklin Roosevelt. For the years 1876–1900, however, such an approach is not feasible if only because of the absence of commanding political leaders. In fact, the politics of those years have often been perceived as almost peripheral to the "real" history of the times. To provide the reader with an essential structure of this historical period, the best organizing principle is the way in which American society was transformed from a predominantly agricultural to an industrial economy.

The Economic Revolution in the title refers to a series of interrelated economic, technological, and social developments that made the United States at the end of the nineteenth century the leading industrial country in the world. The large, integrating theme of this book is that the Economic Revolution shaped the social, intellectual, and political life of the American people. For that reason, if for no other, the industrialization and urbanization of the United States must be included among the most important developments in the nation's history, comparable only to the American Revolution, which established the nation's independence, and the Civil War, which assured its survival.

Each chapter of the book addresses itself, in effect, to the question: How did the coming of the factory and the city alter and shape the United States? Always, attention is focused on relationships between the Economic Revolution and developments in politics, ideas, and society. Therefore, even in the chapter on the cultural and intellectual developments, the emphasis is upon writers and thinkers whose works can be related to the economic changes through which the country was passing.

Above all, the book seeks to explain how the United States was transformed from an agricultural to an industrial society within a single generation, and what it meant for the people of the United States. The story of The Age Of The Economic Revolution is a part of today's history because many countries are going through a similar transition from agriculture to industry.

Although the Second Edition follows the organization and approach of the first, a number of changes have been made. The pictorial essays of the First Edition have been replaced by new illustrations that are now spread throughout the text. All of the text has been scrutinized in detail, with new material added where necessary to bring it into conformity with the latest scholarship. New material has been added, for example, on the social and cultural bases of political parties in the

1880s and 1890s. New findings regarding social mobility in the cities have been integrated into the text along with an expanded treatment of women's influence on social thought and the economy. The most recent interpretations by economic historians for the growth of the economy have been added to the chapters on industrialization. And, of course, all of the the bibliographies have been brought up to date.

In carrying out this revision I have been fortunate in having the advice of a number of people who either worked with me in the process of revision, or kindly informed me of errors in the First Edition, or offered new ways of interpreting and organizing the material. I especially appreciate the help of Professors Walter R. Griffin, H. Wayne Morgan, Jon A. Peterson, and Carl V. Harris, all of whom took time to give me their considered judgments on a variety of subjects, though they must not be held responsible for any errors of fact or interpretation that may remain. David Ebbitt, as in the past, has contributed penetrating editorial skills, which helped me make this edition as precise and concise as I am capable of. My thanks go, also, to Mildred Perrin, whose editorial assistance in seeing the book through the press has been expeditious, careful, and informed. Obviously, all errors of both fact and interpretation that remain are mine; I welcome any corrections or disagreement that readers may care to point out to me.

Finally, it is only proper to acknowledge my indebtedness to the man to whose memory this book is dedicated—David M. Potter. Although Potter died before this Second Edition was even contemplated, he played an important role in the creation of the basic plan of the First Edition, from which the second so heavily derives. His vision of what this book might be alternately inspired and discouraged me. His high standards of historical interpretation and writing, and his careful work as editor, colleague, and enlightened human being helped shape the book more than his modesty ever permitted him to recognize. Whatever originality of conception the book contains is as much his doing as mine. His death was not only a poignant personal loss but an incalculable intellectual one as well.

Stanford, California   C. N. D.

CONTENTS

CHAPTER I   THE GREAT TRANSFORMATION

Growth of an Industrial Society   *1*
New Era, New Concerns   *6*
New Voices of Protest: George and Bellamy   *12*

CHAPTER II   THE ECONOMIC REVOLUTION:
RAILROADS, FACTORIES, AND CITIES   16

The Age of the Iron Horse   *18*
The Causes of the Second Industrial Revolution   *28*
The Growth of Big Business   *36*
The Antitrust Movement   *40*
The Rise of the Industrial City   *43*

CHAPTER III   THE ECONOMIC REVOLUTION: THE WEST,
FARMERS, AND INDUSTRIAL WORKERS   52

The Challenge of the Far West   *53*
Far Western Frontiers: Molders of a New Breed   *62*
The Agricultural Revolution   *64*
Cash Crops: Development of Commercial Farming   *68*
The Recruitment of an Industrial Labor Force   *73*

CHAPTER IV   NATIONAL POLITICS LAG BEHIND, 1877–1892   88

Candidates and Campaigns   *89*
Republicans Search for a National Base   *95*
Politics and the Economic Revolution   *98*
An Age of Whiggish Presidents   *107*

CHAPTER V   THE NINETIES: THE FIRST DECADE
OF MODERN AMERICA   114

Portents of Change   *116*
And the Earth Shook   *121*
Revolution in Politics: Act I   *126*
Revolution in Politics: Act II   *129*
Revolution in Politics: Act III   *133*

Removal of Blacks from Southern Politics   *137*
The Great Departure   *140*
"A Splendid Little War"   *148*

CHAPTER VI   THE SECULARIZATION OF AMERICAN SOCIETY
                    AND THOUGHT   156

The Secularization of Protestantism   *157*
The Growth of Catholicism   *163*
New World Judaism   *166*
A New Position for Women   *168*
Secularizing Force of Darwinism   *173*
Influence of Darwinism on Social Thought and Philosophy   *175*
The Secularization of Culture: Realism in Literature,
    Art, and Architecture   *180*

MAPS, CHARTS, GRAPHS

European Immigration to the United States, 1870–1900   *8*
Major Railroads in the United States, 1870–1900   *21*
Iron, Coal, and Steel Production, 1870–1900   *29*
Population Distribution, 1870–1900   *44*
Population in Urban and Rural Places, 1870–1900   *47*
Number of Urban and Rural Places   *47*
Physical Regions of the United States   *57*
Exports and Imports, 1870–1900   *68*
Labor Force Distribution   *76*
Presidential Elections, 1880–1896   *94–95*
Business Activity, 1876–1901   122
Spanish-American War, Philippine Campaign, 1898   *149*
Spanish-American War, Cuban Campaign, 1898   *150*
American Education, 1870–1900   *169*
Selected Travel Time and Cost, 1870–1900   *176*

THE AGE OF THE ECONOMIC REVOLUTION, 1876–1900
Second Edition

CHAPTER ONE

THE
GREAT
TRANSFORMATION

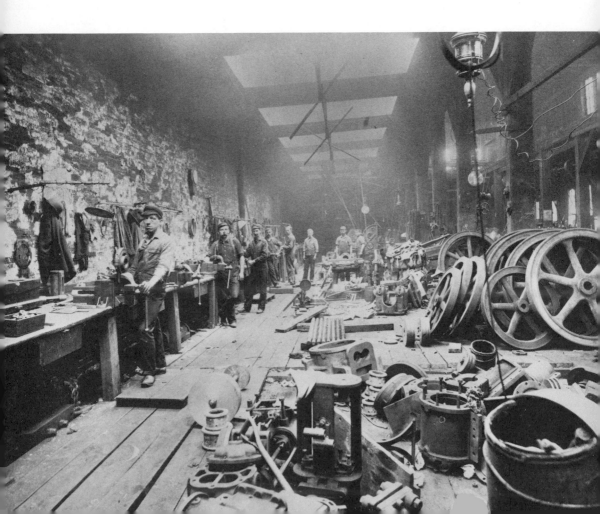

T HE UNITED STATES in 1876 celebrated its first century of independence. In the course of that period the American people had faced numerous issues and problems. Some of them, such as the struggle over neutral rights in the 1790s and the War of 1812, were disposed of relatively quickly, if only because they arose from temporary difficulties with foreign powers. Others, like the steady peopling of a continent, continued to occupy a large part of the nation's energies throughout the century and beyond. One issue—slavery—mounted in intensity until it virtually crowded out all others and split the nation asunder. From at least 1850 until the end of Reconstruction, slavery and its corollary, the future of the freed slave, dominated the politics and much of the thought of the American people. After the withdrawal of the last federal troops from the South in 1877, however, the question of blacks, though still unresolved, swiftly passed from the national stage. Other, fresh concerns began to take its place. The centennial year 1876 therefore marks a dividing line in the history of the United States and a suitable beginning for this book.

Appropriately, the nation celebrated its Centennial in 1876 with a mammoth exposition in the city of Philadelphia, where independence had first been declared. In the light of subsequent developments, the Philadelphia Exposition was doubly fitting, for on display were numerous American-made industrial machines, engines, and inventions, including an operating model of Alexander Graham Bell's newly invented telephone. By 1876, the United States was already in a new phase of its history, of which the symbols would be machines and factories, and the hallmark a high rate of industrial production.

Growth of an Industrial Society

A New Industrial People. The Economic Revolution of the last half of the nineteenth century was more than a proliferation of factories and machines; it can also be seen as a transformation of a society. Within a span of years no longer than a newborn infant takes to become an adult, a nation of small-property owners (the majority of whom were self-employed farmers) became a nation in which most men had little or no connection with the land, were largely without property, and worked for other men. The pattern of their lives was now determined not by the rising and setting of the sun and the slow, steady cycle of the seasons but by the sharp blast of the factory whistle and the relentless tempo of the machine. Increasingly, Americans no longer lived among the unchanging hills and valleys but within the crowded and ever changing confines of the city. (Although a majority of Americans did not live in cities until 1920, by the end of the nineteenth century the city and the factory dominated the affairs of the nation.) Moreover, even those left behind on the land felt the transforming effects, for by the close of the nineteenth century the farm would be mechanized and the farmer would be a businessman, as

The transition of the United States from an agricultural to industrial society was substantially complete by 1890. By then 57 percent of the nation's labor force worked outside of agriculture. *Jones & Laughlin Steel Corporation* tightly enmeshed in the web of the market as a Pittsburgh steelworker or a Boston banker. What that Economic Revolution was, how it came about, and how it affected the lives and thought of people in the United States are the principal themes of this book.

Since the story of this revolution is as complex as it is fascinating, this introductory chapter will set forth its main outlines and call attention to some of the broader implications which cannot easily be discussed in the rest of the book. Subsequent chapters will fill out the story and show how the Economic Revolution affected politics, society, and thought, making the period the Age of the Economic Revolution.

America's Place in the Industrialization of the Modern World. The great transformation was not unique to America. In the eighteenth century, England led the way; during the nineteenth century, she was followed by the United States, Japan in Asia, and Germany and other countries in Europe. In the twentieth century, Russia, the backward giant of Europe, also made the leap from underdevelopment to industrial maturity. Today, still other nations in Latin America, Africa, and Asia are girding themselves for a similar effort. In general, each of the industrialized nations shared a common experience, though some, like England and Russia, probably found the social and human costs higher than did the United States. In the impact of the transformation, however, each country's experience was unique.

Perhaps the distinguishing features of the American Economic Revolution were its astonishing success and the rapidity with which it was accomplished; by the 1890s, the United States had become the greatest industrial power in the world. Although it is always hazardous to attempt to pinpoint the exact time span of any economic and social transition, the pattern of events strongly suggests that the years between 1876 and 1890 were crucial in the transition of the United States from an underdeveloped nation to a mature industrial society. Industry and cities were in a far more advanced state in the 1890s than they were in the 1860s or 1870s. Politically, socially, and industrially the 1890s were actually a part of the twentieth century; the problems and the aspirations of Americans then were already those of people in the 1900s. For example, the issues that engaged the attention of Republican leaders like Theodore Roosevelt and Robert La Follette in the 1890s were much the same as those they would wrestle with in the early twentieth century. These concerns bore little resemblance to the issues that earlier Republicans, such as Abraham Lincoln and Ulysses Grant, had dealt with. Lincoln, after all, had no occasion to handle the problems of labor unions, industrial monopolies, or farm credit—the staple concerns of Democrats and Republicans alike in the 1890s and for many years thereafter.

The Triumph of Urban Industrialism. Let us look now at some of the reasons for regarding the transition of the United States to an industrial society as substantially complete by 1890. That year the annual value of manufactured goods surpassed the value of agricultural commodities for the first time in American history, even though farming was still setting production records almost every year.

By then 57 percent of the nation's labor force worked outside agriculture, whereas only twenty years earlier farmers had comprised more than half the working population. During the decade of the 1880s alone, the number of industrial workers jumped 50 percent, while the capital invested in manufacturing rose 137 percent. The total value of manufactures produced in that ten-year span increased 75 percent as compared with a 60-percent advance in the previous decade. The number of miles of railroad track laid in the 1880s was greater than for any other decade in American history. As many miles of track were laid in those ten years as from 1828, the beginning of railroading in this country, to 1870; in fact, in 1885 and 1886 alone, over 21,000 miles were added to the nation's trackage, or over two thirds the mileage that existed in the whole country in 1860. By 1890 the railroad net of the United States, though not yet complete, was more extensive than that of all of Europe, including Russia.

Not surprisingly, the 1880s also witnessed a rapid growth of cities—the site of factories and the terminals of railroad lines. Cities, it is true, were not new in America; some, like New York, Boston, Philadelphia, and New Orleans, had been important and flourishing ports and even centers of manufacturing for decades. But the growth of most of the great cities of the interior awaited the expansion of manufacturing and railroads in the years after the Civil War. Between 1860 and the present no decade has registered as high a rate of urban growth as the eighties. In that crucial period, eighty-eight cities doubled their populations. Significantly, many instances of that rapid urban growth were to be found in the Middle West, where manufacturing was leaping forward. Chicago's population rose from half a million to more than a million; St. Paul and Minneapolis doubled in size between 1880 and 1890. Milwaukee, Detroit, Columbus, and Cleveland increased at least 60 percent. In 1880, one out of every five Middle Westerners lived in cities of 4000 or more; by 1890, one out of three did.

The Indian: Casualty of the Economic Revolution. The 1880s witnessed not only the growth of factories and the building of cities but the termination of issues that once had loomed large in the affairs of Americans. Ever since colonial days, Americans had fought the Indians for possession of the continent; in the 1880s the long battle came to an end. Throughout that conflict between two cultures, misunderstanding, violence, and injustice by whites were common. Regardless of the good or bad intentions that may have underlain the various Indian policies of the United States, all of them seemed to have had the same result: Steadily the Indians were pushed into the least desirable parts of the country. By the time of the Civil War, only the semiarid Great Plains and the dry, desolate Great Basin region west of the Rocky Mountains remained open without restriction to Indians. But even there the Indians did not rest unmolested, for soon after the war, the Economic Revolution enabled white men to exploit and settle those once-scorned regions.

As we shall see in a subsequent chapter, the new technology of railroads, barbed wire, and steel plow, and the growth of urban markets permitted the first settlement of the "Great American Desert," as distinguished from its mere military occupation. In that sense the Economic Revolution destroyed the last vestiges of the Indians' isolation and opened a new chapter in the relations between the aborigine and the white American. Miners, cattlemen, and farmers invaded the last refuge of the Indian in the 1870s and 1880s. Sportsmen and buffalo skinners came too and wantonly slaughtered the shaggy beasts that roamed the plains in gigantic herds. Perhaps as many as three million bison were killed annually during the 1870s; by the middle 1880s the orgy had almost exterminated them. Since the buffalo provided Indians of the plains food and clothing, the slaughtering of the great herds was as important indirectly in overcoming Indian resistance as the direct military actions by the United States Army. Gradually, always painfully, in an almost uninterrupted series of skirmishes and wars during the 1870s, the Army herded the remaining Indians onto reservations. By the 1880s the struggle was over. The last significant encounter between Indian warriors and the Army took place in 1876 at the Little Big Horn River in Montana, where General George A. Custer and over 250 men of the Seventh Cavalry were wiped out by the Sioux under Sitting Bull and Crazy Horse. During the 1880s only the embittered Apache chief, Geronimo, and a few of his warriors still eluded the Army's relentless efforts to place all Indians on reservations. In 1886 Geronimo surrendered.

The almost continual warfare required to maintain the reservation policy in the 1870s and 1880s is one of the saddest episodes in the long and troubled history of relations between whites and colored Americans. The details of each Indian war may have differed, but the cruelty, treachery, and ruthlessness on both sides, but especially by whites, were constant factors. What was novel in the history of the relations between the two cultures was the emergence in the 1880s of a new attitude toward the Indians: Only after they were thoroughly subdued could white Americans shake off the mixture of fear and hatred that had been both a cause and an effect of a long history of conflict between the two races.

In the 1880s white Americans began to admit their treachery and cruelty toward the Indians. A landmark in the rise of the Indian rights movement was Helen Hunt Jackson's *A Century of Dishonor,* published in 1881. Because the book was drawn from the records of the Indian Bureau itself, Jackson's indictment of official government policy toward the Indians was tellingly effective. The book aroused wide popular support for better understanding of Indians and revealed the numerous betrayals of agreements with the Indians by the American government. It also encouraged the formation of Indian rights organizations by whites, which became increasingly influential during the 1880s. The agitation in behalf of the Indians culminated in 1887 when Congress passed the General Allotment (Dawes) Act; this act sought to bring the Indians into the mainstream of American life by making them citizens and small land-owning farmers. The law provided that the reservation lands, then held collectively by the tribes, would be distributed among and owned by individual Indian heads of families. The purpose was to end the segregation of Indians, which the policy of the reservations fostered. Such an individualistic solution to the future of the Indian in white America was quite in keeping with the philosophy that underlay the Economic Revolution.

Buffalo Bill Cody is shown clasping the hands of two proud Indian chiefs. In the course of the 1870s, wars between the Indians and U.S. Army resulted in the Indians being herded onto reservations. *Library of Congress*

Time would show, however, that this approach to the Indians and their culture was not what the Indians wanted or needed. Although the Indians were recognizable by skin color, their relationship with whites, seemingly analogous to black/white relations, stemmed from more than just being of a different race. Theirs was a different culture as well. Unlike the former slaves, the Indians were neither interested in nor prepared to participate in white society. Blacks, after all, even as slaves, had acquired much of the culture of white people: They knew how to farm, they could speak the language of Europeans, they were accustomed to European ways, and, most important, they wanted to be included on an equal basis in white society. That was the goal of most blacks after slavery, but it was not the goal of Indians, who continued to see themselves as Indians, who wanted above all to be left alone. Therefore, when they were forced to adopt the ways of white Americans under the policy enunciated by the Dawes Act, they lost both their lands to white men (some 90 million acres by 1930) and some of their will to survive as a culture. The Indian population by the 1890s and early twentieth century began to decline ominously. In 1934 Congress reversed the policy introduced by the Dawes Act, thereby halting the breakup of the reservations and protecting and encouraging, rather than destroying, what remained of Indian cultures. But white Americans could not easily accommodate a social group that did not seek ultimate integration into American society. Consequently, the future of the first Americans in modern American society would once again be a live question in the last quarter of the twentieth century.

Subordination of Negro Rights. If the onset of the Economic Revolution marked a shift in Indian policy, it also brought about a noticeable decline in the public concern for Negro rights. At one time the concern for blacks had put three amendments into the U.S. Constitution and sparked the passage of several civil rights acts by Congress. But by the 1890s the Economic Revolution was causing old issues to be abandoned and new ones to come to the fore. In 1890 Senate Republican leaders refused to permit a vote on a House-passed bill to protect blacks voting in the South, partly because they wanted the votes of southern senators to help pass the McKinley Tariff. In choosing to work for the tariff instead of the Negro-voting bill, the Republicans, once the champions of blacks, clearly demonstrated the powerful influence of the Economic Revolution upon politics and the eclipse of other issues that had once commanded the attention of party and nation.

The tariff, to be sure, was an old chestnut in politics, but unlike blacks' rights, it was relevant to economic growth. As industry spread throughout the country, the traditional, sectional attitudes toward the tariff changed. A number of southern senators, for example, urged higher rates in the tariff of 1894 now that the South was beginning to manufacture goods as well as grow crops. Unlike Indian or Negro rights, however, the tariff was not a dead political issue; then and later it was either hotly denounced as an abuse of corporate influence on Congress or defended as essential to economic growth. In either case, it remained a live political question because it was relevant to the Economic Revolution.

New Era, New Concerns

The Coming of Railroad Monopoly. This revolution created new problems at the same time that it superseded old ones. The extensive railroad lines and the large business enterprises of the period, for all their economic advantages, constituted aggregates of power that could not be controlled in the traditional manner. Competition among producers, the traditional device under a capitalist system for protecting consumers against high prices, poor quality, and inferior services, was not effective when the size of firms became so great that no genuine economic rivalry existed. In the case of the railroads, furthermore, competition could not be used for the control of rates, since in most instances the building of parallel or otherwise competing lines would have been too expensive to be practical or would have resulted in more competition than the traffic would support.

Faced with the new problem posed by industrial and railroad monopoly, Congress and the political parties in the course of the 1880s debated various solutions. In 1888 the platforms of all the parties, minor as well as major, pledged some action to control the abuses of economic power. As will be seen in the next chapter,

Congress in 1887 attempted to handle the question of railroad power through the establishment of the Interstate Commerce Commission, and in 1890 it passed the Sherman Antitrust Act to maintain competition among industrial firms. Although both measures proved inadequate, their enactment bespoke the rising concern of Americans with one class of problems that arose out of a developing industrial society.

Increased Immigration: Diminished Welcome. During the 1880s the Economic Revolution also caused Americans to alter their view of immigration. Earlier the nation had generally welcomed immigrants, if only because they were indispensable in peopling an empty continent and supplying labor for an expanding economy. Even during the days of the Know-Nothings in the 1850s, objections had been centered not upon unrestricted immigration but only upon the participation of the newcomers in politics. But as the Economic Revolution drew more and more people from all over the world and the empty lands of the West began to fill up, Americans had second thoughts about the value of unlimited immigration. Workers began to fear that excessive immigration might endanger their jobs or their economic future. Others feared that traditional American values would be lost or diluted. The immigration of the 1880s, which reached peaks not duplicated at any other time in the century, intensified these apprehensions. The number of

Italian bread peddlers in New York's Lower East Side. *Library of Congress*

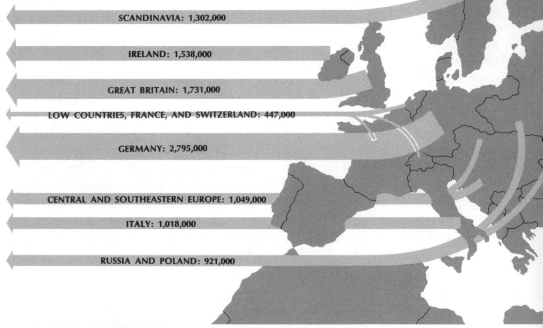

EUROPEAN IMMIGRATION TO THE UNITED STATES, 1870–1900
Figures are approximate

SCANDINAVIA: 1,302,000

IRELAND: 1,538,000

GREAT BRITAIN: 1,731,000

LOW COUNTRIES, FRANCE, AND SWITZERLAND: 447,000

GERMANY: 2,795,000

CENTRAL AND SOUTHEASTERN EUROPE: 1,049,000

ITALY: 1,018,000

RUSSIA AND POLAND: 921,000

Until 1896 a majority of the immigrants who came to the United States each year were from Northern and Western Europe; in the peak year of 1882, for example, 250,630 Germans alone arrived. But in 1896 immigration from Southern, Eastern and Central Europe became predominant.

immigrants who entered the United States in 1882, for example, was not equaled in any one of the succeeding twenty years.

The first manifestation of this new hostility toward immigrants was directed against the Chinese, who came to the United States in large numbers in the 1860s and thereafter to help build the transcontinental railroads. Most of them settled in the western states and territories, particularly California. In response to anti-Chinese violence in the West, as well as to agitation by labor organizations and by demagogues like Denis Kearney of the San Francisco "sandlots" (a group of workingmen, who, like their leader, were mostly Irish born), Congress passed the Chinese Exclusion Act in 1882. This was the first federal limitation on immigrants and the first (but not the last) measure to discriminate against an immigrant nationality. In that same year Congress enacted another measure which prohibited the immigration of paupers, the insane, and the feebleminded, and placed a head tax on all immigrants. In the twentieth century immigration reached even greater heights than it had in the nineteenth, and demands for its limitation grew correspondingly stronger until, in 1924, Congress ended the historic policy of unqualified welcome for all peoples. (In 1965 discrimination against Asians and Eastern and Southern Europeans was ended.)

The Great Strike of '77. The impact of the Economic Revolution was also felt outside the halls of Congress. In the summer of 1877 a great strike of railroad workers protesting wage cuts erupted. It spread rapidly from West Virginia and Maryland to Pittsburgh, through the Middle West, on down into Texas, and out to the Far West. Strikers clashed with militia, burned trains, destroyed property, and set fire to roundhouses in a score of cities and a half dozen states. The great upheaval also ignited strikes by steel workers, coal miners, and canal boatmen in several states. Before the violence ended, lives were lost, and President Hayes had to send federal troops into a number of areas to restore order and protect property. When measured by the number of men involved and amount of property destroyed, the strike of 1877 was the greatest in the nineteenth century. In its fitful light, thoughtful persons suddenly caught a glimpse of a more troubled future for the United States. "The youth of the American Republic is over," wrote a Canadian observer. "Maturity with its burdens, its difficulties and its anxieties has come." When James Ford Rhodes, a former businessman who lived through the strike, wrote his multivolume history of the period, he remembered that the violence of the strike "seemed to threaten the chief strongholds of society and came like a thunderbolt out of a clear sky, startling us rudely. For we had hugged the delusion that such social uprisings belonged to Europe and had no reason of being in a free republic where there was plenty of room and an equal chance for all."

Haymarket Riot: Foreshadower of an Era. The strike of '77 was only the first of the labor upheavals that dramatized the human consequences of the Economic Revolution. While less impressive in size and less costly in damage, the riot in Chicago's Haymarket Square in 1886 was more dramatic and even more significant. It made Americans recognize that they now lived in a new era. The riot began when a large force of police ordered the dispersal of a meeting of workingmen who were protesting the strikebreaking activities of the police on the previous day. Before the workingmen could heed the order, someone who was never identified hurled a bomb that killed one policeman immediately and fatally wounded six others. During the ensuing riot a number of workingmen were killed or wounded, and in the confusion several policemen shot one another. Since the meeting had been sponsored by anarchists, the episode was instantly interpreted as a conspiracy of radical workers against order and property.

Popular fear and anger spread far from Chicago. The *New York Times,* for instance, maintained that "No disturbance of the peace that has occurred in the United States since the war of the rebellion has excited public sentiment throughout the Union as it is excited by the Anarchist's [sic] murder of policemen in Chicago. . . . It is silly to speak of the crime as a riot. All the evidence goes to show that it was concerted, deliberately planned and coolly executed murder." One religious periodical even suggested that all such future demonstrations be met with machine-gun fire. The public outcry was so strong that organized labor cautiously repudiated any connection with the meeting, though its purpose had been to de-

An artist's conception of the bomb explosion in Chicago's Haymarket Square, 1886. *Historical Pictures Service, Chicago*

fend the rights of labor. The eight men who were tried for conspiring with the unknown bomb-thrower were quickly convicted in a patently unfair trial, presided over by a judge determined to see them hang. Four were hanged, one committed suicide in jail, and three had their sentences commuted to life imprisonment. Once fears had subsided, many people admitted that the evidence against the convicted men was shockingly flimsy, and in 1893 a newly elected governor, John Peter Altgeld, pardoned the three men who were still alive.

The significance of the Haymarket riot lies not so much in the violence of the event nor even in the miscarriage of justice that followed. Neither was new. What was novel was the sense of dismay and horror that gripped the minds of millions of Americans. Not even the great railroad strike of 1877 had produced such widespread alarm. With a shock, many Americans suddenly realized that a society they did not know or understand was developing in the United States. The Haymarket affair spelled out their apprehensions all too clearly. The riot had erupted in one of the large and growing cities of the nation, and its perpetrators were anarchists who repudiated the accepted forms of government and the rights of property. Moreover, the criminals were mostly industrial workers who defended the strike as a legitimate weapon of labor, and their names seemed to indicate that most of them were foreign born. The riot symbolized the issues that would become the central concerns of an America transformed by the Economic Revolution:

the factory, the city, the foreigner, and the slum.

In Search of Solutions: Unions and Settlement Houses. The impact of the factory upon society in this crucial decade of the 1880s was also readily apparent in the spectacular growth of national labor unions and in a new militancy on the part of organized labor. Between 1877 and 1890 an organization known as the Knights of Labor rose to national prominence. Its membership reached 700,000 in 1886, a figure unmatched by any other labor organization before the twentieth century. That same year, 1886, witnessed the founding of the American Federation of Labor, destined to be the successor to the Knights in importance and the dominant labor organization of our century. A further sign of industrial labor's militancy in the course of the 1880s was the tripling of the number of work stoppages and the doubling of the number of workers involved in strikes. Furthermore, during that same decade, labor organizations devised and widely used for the first time the weapon of the boycott—that is, the refusal of workers to buy goods from firms believed to be unfair to labor. In short, the Economic Revolution even before the 1890s brought with it industrial conflict unprecedented in scale and intensity.

With their demands for higher wages, labor unions were indirectly attacking

For "5¢ a spot" an immigrant without a family could obtain a place to sleep like this one. *Library of Congress*

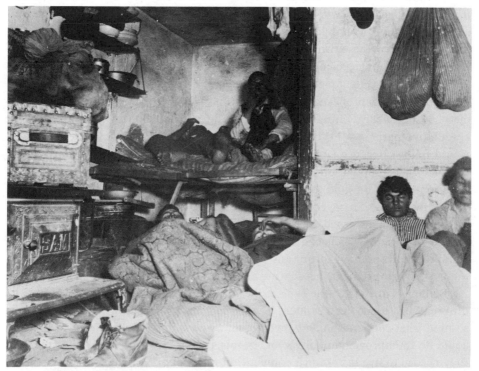

the evils of the urban slums. A more direct assault came from a different source. In 1886 Stanton Coit, a young graduate of Amherst College, opened the first settlement house in the United States in the slums of the lower east-side of New York City. Coit, a middle-class American whose social conscience had been aroused by his investigation of industrial slums in both Europe and the United States, was inspired by Toynbee Hall, an English settlement house. Other middle-class Americans soon followed his lead. In 1889 Jane Addams, Ellen G. Starr, and Julia Lathrop, who also wanted to put their college educations to social use, opened Hull House amid Chicago's teeming immigrant slums. Like the many settlement houses that would follow its pattern, Hull House sought to relieve the impoverishment of body and spirit that the poor, the foreign, and the socially disinherited endured in the crowded, dirty slums of the nineteenth-century American city. It did so through elementary medical care, day nurseries, and other services. With Jane Addams and Hull House began the effort to reduce the high human costs that the Economic Revolution entailed then and still exacts in our own time.

New Voices of Protest: George and Bellamy

The beginning of the intellectual response to the Economic Revolution also dates from the years between the end of Reconstruction and 1890. That response, as exemplified by Henry George's *Progress and Poverty* (1879) and Edward Bellamy's *Looking Backward* (1888), was both a denunciation of the inhumane consequences of the Economic Revolution and a vision of its potential benefits.

In some ways these two influential books were quite different. Though couched in popular language, George's was a serious treatise on economics, while Bellamy's was an excellent piece of persuasion in the form of a mediocre novel. Moreover, the two men proposed different solutions to the problems of an industrial society. Henry George argued that land should not be held out of production for speculative purposes. Force it into use, George advised, and prosperity for all would follow. Because he saw the rise in land values as resulting primarily from the growth of population and society, he did not hesitate to call for the confiscation of rent on land, as distinguished from rent on buildings and improvements, by means of a government tax. All increases in the value of unused land, he insisted, were "unearned increments" to the landholders and legitimately belonged to society, which had created them. Because George thought that a tax equal to the economic value of any piece of land would be sufficient to pay for all the costs of government, his scheme came to be called the Single Tax.

Bellamy's answer to the evils of the Economic Revolution was not only quite different but much less explicit. Describing an ideal society in A.D. 2000, he showed what cooperation and government ownership of the means of production could do to improve humanity's lot. In this society everyone received as much as they needed to live in comfort; competition was therefore unnecessary. Work was easy and retirement early and honorable. Crime was nonexistent, and people worked not for gain but for honor to themselves and society. Bellamy's utopia was a variety of socialism since society owned all the means of production, but because it was devoid of foreign inspiration or connection, it reached and attracted a much wider audience in the United States than the Marxian Socialist doctrine ever did.

Despite the differences between Bellamy's and George's approaches and the inadequacies of both as solutions to the problems of an industrial society, the two books had one important point in common: The basic fact of economic life was that the production of goods was never sufficient to permit more than a small proportion of people to live without persistent hunger, inadequate shelter, and intellectual poverty. Bellamy and George insisted that at last it was possible to change this ancient condition. The true meaning and promise of the Industrial Revolution, they asserted, was that poverty could be ended. Their great indictment of the society of their time was that the promise was not being fulfilled.

Why is it, George asked, that "in factories where laborsaving machinery has reached its most wonderful development, little children are at work"? Why is it that wherever machines are widely used "large classes are maintained by charity or live on the verge of recourse to it"? How paradoxical it is, he went on, that "the fruits of the tree of knowledge turn . . . to apples of Sodom that crumble at the touch. . . . This association of poverty with progress is the enigma of our times." Although George and Bellamy disagreed on the specific causes for this fatal association, they were in complete agreement on its general cause. The paradox of poverty and progress lay not in the immutable laws of nature or of God, but in people and the society they built. As George defiantly wrote in *Progress and Poverty,* "I assert that the injustice of society, not the niggardliness of nature, is the cause of want and misery." After George and Bellamy published their books, the poor could no longer be blamed exclusively for their poverty.

Such ideas constituted economic as well as social heresy; a whole generation of economists, businessmen, and clergymen had been preaching the immutable laws of economics. These laws, it was said, controlled prices and wages and made poverty inevitable no matter how regrettable it might be. Mere men and governments, which were only human, could not alter the principles that controlled the prices and distribution of goods or the cost of labor, and efforts to do so would result in violence and injustice. In fact, any government interference in economic affairs would make matters worse. Though there was a large degree of simple, selfish defense of the status quo in such arguments, there was reason behind them. Under the principles of laissez faire, the American economy, like that of the western world in general, had become more productive than any earlier economy in recorded history. Thus, to many people government interference in, or regulation of, the economic process not only deprived businessmen of what they considered their personal liberty, it also threatened the continued operation of the most productive economic machine ever developed by human beings.

George's and Bellamy's trenchant criticism of the status quo and their disbelief in the immutability of these laws of economics aroused such widespread response that their books launched a whole generation of economic and social reform. *Progress and Poverty,* which was translated into several languages, sold more copies than any other treatise on economics up to that time. Almost overnight, George became a celebrated reformer in both America and England. In 1886 he ran on a workingmen's platform for mayor of New York City, and though he came in second, he ran ahead of the Republican candidate, Theodore Roosevelt, by thousands of votes. Bellamy's book was even more popular, if only because it was cast in the form of a novel. Within two years after its publication, 200,000 copies had been sold and weekly sales had reached 10,000. *Looking Backward* inspired a national magazine, *The Nationalist,* and brought into existence more than 150 clubs to propagate Bellamy's ideas.

Both books proved to be seminal in the thought of many later leaders of industrial reform in both the United States and Europe. Thorstein Veblen, a major critic of the American socioeconomic system, for example, found Bellamy's book a "turning-point" in his life; Norman Thomas, for several decades the foremost spokesman for the American Socialist party, entered upon a lifelong commitment to socialism through the door of *Looking Backward.* Key figures in the Progressive movement of the twentieth century, like Tom Johnson and Clarence Darrow, later testified that *Progress and Poverty* helped focus their attention on the inequities of industrial society.

Thus, by the time the American people entered the last decade of the nineteenth century, they had taken up new issues raised by the Economic Revolution and left behind a whole series of matters which once had engaged their attention but now seemed irrelevant. The new problems constituted the challenge and controlled the shape of the future; for the next half century the nation would struggle with their resolution. Though ensuing years would bring more social changes and fresh problems, few would come as a surprise after 1890. By then the nature of a society of factories and cities and the problems of life that confronted it were already apparent. Even some of the solutions had been suggested.

In the next two chapters we shall examine the character and impact of the Economic Revolution which brought the new age into being.

SUGGESTED READING

The Indians have been a popular subject. An excellent introduction by a leading authority is Wilcomb E. Washburn, *The Indian in America* (1975). A convenient and reliable collection of documents is Virgil Vogel, ed., *This Country Was Ours* (1972). Less authoritative but engrossing is Dee Brown, *Bury My Heart at Wounded Knee: An Indian History of the American West* (1971). Ralph K. Andrist, *The Long Death: The Last Days of the Plains Indian* (1964), is a very well-written account of the shocking story. Stanley Vestal, *Sitting Bull* (1932), is an authoritative biography of the best-known Indian leader of the time. The last "battle" between Indians and whites is authoritatively told in Robert M. Ut-

*Available in paperback edition.

ley, *The Last Days of the Sioux Nation* (1963). Loring Benson Priest, *Uncle Sam's Step-children: The Reformation of U.S. Indian Policy, 1865–1887* (1942), is old but still useful. Informative and important is Henry E. Fritz, *The Movement for Indian Assimilation, 1860–1890* (1963). Harold E. Fey and D'Arcy McNickle, *Indians and Other Americans* (1959), treats the problem of the red American in white society yesterday and today.

On Chinese immigration see Mary Roberts Coolidge, *Chinese Immigration* (1909), and Elmer Clarence Sandmeyer, *The Anti-Chinese Movement in California* (1939). The latter has been largely superseded by the subtle and revealing *The Indispensable Enemy: Labor and the Anti-Chinese Movement in California* (1971), by Alexander Saxton. Background to the hostility is further provided by Gunther Barth, *Bitter Strength: A History of the Chinese in the United States, 1850–1870* (1964).

An excellent study on the eruption of labor problems is Robert V. Bruce, *1877: Year of Violence* (1959). A powerful companion volume is Henry David, *The History of the Haymarket Affair* (1936). The standard labor history is John R. Commons et al., *History of Labor in the United States*, 4 vols. (1918–1936). Donald L. McMurry, *The Great Burlington Strike of 1888* (1956), further underscores the labor trouble of the 1880s.

The best biography of the founder of Hull House is Allen F. Davis, *American Heroine: The Life and Legend of Jane Addams* (1973). Jane Addams, *Twenty Years at Hull House* (1912), tells the firsthand story of the best-known and one of the earliest settlement houses. Broader in scope is Robert H. Bremmer's excellent work, *From the Depths: The Discovery of Poverty in the United States* (1956). Arthur M. Schlesinger, *The Rise of the City, 1878–1898* (1933), also deals in some detail with the rise of the settlement house. Jacob A. Riis, *How the Other Half Lives*, which first appeared in 1890 but has been reprinted several times, is a striking description of tenement life.

A fine introduction to the reform sentiment of the 1880s and 1890s can be found in the opening chapters of Eric Goldman, *Rendezvous with Destiny* (1952). Daniel Aaron, *Men of Good Hope* (1951), has some penetrating remarks on Henry George and Edward Bellamy. A good study of Bellamy is Arthur E. Morgan, *The Philosophy of Edward Bellamy* (1945); it can be supplemented by Sylvia Bowman, *The Year 2000: A Critical Biography of Edward Bellamy* (1958). Undoubtedly the best biography of Henry George is Charles Albro Barker, *Henry George* (1955). George's ideas are examined in G. R. Geiger, *Philosophy of Henry George* (1933). Part I of Henry Steele Commager, *The American Mind* (1950), deals provocatively with the intellectual currents of the 1880s and 1890s. John A. Garraty, *The New Commonwealth, 1877–1890* (1968), deals with the whole period, including reform. A broader and provocative interpretation is the influential Robert Wiebe, *The Search for Order, 1877–1920* (1967).

CHAPTER TWO

THE ECONOMIC REVOLUTION: RAILROADS, FACTORIES, AND CITIES

W HAT WAS THE Economic Revolution and how did it come about? It is perhaps most accurately described as the convergence of three different, though closely interrelated, economic and technological developments in the last half of the nineteenth century.

One of these developments was a revolution in power. The steam engine, though used for decades in both manufacture and transport, now came into its own. As recently as 1860 animals (chiefly horses and mules) supplied almost two thirds of all the nonhuman power consumed in the economy. By 1890, however, the horsepower generated by improved steam engines and steam turbines had increased six times and comprised over 60 percent of all the nation's power, even though the amount of animal power had itself doubled during the same period. By 1900 two new sources of energy emerged: electricity and the internal-combustion engine, the bases of twentieth-century industry.

A second development was the enormous increase in both production (the quantity of goods produced) and in productivity (the efficiency with which they were turned out), principally through the greater use of machines. The growth in manufacturing will be discussed in the second half of this chapter. The upswing in farm productivity not only tripled the output of American farmers but also freed large numbers of workers for labor in manufacturing. This Agricultural Revolution is the subject of the first half of Chapter Three.

A third development, which has been called the Communications Revolution, was a series of technological and economic innovations in transportation and communications which, for the first time in history, linked the four corners of the earth in a gigantic market for bulk as well as luxury goods. It is in the Communications Revolution that the close interrelationships among these three developments can be seen most clearly. One reason the United States made such rapid gains during these years was that its farmers found world markets for their mounting crop surpluses. Without a market of world dimensions, American agriculture would not have expanded as it did; without this marked increase in farm production, American industrial growth would undoubtedly have been retarded; without the development of a highly productive and efficient agricultural-machinery industry, farms could not have boosted their productivity. All three developments interacted to produce the Economic Revolution. Let us turn first to an examination of the Communications Revolution.

In the creation of the world market, improvements in transoceanic transportation and communication were central. The submarine cable, for example, accelerated business communication, while the completion of the Suez Canal in 1869 opened East Asian markets to shipments of bulk goods from America for the first time. Moreover, improved types of ships now carried more goods farther, faster, and at less cost than the old sailing vessels or even the newer wooden steamships. The compound-steam engine, the screw propeller, and the steel hull halved the

The difficulties of terrain that had to be overcome in extending the railroad westward are apparent in this awesome view of the Diablo Canyon Bridge in Arizona. *Santa Fe Railway* amount of fuel a ship needed to carry, a development which doubled freight capacity and reduced rates. While in 1860 it cost 12 cents or more to ship a bushel of wheat from New York to Liverpool, by 1888 the price had fallen to 5 cents. A similar reduction in passenger rates helped account for the great increase in immigration to the United States in the last half of the century. One measure of the increased productivity in marine shipping was the fact that the amount of trade carried by British merchant ships between 1870 and 1880 increased by 22 million tons, while the number of workers involved in shipping actually fell by almost 3000.

The Communications Revolution was also apparent domestically. Such devices as the typewriter and telephone, both invented in the 1870s, found a ready use as the volume and pace of business activity increased. With George Eastman's discovery of the process of dry-plate photography on paper-backed film and Ottmar Mergenthaler's invention of the linotype machine, both in 1884, the cheap, mass newspaper and magazine trade expanded, offering new opportunities for wide-scale advertising and sales promotion among the growing number of urban dwellers.

The keystone in the arch of the Communications Revolution, however, was the railroad. Its role in the economic growth of the United States is sufficiently strategic to warrant careful examination.

The Age of the Iron Horse

The Role of Railroad Construction. As an invention, the railroad was old by 1860, but as a means of transportation, it was not widely used until after the Civil War. Because of the primitive character of the early trains, no railroad in the 1840s or even the 1850s could compete as a bulk carrier with river steamboats or canalboats. However, as more railroads were built, their potentialities as overland bulk carriers came to be recognized. Between 1870 and 1890 over 110,000 miles of railroad track were laid—more than existed in all of Europe. As Sir John Clapham, the British economic historian, has written, "If a single national contribution towards the making of the new era [of industrialization] had to be selected for its world-wide economic importance," it would be the gargantuan railroad construction in the United States. By reducing costs of overland transportation, railroads widened the market for all goods. David A. Wells, an American economist, wrote in 1884 that a ton of goods "can now be carried on the best managed railroads for a distance of a mile, for a sum so small that outside of China it would be difficult to find a coin of equivalent value to give a boy as a reward for carrying an ounce package across the street."

It is possible to exaggerate the effect of the railroad on economic development, as some historians have shown. Railroads, for example, did not stimulate the coal industry, despite what one might think, simply because they principally burned wood in the years before the Civil War. Nor was the consumption of iron by railroads before 1860 as great as by the nail-making industry. Yet railroads did stimulate the development of machine shops, add new demand for cars, steel, and wood, and help in the opening of the West by transporting settlers to the edge of the frontier, even if the settlers did not significantly build ahead of settlement. Certainly the railroads' need for steel helped lower the price, thus attracting new consumers and evoking new uses for the tough and resilient metal. In 1874 the first steel bridge was built across the Mississippi at St. Louis by James B. Eads; others soon followed. By the 1880s American steelmakers were sufficiently versatile that the federal government could use their plate and other products in building a new steel navy.

Despite the undeniable economic advantages of railroads, their construction presented problems to a country short of capital and labor. Railroads take a long time to build, and during that time there is little if any return on capital. Furthermore, the money for financing railroad construction cannot be invested piecemeal, as it can be, for example, in installing spindles in a cotton textile mill where each spindle adds so much to productive capacity. Until at least two important points have been connected by track, no adequate traffic can move. Moreover, even when completed, railroads are not only expensive to operate, but their costs (such as maintenance of the tracks, the engines, and the roundhouses) also continue, regardless of the amount of business. It was these high fixed costs which forced railroads into the excessive competition for traffic that became the bane of the industry in the 1870s and 1880s.

These economic characteristics of railroads also explain government aid to railroad construction in the post–Civil War years. Where there was ample traffic, as on the eastern roads, private enterprise usually could manage the risks and costs of railroad construction. But in the West, where settlement was sparse, railroad building required government assistance. Actually, government aid to economic growth was not new. In the 1840s and 1850s a number of states contributed funds to canal and railroad corporations, and in 1850 the federal government made its first venture in this field by providing land grants for the construction of the Illinois Central Railroad.

Through the Pacific Railway Acts of 1862 and 1864, the federal government encouraged western railroad construction by offering millions of dollars in loans and millions of acres of land to the newly created Union Pacific Railroad Company and others for the joint construction of a road that would connect the East and West Coasts. The act of 1864, typical of a number of such acts, granted the railroad the right to select, on each side of the track, ten alternate sections (that is, pieces of land one mile square) for every mile of track. Thus, the total of twenty square miles of land per mile of track would be arranged in checkerboard fashion. The plots were to be chosen within a strip twenty miles on each side of the right-of-way. While the road was being constructed, these tracts of land could be used by the builders as collateral for loans or supplies; once the railway was completed, they could be sold for cash to settlers. Between 1850 and 1872 the federal government, together with nine states, gave some 70 railroads about 183 million acres of land, roughly the area of the United Kingdom, Belgium, and

Spain combined. Another way of describing it would be to say that the grants were equal to about one tenth of the Sahara Desert, for until the railroad came through, most of the West was a social desert, devoid of people or means for settlement. One economic historian has calculated that the building of the Union Pacific Railroad alone added roughly $16.5 million a year to the national income between 1870 and 1880.

The federal government also encouraged railroad construction by means of cash loans amounting to millions of dollars. Because the railroads obtained capital from the government instead of competing in the money market, federal loans saved them interest charges of as much as $48 million. Loans from fourteen states probably netted the roads another $90 million. Furthermore, local communities often encouraged railroad construction by granting tax exemptions or by guaranteeing railroad bonds. Their reasoning can be found in the words of a public meeting in Iowa in 1865: "Resolved, that Johnson County donate half a million dollars rather than this Rail Road should be made twenty miles east or west of us." Whether a railroad came to a town or not often meant the difference between future prosperity and mere survival.

Railroad construction was a risky business at best, and the insecurity was magnified in an age of speculation and business recklessness. Hence, devices that now appear unscrupulous were often employed in an effort to compensate for the high risk. One such practice involved direct ownership of the construction company that built a railroad by some of the principal stockholders in the railroad company. The most famous of such construction companies was the Crédit Mobilier, founded in 1864 to complete the Union Pacific Railroad. Since many of the same men were executives in both companies, the "insiders" in the railroad were able to turn over the assets of the road to themselves, as constructors, through contracts to build at high prices. The result was that the construction company often obtained very high profits while the railroad was milked dry. In fact, the enormous profits of the Crédit Mobilier created a national scandal when the distribution of its stock to some congressmen was exposed in 1872. Despite the notoriety of that particular scandal, the widespread use of the construction company in the building of railroads was more indicative of the difficulties of accumulating capital than of general thievery in railroading. Indeed, like the government land grants and loans, such construction companies were probably indispensable in accumulating capital for building railroads in the sparsely settled regions of the country. By the time the last of the four pioneer transcontinentals, James J. Hill's Great Northern, was constructed in the 1890s, private capital was able and ready to do the job unassisted by government.

Forging a Modern Railroad Network. For a quarter of a century after 1860, the railroads of the United States occupied themselves not only with laying track, but also with forming a network of rails, usable without interruption from one line to another. On a railroad map of the 1860s, the United States appeared to possess an impressive web of lines, but in fact, the absence of bridges over the major rivers, the diversity in gauges (the width between the rails), and the small size of engines

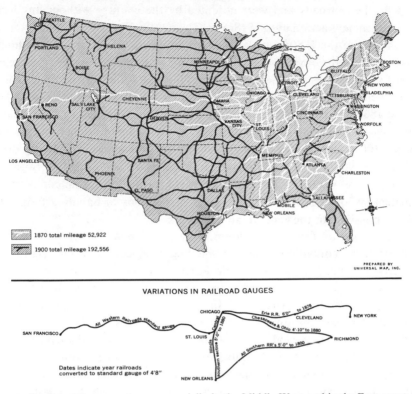

MAJOR RAILROADS IN THE UNITED STATES 1870-1900

1870 total mileage 52,922

1900 total mileage 192,556

PREPARED BY
UNIVERSAL MAP, INC.

VARIATIONS IN RAILROAD GAUGES

Dates indicate year railroads
converted to standard gauge of 4'8"

While not all railroad lines are shown, especially in the Middle West and in the East, most of the period's nearly 300% growth in track mileage did occur west of Chicago and New Orleans, thereby stimulating growth in all areas.

and cars prevented railroads from effectively challenging canalboats and steamboats as long-distance freight haulers. Over four fifths of the traffic carried by the Pennsylvania and the Baltimore and Ohio railroads did not travel beyond their own tracks. Moreover, in the absence of double-tracking, speed was sacrificed and safety threatened.

By the 1880s double-tracking, smoother roadbeds, steel instead of iron rails, and freight cars twice the previous size speeded up service and increased freight loads. Bridges now spanned the major rivers, and in 1886 the standard gauge of 4′ 8½″ was finally adopted by every railroad line in the country. By the end of the 1870s almost half the nation's trains were equipped with the new Westinghouse air brake, which provided a quick and efficient means of halting a whole line of cars, thus permitting greater speed while ensuring safety. The railroad by then had completely surpassed the canalboat and the steamboat as a long-distance hauler. Symbolic of the new long-distance function was the growing use of the Pullman sleeping and dining cars on passenger trains and the adoption in 1883 of uniform time zones across the country to avoid confusion in schedules. It was indicative of the importance of the railroads and of the influence of pri-

THE AGE OF THE IRON HORSE   21

vate institutions on public life that the time zones, still in use today, were first devised by the railroads and were accepted by the country without any legislation or government action until 1918.

By the end of the 1880s a train could cross the continent virtually without interruption. The most obvious and important consequence was a steady decrease in transportation charges. On the run between New York and Chicago, for example, rates on the four highest classes of goods dropped more than 50 percent between 1865 and 1888. On raw materials from the West, rates also fell sharply. The cost of shipping wheat from Chicago to New York declined from 65 cents to 20 cents per 100 pounds between 1866 and 1897. The expense of moving dressed beef fell from 90 cents per 100 pounds in 1872 to 40 cents in 1899. Since rates dropped 10 to 50 percent even on local runs where there were no competitors, it is evident that lower costs and more efficient methods of handling freight were largely responsible for the general fall in charges.

The Railroad as Enterprise: Incentive to Fraud and Corruption. Railroads were more than economic institutions, binding producers and markets together; they were also the creation of human labor, ingenuity, business acumen, and, sometimes, chicanery and greed. The prevalence of the last two elements has often been exaggerated. Daniel Drew and Jim Fisk, who earned lasting notoriety by their manipulation of the stock of the Erie Railroad in the 1870s, were not typical of railroaders in this period, because they were not railroad men. They were swindlers who happened to be in railroading. Yet something in this business more than in others encouraged fraud and corruption. What one economic historian has described as the railroads' "insatiable and urgent demands for capital" led to many kinds of schemes to secure the necessary funds. For instance, in order to attract capital, railroad leaders were often tempted to declare dividends larger than good management permitted or, as happened with the New York Central under Commodore Vanderbilt, to maintain dividends even if it could be done only by gouging the public with higher rates. The extraordinary appetite for capital also meant that railroads were usually corporations, which were able to issue stocks and bonds as dividends or as means of securing favors. Cornelius Vanderbilt, in building the New York Central system, often issued "watered stock," shares in excess of the value of assets, to buy out competing or connecting lines. In time the more responsible roads, like the New York Central, squeezed out the "water" by reinvesting earnings in improvements.

In their stock manipulations, railroad men also provided the first great example of separation of ownership from control in American corporations—a phenomenon now quite characteristic of American business. Ostensibly and legally the stockholders owned the railroad, but stock watering and other financial manipulations revealed that the managers often ran the company and disposed of its assets as they saw fit. In short, the public can own but not manage a large corporation.

Railroading was a risky business, but for those companies that did succeed, high profits were not uncommon. The promoters of the Union Pacific, to cite one case, received profits of between $14 and $15 million simply for building the road, though actual construction costs totaled less than $60 million. The great hazard of railroading was that the traffic might not justify the costly investment, and the history of the 1870s and 1880s is filled with stories of fierce competition for traffic. John W. Garrett, who developed the Baltimore and Ohio into a major system, virtually ruined the road financially in the course of his titanic struggle with the Pennsylvania Railroad. In order to secure traffic, he cut rates so sharply that the road was kept financially afloat only by falsifying the records and by borrowing money at exorbitant rates of interest.

Not all railroad companies necessarily succumbed to dishonesty in order to survive and grow. J. Edgar Thomson's Pennsylvania Railroad managed to grow without scandal from a small line between Pittsburgh and Philadelphia in the 1850s, to a thousand-mile giant stretching between the Atlantic coast and Chicago in the 1870s. The Pennsylvania made a name for itself as one of the first to introduce new techniques into railroading such as the use of Bessemer steel rails, air brakes, the block signal system, and the overhead crane.

The Great Race. To people of the time the great work of the age was the spanning of the continent by the Union Pacific and Central Pacific. Well before the Civil War decade Americans had dreamed of building a line to the Pacific Ocean, but political rivalry between the North and the South had prevented it. After the war began, the North was free to ignore southern wishes for a terminus in New Orleans or Memphis. Acts of Congress in 1862 and 1864 authorized the Central Pacific to build eastward from Sacramento, and the Union Pacific to work westward from Omaha. Aside from the heavy costs, which the transcontinentals encountered to an even greater degree than other roads, the engineering problems alone were formidable. The Central Pacific ran into difficulties of terrain almost immediately. Since at that time there were no power drills to expedite railroad construction through the Sierra Nevada, the roadbed was carved out of the rock, mainly by nine thousand recently imported Chinese laborers using hand chisels and hammers. When gigantic snowslides covered the construction sites in the mountains, long sheds had to be thrown up so that work could proceed. After two years of heartbreaking labor in the mountain passes, the Central Pacific workers finally broke through to the Nevada plateau. Once in the open, the company drove the workers to prodigious efforts; they put down 362 miles of track in a single year—almost a mile a day.

The men behind the Central Pacific were the big four of nineteenth-century California history: Leland Stanford, later governor and founder of the university that bears his son's name; Collis P. Huntington; Mark Hopkins; and Charles Crocker. All four were recent immigrants to the West, attracted by the profits to be gained from selling supplies to the gold miners. Moderately successful as merchants, they seized upon the railroad venture as a chance to acquire substantial fortunes and fame.

The Union Pacific's task was only slightly easier. Although no mountains had to be scaled before reaching the Rockies, Indians were a menace. When the armed guards who accompanied the construction crews could not always provide sufficient protection, the workers had to drop shovels and pick up rifles to assist in repelling the attacks. Until 1867 construction was slow, but as the ribbon of steel and wood gradually grew longer and gave evidence that the road would in fact be completed, tracks went down with astonishing rapidity. At the end of 1867, with the Union Pacific crews on the eastern edge of the Rockies and the Central Pacific on the Nevada plateau, competition became so keen that neither would take the usual winter break. The spring of 1869 found both crews working furiously in western Utah. Neither company, however, was willing to make the expected juncture, since government loans were paid on the basis of each mile of track laid. As a result Congress had to intervene and designate Promontory Point, six miles west of Ogden, Utah, as the meeting place. There, on May 10, 1869, a golden spike (since removed) was driven into the last tie, while telegraph lines literally flashed the blows of the sledgehammer across the nation.

A second line to the West Coast was not constructed until 1883, when the Northern Pacific was completed from St. Paul to Portland. Meanwhile, the Atchison, Topeka and Santa Fe joined with the Southern Pacific at Deming, New Mexico, in 1881, and a year later the latter road completed a juncture with New Orleans, thus giving the South its long-sought western connection. A fourth transcontinental line—James J. Hill's Great Northern, from St. Paul—was completed to Tacoma in 1893.

The Railroad as Menace. The growing public interest in some kind of government regulation of railroads in the 1870s and early 1880s stemmed from two causes arising from the nature of railroads. First, where traffic was so limited that only one railroad was economically practical, it enjoyed a natural monopoly. In such situations railroads could, and often would, charge what seemed to be excessive rates, though these were sometimes only an effort to make up for losses incurred at shipping points where they were forced to compete. Throughout the period there was public demand for government regulation of rates to cope with this situation. The more frequent and bitter complaints against the railroads centered on discrimination in the rates charged different classes of shippers. This practice of the railroads, which was usually stigmatized as an abuse by those who had to pay the higher rates, resulted not so much from monopoly as from excessive competition. In its pursuit of traffic a railroad would allow lower rates to large, through-traffic shippers than to small, local-traffic ones, or would offer the through-traffic shippers rebates (refunds of part of the charge), which amounted to the same thing. This practice was so common that a railroad executive appearing before a Senate investigating committee in 1886 said that discrimination through "rebates is a part of the present railroad system. I do not believe the present railway system could be conducted without it."

Another form of discrimination in favor of the big shipper was to charge less for a long haul than for a short haul (included within the longer haul). This practice was justified by the railroads on the ground that long hauls cost less because they involved fewer stops, unloadings, and storage facilities en route, and because

An example of the popular hostility toward railroads in the West. The phrase 'The Public Be D____!' was reputedly said by William Vanderbilt of the New York Central; he is presumably the "robber baron" astride the locomotive and dominating the workers and citizens around him. Courtesy of *The New York Historical Society*

they were usually for large quantities of goods. But in the eyes of the small, local shippers, who were usually individual farmers and local merchants and business-men, it seemed like simple favoritism to large manufacturing and mining firms.

Excessive competition among roads also resulted in drastic rate wars that may have benefited shippers for a short time by cutting rates, but over the long term were disastrous to shippers as well as railroads. In fact, constantly changing rate schedules confused shippers, disrupted their marketing plans, and aroused suspi-cion of discrimination. Moreover, rate wars could easily end in the bankruptcy of at least some of the railroads involved, and the consequent disruption of service further weakened public confidence and deprived shippers of service. Some specu-lators in railroading in the late 1870s and 1880s deliberately sought to profit from excessive competition by increasing it. They constructed competing lines just to sell them at a profit to the established roads. William Vanderbilt dubbed a railway paralleling his own along the shore of Lake Erie the "Nickel Plate Line" because the purchase price was so high he could not believe that its rails were made of mere iron.

The rate wars and the drive for traffic during the 1870s and early 1880s made it apparent that competition neither provided protection for the public nor was it conducive to the efficient functioning of a transportation system.

Sometimes, especially when they dominated a state or region, the giant railroad companies used their power in politics. Such activities often resulted in popular hatred of the railroads and political attacks against them. The political machination of the Union Pacific in Wyoming and the Southern Pacific in California made them the objects of public animosity. Some railroads, like the New York Central under Commodore Vanderbilt, did not hesitate to bribe state legislators or corrupt judges if it served their purpose.

Government Regulation. The movement for regulation of the railroads did not stem primarily from such political activities, unsavory as they may have been. It resulted both from the much more widespread discriminatory practices and from the belief that rates were excessively high even when they were not discriminatory. (Actually, as has been noted, rates in general fell during the whole period, but never as much as shippers, especially farmers, would have liked.) As early as the 1870s many businessmen and farmers, finding themselves dependent upon railroads yet ineligible as small shippers for rebates or the benefits of the long-haul discrimination, began to agitate for state regulation. The beginning of the long decline in farm prices compounded the farmers' dissatisfaction with railroad rates, for the farmers' prices fell faster than the railroads'. The railroads vigorously opposed state interference (although not always successfully), usually defending their position on the grounds of laissez faire and lack of sufficient traffic to meet costs.Because of the pressure from businessmen and farmers a number of midwestern states did enact regulatory legislation, known as the Granger laws.

At first, this legislation received support from the U.S. Supreme Court. In 1877, in the case of *Munn* v. *Illinois,* the Court upheld the right of an Illinois regulatory commission to set maximum rates for a grain elevator. The principle enunciated by Chief Justice Morrison Waite in that decision was equally applicable to railroads. Property "clothed with the public interest," the Chief Justice declared, "when used in a manner to make it of public consequence . . . must submit to be controlled by the public for the common good. . . ."

Nine years later, however, the Court, somewhat changed in composition and radically altered in economic philosophy, substantially modified the Munn interpretation of the interstate commerce clause of the Constitution. Waite in his 1877 decision had recognized that Congress possessed the paramount power over interstate commerce, but in the absence of Congressional action, he said, the state could regulate. Now, in 1886, the Court ruled that the power of Congress was exclusive and that any traffic moving into, out of, or through a state was beyond state regulation. Inasmuch as over three quarters of the nation's rail traffic was interstate in character, the decision in *Wabash, St. Louis and Pacific Railroad* v. *Illinois* effectively ended state regulation.

By the same token, however, the *Wabash* decision challenged Congress to adopt some form of federal regulation of railroads, as advocates of regulation had been proposing for more than ten years. The proposed bills attacked the problems both of monopoly and of discriminatory rates. The most obvious form of monopoly was the pool—an agreement among supposedly competing railroads to divide the traffic. From the railroads' standpoint a pool was a necessary protection against ruinous rate-cutting and, as recent historians have shown, this was not as self-serving as it sounded to many shippers. Given the pattern of traffic and amount of rolling stock, some kind of division of business was imperative if rates were to be stable and predictable for shipper and carrier alike.

Despite this, in Congress there was general agreement upon the need to pro-hibit pooling, which was viewed as an unconscionable aggregation of private eco-nomic power. It was the means of accomplishing this end that was disputed. The House, led by John H. Reagen of Texas, favored simple prohibition of dis-criminatory rates and pools, while the Senate, more aware of the nature of the railroad business and less responsive to the shippers' demands, preferred an ad-ministrative commission that would oversee railroad practices and thus be less rigid in dealing with them.

The final Interstate Commerce Act, passed in 1887, was a political com-promise, accommodating both approaches. The act set up a five-man commission to regulate the railroads and determine rates in interstate traffic. No more than three members could be drawn from one political party. All railroad rates were to be reasonable and just, though the new Interstate Commerce Commission re-ceived no guidelines for judging them. The act categorically banned pools but mentioned no other forms of monopoly or combination. With some exceptions it also outlawed discriminatory practices, such as rebates and the long and short haul. To eliminate undercover arrangements, the act required the public posting of all rates and permitted changes only after the Commission had been given ten days' notice.

The Interstate Commerce Commission was the first of a long line of similar administrative agencies which the federal government would find indispensable in dealing with the new problems of an industrial society. From that beginning came the Federal Trade Commission (1914), the Federal Communications Commission (1934), and the Securities and Exchange Commission (1934).

A Paper Tiger. If the act seemed to be a victory for those who opposed some of the practices of the railroads, for a time many railroads welcomed the stability that the Commission brought to transportation. Moreover, a modicum of regu-lation—and that is all the act contemplated—relieved some of the public pressure on the railroads. But the honeymoon was soon over. Many railroads did not want to abandon rebating, for example, since it constituted an important competitive advantage. The inexperienced Commission found it difficult to cut its way through the complications of rate determination and to overcome the refusal of an increas-ing number of roads to supply information. Furthermore, as a result of inter-minable appeals to the courts, the orders of the Commission often were not car-ried out.

Indeed, the judiciary, which could review the Commission's orders, soon re-vealed itself as a quagmire that gradually reduced the Commission to impotence. This became clear in the Maximum Freight Rate case decided by the Supreme Court in 1896. For almost ten years the lower courts, despite a general friendliness toward the railroads' position, had recognized the Commission's claim to rate-setting powers. But in 1896 the highest court decided that the Interstate Commerce Act bestowed only the power to prohibit unreasonable rates, not the power to set new ones. Such a narrow definition of the Commission's power virtually ended any possibility of its maintaining effective controls over rates. The Maximum Freight Rate case was only the most outstanding instance of the courts' unsympathetic attitude toward the Commission's activities. In the first fifteen years of the Commission's existence, over 90 percent of the court cases involving rates went against it. The courts simply did not want to allow an administrative tribunal so new in federal law to assume control over important economic matters. Only time, experience, and further Congressional legislation would give the regulatory commission a chance to play its proper and full role in controlling the new forces released by the Economic Revolution.

For all its importance in the Communications Revolution, the railroad was still only a part of the Economic Revolution. Of equal if not greater significance was an upsurge in manufacturing after 1870 which so dwarfed even the substantial industrial growth of the pre–Civil War years that it deserves to be called a Second Industrial Revolution.

The Causes of the Second Industrial Revolution

During the second half of the nineteenth century the United States became the greatest economic power in the world, toppling Britain from her long-held position of industrial preeminence and far outdistancing all other rivals. At the end of the century, for example, American steel production, the most convenient single measure of industrial power, was double that of Great Britain and almost twice that of Germany, England's most recent European rival. Other figures that measure the strides over the years are equally impressive. Between 1860 and 1900 the number of workers employed in manufacturing and construction quadrupled and the value of manufactures increased over five fold, yet the population of the country advanced less than 2.5 times. In the thirty years after 1870 the average annual per-capita gross national product rose 82 percent in constant dollars, or at an annual rate of about 4 percent. The reasons for this burst of economic activity are many; they merit examination because together they account for the most important single influence in American history since the Civil War.

Natural Riches. The story should begin with the land. Geographical circumstances do not in themselves cause industrialization, but they can facilitate or hinder that process. The United States not only had a vast expanse of territory, which prevented population pressure upon the land, but also encompassed great stretches of rich farmland and ample, sometimes almost inexhaustible, deposits of most of the principal mineral resources needed by an industrial economy. Coal and iron ore were to be found in abundance. Americans did not have to import such raw materials, as did the Japanese and the French, for instance, in their rise to industrial power. Moreover, the Rockies and Sierra Nevada contained large deposits

IRON, COAL, AND STEEL PRODUCTION, 1870-1900

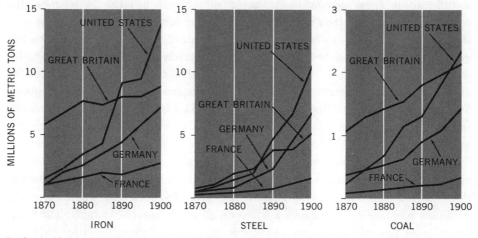

In the rapid rise of the United States to first place among the world's industrial powers, the achievements of the 1880s played a key role (see p. 122). By 1890, America had surpassed all contenders in iron and steel production.

of the precious metals, gold and silver, and impressive stores of such industrial metals as lead, zinc, and copper. Petroleum, destined to be the great fuel and lubricant of the twentieth-century industrial age, existed in large quantities in western Pennsylvania, and in gargantuan amounts in Texas, as the spectacular gusher at Spindletop near Beaumont proclaimed in 1901. By the middle of the nineteenth century, the largesse of nature in America attracted and amply supported a rapidly growing population, which in turn constituted an enormous market undivided by tariffs, political boundaries, or language barriers.

Early Roots of Industrial Development. In attempting to account for the surge of industrial growth after the Civil War, the preceding years of industrial development need to be recognized. Recent investigations by economic historians emphasize that the 1850s constituted a period of sustained economic growth, with a substantial industrial component. By 1860, for example, American production of manufactures was over the billion-dollar mark and rising each year. States like New York and Pennsylvania had surpassed Massachusetts and the rest of New England as manufacturing centers. The rapidly lengthening internal waterways of canals and navigable rivers, supplemented by a developing railroad system, already marked the United States as a coming industrial power. Moreover, the highly productive cotton economy of the South provided substantial impetus to the economy as well as a majority of American exports to Europe.

The Civil War—in some respects, at least—interrupted that economic growth. Production continued to increase, but the rates of growth in production of important commodities like iron, cotton textiles, and railroads fell off between 1860 and 1870, presumably because of the war. However, the interruptions were not uniform. The rates of growth in the production of coal and woolen goods, to cite two examples, were unaffected by the conflict. In fact, the war inflation probably gave a fillip to business expansion, reflected in a great upsurge in business incorporations between 1860 and 1865. In Ohio the number of incorporations rose from fewer than forty in 1860 to over three hundred in 1865. War orders by the government also stimulated standardization of production, since the Army, the greatest single consumer, favored uniformity. Rocketing federal expenditures gave a new push to the economy. Before 1860 the federal budget averaged about $60 million annually; during the war it reached $1.3 billion. Thereafter it seldom fell below $300 million. Thus the federal budget continued to support economic growth.

The war also made it politically possible for the Republican administration to enact legislation favorable to industrial growth, though the quantitative impact is difficult to assess. The banking acts of 1863 and 1864 secured a stable currency, while the issuance of greenbacks assured an adequate currency supply. The Contract Labor Law of 1864 encouraged the importation of cheap labor for industry, and the tariffs of the war years initiated the high protective policy of the late nineteenth century. The contribution of the tariff to the creation of the American industrial machine is open to controversy. The question is not whether the tariff encouraged industry—which no one disputes—but whether that encouragement was essential to economic growth. While the British economy industrialized without the aid of tariffs, it did not meet, at the outset, the international competition which the United States had to face as a late starter.

Equal Opportunity for All. Another important factor contributing to industrial growth was the general climate of opinion. In the middle of the nineteenth century and for many years thereafter, most Americans (not just businessmen) believed that unfettered, individual self-interest was and ought to be the prime mover in the economy. Equal opportunity for all, special privileges for none, had been the Jacksonian motto, and so long as there was competition to protect society, most Americans believed in the practical consequences of the slogan. It seemed the best way to encourage rapid economic growth, even if it sometimes resulted in fortunes made in questionable ways or if it wasted natural resources. In the long run it would help the country grow. As one small-town newspaper stated the issue in 1871, "We can stand a pretty good 'steal' if we can get railroads in the state."

Economic enterprise was also encouraged by the sure protection of property, a principle that had been built into the American political and judicial system from the beginning. The Revolution, after all, had been largely about the protection of property rights—against unjust taxation, for example. And early decisions of the Supreme Court like *Fletcher* v. *Peck* (1810) and the Dartmouth College case (1819) had emphasized the need to protect property rights. Yet a decision like that in the Charles River Bridge case (1836) had shown that property rights could not take precedence over the economic needs of the society as a whole.

In practice, business, spurred on by the carrot of high profit and the stick of bankruptcy, enjoyed a great deal of freedom and even government aid. As the agent of society, government sometimes assisted economic development when private enterprise could not do the job alone, as in the building of the transcontinental railways. Yet in doing so, government did little to restrict individual enterprise or to add to the costs of business operation. Even when government helped pay for the building of railroads, as it did for some of the transcontinental lines, it did not ask for a share in the ownership or operation but made grants of land and money to private corporations, vesting complete ownership in the companies. Regulatory measures like the Interstate Commerce Act were few on the federal and state levels, and those few did not add to costs of operation, as did workmen's compensation (for injuries sustained on the job) and sanitation laws in nineteenth-century England. The first workmen's compensation laws in the United States were not passed until the twentieth century—in Maryland in 1902 and in Montana in 1906.

Mechanization: The Key to Industrial Growth. The heart of the industrial process is mechanization. Thus, those general and particular factors that encourage a wider and more intensified use of machinery are crucial in explaining rapid industrial growth. Among such factors were the high wages in America relative to Europe—a result, probably, of the availability of land in the United States. In order to compete with cheaper European labor, American manufacturers had to cut the costs of production without cutting wages; this they did by introducing machines. The availability of immigrant labor, which was mostly unskilled, also encouraged the use of machines in place of, or in the absence of, skilled labor. The more an employer depended upon unskilled labor, the more he became committed to machines in his production.

To many Europeans who visited the United States around the turn of the century, the acceptance of the machine by both workers and management seemed to be the key to American industrial success. A group of British trade-union leaders who toured the United States in 1902 seeking the "secret" of American productivity thought they found it in the wide use of machinery in American factories. "The number of labour-saving appliances in use for almost everything is perfectly astounding," wrote one of them in his report.

The widespread use of machines required more than a large number of technological improvements; it also necessitated what economists refer to as an investment in human capital. For as a Commissioner of Patents wrote in 1900, "to employ these devices [inventions] to the best advantage requires the intelligence of the American workmen, and the result is due to the combination of witty inventions and thinking men. Witless men behind witty machines would be of no use." One authority has estimated that American investment in popular education jumped from $60 million in 1860 to $503 million in 1900. Already in 1870 about 90 percent of white adult Americans could read and write, though only about 20 percent of adult blacks—most of whom had been slaves five years before—were literate. By 1910 about 70 percent of adult blacks and 95 percent of adult whites were literate.

Reaping the Benefits of Old World Technology and Capital. One reason American industrial production surpassed that of Great Britain was that America profited from English innovations and mistakes, just as Germany, Japan, and

Russia—latecomers to the Industrial Revolution—in turn learned from American advances and errors. The Bessemer and the Siemens-Martin open-hearth processes in steel production—European inventions—were easily adopted by Americans. (William Kelly, an American, preceded Bessemer in using a blast of air through molten iron to produce steel, but Bessemer's process was used in American steel mills in the 1860s and after.) Europeans also invented the internal-combustion engine, which, in the automobile, was to play a central role in the American economy during the twentieth century. The wide acceptance of machinery resulted in a great advance in American productivity and wages over those of Europe. By 1900 the productivity of the *average* American worker in the steel industry was twice that of the *best* European.

Machines are only a part of what economists call "capital stock," which is necessary for economic growth. Capital stock includes all the permanent structures and equipment that facilitate production. Between 1869 and the First World War the capital stock of the United States increased at an annual rate of around 4 percent. Since the labor force increased more slowly, capital stock grew from $2110 per worker in 1869 to $3790 per worker in 1899. This, too, was a measure of why American workers produced so much; they had a good deal of help.

Because the United States entered upon industrialization after Britain and France, it was able to draw upon Europe in another way. In addition to its own accumulation of wealth, the United States had access to European financial capital (mainly English). By 1900 Europeans had invested over $3.4 billion in this country, principally in railroads, mines, and state bonds, thereby releasing American capital for manufacturing. European capital was readily available to American enterprise largely because the years 1815 to 1914 afforded the western world an unprecedented era of peace. For even conflicts like the Crimean War or the Franco-Prussian War were either outside Europe or of very short duration. Rapid communications, profitable industrialization, and an international gold standard permitted capital to flow across international boundaries more easily and safely than at any other time in history. The resulting availability of capital is one reason why Americans faced fewer difficulties in building an industrial society than the Russians, the Indians, or the Communist Chinese. It has been estimated, for example, that Americans had to invest only 11 to 14 percent of their national income during their years of industrialization as compared with the 20 percent the British and the Russians had to save during their period of industrial growth. Western scholars estimate that Communist China in 1956 invested as much as 23 percent of its total national income in industrial growth.

The Power of Machines. Along with the acceleration of communications, the invention of new machines was one of the principal causes for industrial growth after 1870. Sometimes inventions spawned completely new industries, as in the case of the telephone, invented by Alexander Graham Bell in 1875. By the end of the century telephone communication was a major industry, and the Bell Telephone Company had become one of the giants of big business. Thomas A. Edison's invention of the phonograph (1877) and the electric light bulb (1879) also created new industries. Indeed, Edison's discovery of a proper filament for an incandescent lamp itself created several industries, for in order to utilize his invention, Edison and his associates also had to invent machinery for generating electricity and new devices and techniques for transmitting and applying the new source of power. By 1890 the three electrical companies in the United States operated more than a thousand central power stations which lighted 1.25 million lamps.

George Westinghouse expanded the use of electricity through the introduction of alternating current. Using the inventions of a recent immigrant, Nicholas Tesla, Westinghouse showed that, because alternating current (unlike direct, which Edison favored) could be transmitted over long distances, it permitted the tapping of sources of hydroelectric power, such as Niagara Falls. Before the century was out, the great falls at Niagara were harnessed for electric power.

The introduction and use of electric motors in manufacturing made electricity the most convenient as well as the cleanest form of industrial power the world had known. By the 1890s electric power was widely used in transportation. In Richmond in 1888 Frank J. Sprague successfully demonstrated the first electrically driven streetcar, which filled a definite urban need and was soon used in many other cities. It was rapid, cheap, easy to operate, and did not pollute the air or present a fire hazard as steam trains did.

In 1881, "Hello Girls" work at a New York telephone office. By the end of the century, telephone communication gave rise to a major industry. *American Telephone & Telegraph Company*

While not all inventions that advanced industrialization were as dramatic as these, many were as instrumental in expanding production and lowering prices. One example was the invention of the sterile tin can and Gail Borden's development of sanitary canned milk, which not only sparked a new food-processing industry but stimulated a canning industry as well.

The machine-tool industry provides a good example of the importance of small, unspectacular inventions, for the advance of this business was central to rapid mechanization. Machine tools, which are power-driven contrivances that cut, shape, and mold metal, are machines that literally make other machines; lathes and milling machines are the most common examples. They also involve a "transfer of skills," since with them unskilled workers can make parts for machines that otherwise only highly skilled metal-craftsmen could cut or shape. Their use on a wide scale waited upon two developments, both of which came only after the middle of the nineteenth century. The first was the production of high-quality steel at low cost, made possible by the Bessemer process. The second was the invention of devices to cut and shape metal with speed and precision. One of the many innovators in this field was Frederick W. Taylor, who in the 1880s and 1890s invented a whole series of important machine tools, but whose major contribution was the development of techniques for making high-speed machine tools. The higher the operating speed of a machine tool, the greater the amount of work it could perform, but high speeds also heated the tool to the point where it softened and lost its cutting ability. Working with J. Maunsel White at the Bethlehem Steel Company, Taylor in 1898 developed a process whereby the steel tool retained its hardness even when running very fast and hot. Taylor's processes and tools are still standard in the machine shops of the world.

Innovators and Organizers. American industrial growth was not accomplished by machines and inventions alone; indispensable in that process were men—the entrepreneurs who organized the businesses, gathered the capital, recruited the labor, systematized the production, and sold the finished products. The most famous, like Andrew Carnegie, Philip Armour, Gustavus Swift, John D. Rockefeller, George Westinghouse, and John S. Pillsbury, are remembered today, if only because their industrial creations sometimes carry their names. These were the true innovators, the men who broke with the old patterns of industrial production and distribution to strike out in new directions. Sometimes the contribution of these giants was in accumulating capital and organizing vast new enterprises, as did J. P. Morgan with United States Steel and Edward Harriman with railroads. Partly because these entrepreneurs were innovators, the American historians Charles and Mary Beard once argued that they were a new social class come to power. The Beards saw the typical industrial leader as a farm boy of poor social origins who rose to power without the advantages of much education.

Reassessment of the Entrepreneurs. A larger sample of industrial leaders, however, reveals a quite different composite picture of the social character of the new men of power. An investigation of the background of fifty-one railroad leaders, for instance, indicated that twenty-six of the men attended college and that all but six had attended high school. This is especially striking since few Americans at the time could boast more than a grammar-school education. None of these railroad leaders came from the working class. An even broader investigation of 300 industrial leaders of the 1870s concluded that the typical magnate was: native born; Congregational, Presbyterian, or Episcopalian; and had a New England father who was a businessman of English descent. The majority of these leaders came from well-to-do homes. Instead of going to work at an early age, as the myth would have it, most of them took their first regular jobs at eighteen and then only after educations far above average for the time.

If the concept of the self-made man as the typical entrepreneur of the period needs some modification, so does its corollary that these men were simply "robber barons" who ruthlessly crushed their competitors, exploited their workmen, and defrauded the nation. Certainly it is true, as one historian has shown, that many of these industrial captains, such as John D. Rockefeller, Cornelius Vanderbilt, and Andrew Carnegie, went to almost any lengths to expand their enterprises. Thirteen of the forty-six leaders examined by this historian gained favors through political corruption, and sixteen profited at the expense of their own companies. Nor can one deny the power and ruthlessness of an individual organization like the Standard Oil Trust, which Rockefeller formed in 1882 and which, thereafter, virtually monopolized the oil-refining industry. Certainly, Standard Oil, with its undisguised threats of economic extermination, compelled small oil-refiners to sell out at a low price. Rockefeller also took advantage of the railroads at every opportunity. In the notorious (if short-lived) South Improvement Company episode, he actually secured rebates not only on the oil his own company shipped but on the shipments of his competitors as well. With unmistakable ruthlessness, John D. Rockefeller admitted that in the Standard Oil Trust he wanted "only the big ones, those who have already proved they can do a big business. As for the others, unfortunately, they will have to die."

Yet even after recounting such examples, there remains another side to the activities of the robber barons, as Matthew Josephson called them in a book by that name. Rockefeller's management of the Standard Oil Company marked the beginning of order and stability in an industry notorious for chaos. Prices, the supply of raw materials, and the employment of labor fluctuated so widely and wildly that companies rose and fell abruptly, leaving production neither systematized nor dependable. Consumers, especially, suffered from such instability. In 1873 illuminating oil sold for 17.9 cents a gallon wholesale in New York; a year later the price was 13 cents. In 1876 it was back up to 19 cents. After Standard Oil took over the industry, however, the price never rose above 8.5 cents for the remainder of the century, and sometimes it fell below that point. (At the same time, it should be noted that Standard's rate of profit during the last twenty years of the century was very high, between 15 and 20 percent of the net assets annually.)

The social implications of an example like Standard Oil are broader than mere reduction in consumer prices, though that is certainly important. At a time when the public was acutely suspicious of any government regulation of industry, certain powerful corporations imposed private regulation to instill order in an excessively competitive economy. Defenders of private enterprise have traditionally denounced collectivism; yet private enterprise itself imposed a kind of collective control over some American industries during the late nineteenth century.

The Growth of Big Business

The giant corporate enterprise has been the hallmark of American economic development. In the nineteenth century no other industrialized people used the corporation so widely as Americans, and no nation, except perhaps Germany, was so well known for the large size of its industrial firms.

The business corporation is an old legal institution that stems from the English joint-stock company of the sixteenth century. In the 1800s the corporation replaced the partnership or the individually owned company for several sound business reasons. Being a permanent legal entity, the corporation, unlike the partnership, is not disrupted by the death of one of its members. It enjoys limited liability; that is, those who invest (buy stock) in it are not legally liable, as partners are, for the debts of the corporation beyond the amount of their investment. Furthermore, the attributes of the corporation provided the means necessary to attract the very substantial investment capital required by large enterprises of the time.

The corporation did not become a prominent form of organization in manufacturing until after the Civil War, though it had been used widely in canal and railway construction. By 1900 the corporate form dominated American business; 86 percent of the output of mines and quarries and two thirds of manufactures were produced by corporations. Considering the English origins of the joint-stock company, British manufacturers, unlike those in America, made surprisingly little use of the corporation; in fact, before 1862 not all kinds of economic enterprises were legally entitled to enjoy limited liability. Until the end of the nineteenth century most British industrial firms were owned by individuals or by partnerships.

But it is the size of the enterprise, rather than its form, which distinguishes American business, for the British did not develop the giant company even when the corporate form became more popular. (The British, as a result, never engaged in the battles over monopoly and concentration of industrial power so prevalent in American economic and political controversy during the late nineteenth century and after.) Large-scale enterprise in Britain became prominent only after 1914.

Before 1870 American industry was made up chiefly of small firms, whether incorporated or not. By the opening of the new century, however, the picture had altered substantially; the great company, grown large either by expansion or by buying out competitors, had become prominent, foreshadowing an even larger role in the future. In the iron and steel industry, to cite one example, the capital and production per firm increased 500 percent in these three decades, while the number of firms actually decreased 5 percent. In some industries, giant enterprises like Standard Oil, the American Sugar Refining Company, United States Steel, International Harvester, and Armour and Company controlled 50 percent or more of the total production. Moreover, many of these giant companies were vertically integrated—that is, they owned everything they needed, from sources of raw material (oil wells, sugar plantations, and coal and ore mines) to transportation facilities (railroads, pipelines, steamship companies, Great Lakes ore boats) and marketing facilities (warehouses, retail stores, and wholesale distributing agencies). This kind of ownership is contrasted to horizontal integration in which a company controls only one phase of production.

Basically, the reasons for the growth of the giant industrial enterprise in the United States lie in the enormous market created by the railway network and the burgeoning cities. Cities contained not only millions of consumers for "soft"

Railroads stimulated the steel industry and were a major contribution to America's economic growth. These rails await shipment from an American steel mill. *National Archives*

goods but, in their construction, created a large demand for concrete, brick, iron and steel, transportation equipment, and other capital goods. Aside from this general basis for growth, individual firms had their own motives for expansion. Sometimes, as in the case of Standard Oil, growth resulted from the desire to cut competition; hence, small firms were bought out and joined to the big ones. At other times, vertical integration promised greater efficiency and cheaper access to raw materials, which also resulted in growth. This, apparently, was the motive behind the purchase of the ore-rich Mesabi range in Minnesota in 1896 by the Carnegie Steel Company and the purchases of ore fields by the Anaconda Copper Company. In such other industries as explosives, paper, and coal mining, mergers were prompted by a desire to lower production costs through the wider use of existing machines and techniques.

Development of a Nationwide Market. The careers of Gustavus Swift and Philip D. Armour in meat-packing reveal the difficulties that confront entrepreneurs seeking to build a nationwide industry, as well as some of the reasons why these businesses soon mushroomed into large-scale ventures. Prior to the invention of the regrigerator car in the 1870s, a nationwide fresh-meat-packing industry was not possible; only pickled or salted meat could be shipped long distances. Cattle and hogs, brought to the city by train, were slaughtered in evil-smelling abattoirs on the outskirts, and the meat was then distributed through local butcher shops. But even the ice-cooled refrigerator car did not solve all the problems of a fresh-meat industry seeking a national market. Finding local outlets for such an industry was not easy; butchers and abattoir owners vigorously fought the introduction of meat that had been shipped from other vicinities, and the public could not be persuaded that such meat was either as fresh as or as sanitary as that from recently slaughtered animals. A cookbook compiled in 1889 by a chef at Delmonico's, a fashionable New York restaurant, for example, advised that refrigerated beef was unsatisfactory for good cuisine, and in the nineties many a New York butcher proudly displayed a sign reading "No Chicago beef sold here."

To surmount this and other opposition, Swift and Armour set up their own distribution and transportation agencies. They sent out salesmen, bought out butcher shops, and opened retail outlets. Because the railroads refused to introduce refrigerator cars, the packinghouses bought and maintained their own. To be able to undersell local butchers and abattoirs, the meat-packers cut costs by making use of waste products, thereby projecting themselves into new fields. Buttons were made from bones, glue from hoofs, combs and ornaments from horns. By the 1890s both Armour and Swift owned glue, soap, glycerine, and fertilizer factories. And because waste products constituted 35 percent of an animal's weight, the packers saved on transportation costs. This, in combination with vigorous selling, permitted them to undersell locally dressed meat virtually anywhere in the United States. By the 1890s most of the abattoirs had been eliminated by the competition; it was clear that only large firms, necessarily few in number, would dominate the industry thereafter.

Other consumers' goods firms, like the American Tobacco Company, United Fruit, and the National Biscuit Company, followed the same pattern. If size was often the result of trying to buy out competition and stabilize production, continued growth just as often stemmed from the need to find markets for the enormous potential output of the machines.

At the same time that American business was developing its capital goods industry, it was also building a giant consumers' goods industry, to satisfy the market created by the growing urban population. Thus, as a result of industrialization, America became a land of plenty, and Americans, a people of power.

Corporate Organizational Experiments. Historically, it took a number of decades for the giant industrial combinations to discover the most practical organizational structure. One of the earliest devices, the pool, proved to be among the least satisfactory, as we have seen in the case of the railroads. A pool in the distilling industry in 1881, for example, lasted scarcely a year before one of the companies broke away—a common danger since no pool agreement was legally enforceable. A device almost as transitory was the trust, which John D. Rockefeller introduced in 1882 with Standard Oil. Although the name "trust" later came to stand for any large firm of whatever legal form, it originally had a quite restricted meaning. It was simply a group of men who held in trust, on behalf of the stockholders, the stocks of a number of companies. This arrangement allowed the trustees to coordinate the operations of what otherwise would have been competing firms. The trust was obviously superior to the pool as a device for checking excessive competition and production. As its popularity grew, this organizational structure found favor in other industries besides oil, notably distilling, which had experienced disastrous results with the pool. As a form of industrial organization, however, the trust soon was severely limited by the state courts, particularly in Ohio and New York, which declared it contrary to the prohibitions of the common law against restraint of trade.

The legal device that superseded the trust and has remained the typical form of organization of the giant firm is the holding company, which is simply a corporation empowered to hold the stock of other corporations. However, this type of organization was not legal until New Jersey made it so in 1888. Soon thereafter New Jersey earned the reputation as the home of trusts, since so many big companies used its permissive incorporation provisions. In time other states followed New Jersey's lead, if only to secure the incorporation fees.

Corporate Financing: The Investment Bank. Like the development of industrial enterprises, the growth of investment banking was at once a measure and a characteristic of industrial evolution in the United States. Investment banks are companies that devote themselves to marketing the securities of railroad and industrial properties, some of which by the late nineteenth century had become too large to be financed by direct appeals to the public. Large accumulations of capital were especially important in financing the mergers and the purchases of other firms that were essential to business expansion of the late nineteenth century. Foremost among investment houses was J. P. Morgan and Company of New

York, which played a central role in the reorganization of a number of railroads and other companies in the 1890s. Obviously the growth of such investment houses was both a consequence and a cause of the large size of American businesses.

Investment bankers were heavily involved in financing American industry and exerted a strong influence upon its development; usually they decreased the amount of competition. Once a house like J. P. Morgan had secured an interest in a firm, it also acquired some control over that firm's operations, perhaps by naming a member of the banking establishment to the firm's board of directors. Often the representatives of the House of Morgan would sit on the boards of two or more competing firms, in which case the degree of competition would obviously be muted. Such interlocking directorates, as they were called, became common in the twentieth century as investment houses played an increasing role in the financing of American industry.

Not all American industrial firms, of course, were compelled to look to the bankers for funds; the Ford Motor Company was the classic instance of one which did not. But there were enough such financial arrangements to arouse concern over their threat to competition. Many public figures in the early twentieth century began to denounce the "Money Trust" for reducing competition in industry and having a near monopoly on capital. In 1911 Congress finally undertook a major investigation of investment banking for just those reasons.

The Antitrust Movement

Despite the ability of the large industrial enterprises to produce great quantities of goods, often at reduced prices, their rapid growth and great power aroused hostility and fear among broad segments of the public. Small businessmen suffered from their competition, workers felt overwhelmed by their domination of the labor market, and farmers protested their control of transportation facilities and monopolization of the manufacture of agricultural machinery. Moreover, political leaders and others saw them as potential monopolies capable of destroying small businesses and victimizing the consumer through excessive prices. And it was a fact that the size of the giant corporation often permitted it to operate beyond the controls of competition, since three or four big enterprises might produce almost the entire output of a whole industry. In such cases, it was asked, what would prevent them from agreeing on prices far above the cost of production and realizing large profits at the expense of the public? In government and politics, Americans had long been accustomed to thinking that power needed to be constantly checked and that diffusion of power was one of the best ways to do it. It was natural, therefore, for them to demand that similar checks be placed upon the unprecedented economic power of the new and rapidly growing industrial combines.

During the 1880s public concern over the burgeoning trusts reached a high point. The Cullom Committee of the Senate, investigating railroad abuses, concluded in 1885 that "no general question of governmental policy" was more prominent among the people than "that of controlling the steady growth and extending influence of corporate power and of regulating its relations to the public. . . ." Already a dozen or more states had written prohibitions against monopolies and trusts into their constitutions, and several others had passed statutory prohibitions. Most of these states were in the West or the South, where declining farm prices had made the dominant agricultural population particularly sensitive to the power of the railroads and the industrial combinations. Legislative investigations by state and federal authorities publicized new and sometimes shocking examples of monopolistic activities by some of the giants. An investigation of trusts in New York in 1888, for instance, turned up evidence of such ruthless suppression of competition that it inspired a suit against the Sugar Trust in that state and one against Standard Oil in Ohio; the result was the legal dissolution of trusts. President Harrison, in his first annual message in December 1889, urged Congress to take action against combinations that crush competition, for "they are dangerous conspiracies against the public good, and should be made the subject of prohibitory and even penal legislation."

The Sherman Antitrust Act. At the first meeting of the Fifty-first Congress in December 1889, Republican John Sherman of Ohio proposed an antitrust measure, Senate Bill No. 1. The people, Sherman said in defending his bill, were anxious about "the concentration of capital into vast combinations to control production and trade and to break down competition." In view of the size of these organizations, he went on, "Congress alone can deal with them." After five days of debate the bill passed overwhelmingly, and a short time later it passed the House without dissent, though some eighty-five members did not vote. It became law on July 2, 1890.

The Sherman Act, as the first antitrust statute came to be called, declared illegal "every contract, combination in the form of trust or otherwise, or conspiracy, in restraint of trade or commerce among the several states. . . ." Conviction under the law could bring a fine of $5000 and one year's imprisonment. Section 7 authorized private persons to institute civil suits for injuries arising from unlawful combinations and provided that triple damages, including court costs, might be awarded a successful plaintiff.

The vagueness of the definition of monopoly in the law has occasioned much subsequent criticism, including the accusation that the ambiguity reflected an insincere motivation on the part of the sponsors. But the vagueness was apparently deliberate. The language was actually that of the common law, which had traditionally forbidden monopolies and restraints on trade. By bringing the common law definition into the federal courts, Sherman and his supporters hoped to utilize its flexibilities and thus avoid spelling out in the act all the varieties of illegal industrial combinations. As a senator pointed out at the time, 68 of the 82 senators were lawyers, and "I suppose no lawyer needs to have argument made to him that these combinations and trusts are illegal without statute." Unfortunately, this approach depended upon the courts, and they did not cooperate. Instead they chose to interpret the statute narrowly, thus necessitating further antitrust legislation in the twentieth century.

The Sherman Act, which, after the Interstate Commerce Act, was the second attempt to deal nationally with some of the new problems of an industrial society, offered a quite different solution. In place of a regulatory commission, Congress simply used the power of government to enforce competition, the traditional protector of the consumer. The different approach of the new act can be explained by the contemporary belief that railroads were public utilities and therefore subject to regulation by public authority, while manufacturing enterprises were not and thus should continue to be controlled by competition. Moreover, the provision for triple damages to injured parties suggests that the sponsors of the act thought prohibitions of monopolies would be self-executing and not actually dependent directly upon government action. In this regard the Sherman Act reflected the prevalent belief in the social virtues of individual self-interest as well as the popular distaste for government intervention in the economy.

Until American influence in Germany after World War II inspired the enactment of a similar antitrust statute, no other industrial country followed the United States example of legislating to ensure competition. Pre-war Germany, for instance, was so unconcerned with the question of the concentration of economic power that it officially encouraged large enterprises, called cartels, and other forms of combination.

For ten years or more after its passage, the government rarely invoked the Sherman Act and was seldom successful when it did. Of the twenty-six suits instituted between 1890 and 1903, only ten were won by the government, and four of those were against labor unions and not business corporations. The administration of President Grover Cleveland saw little reason for the act, and at first the Supreme Court was not much more enthusiastic. This attitude is well illustrated by the case against the Sugar Trust, *United States* v. *E. C. Knight Company*, decided in 1895. The government lawyers presented an unnecessarily weak argument, and the Court took an incredibly narrow view of the meaning of the act. Although both sides in the case admitted that the company controlled 98 percent of the production of sugar in the country, the Court announced that manufacture was not trade and that therefore the virtual monopoly of production was not a restraint of trade prohibited by the act. Upon learning of the decision, Attorney General Richard Olney, who was responsible for the government's case, wrote privately, "You will have observed that the government has been defeated in the Supreme Court on the trust question. I always supposed it would be and have taken the responsibility of not prosecuting under a law I believe to be no good. . . ." Therefore Olney employed the act solely against labor unions. The Attorneys General under the succeeding McKinley administration were scarcely more active; they entered three suits in four years.

In two cases at the end of the decade, however, the Supreme Court put back into the Sherman law some of the teeth it had drawn in the Knight case. In *United States* v. *Trans-Missouri Freight Association* (1897) the Court applied the Sherman Act for the first time to railroad combinations by upholding the government's argument that combinations to fix rates were illegal. Then in 1899, in *Addystone*

Pipe and Steel Company v. *United States,* the Court unanimously held that a pool among manufacturers of steel and iron pipes was illegal even though, in this instance, the pool controlled only 30 percent of the nation's production of pipe. This decision, when taken together with the Knight decision, which the Court did not overrule, made the judicial definition of monopoly ambiguous. In effect, the Court said that combinations among independent companies to fix prices were illegal *(Addystone)* but that if a single company monopolized production in a given industry, such an action did not restrain trade and therefore was not a violation of the Sherman Act *(Knight).*

Such an approach possessed a certain narrow logic, but it evaded the intention of the Act to deal realistically with economic monopoly. Not until well into the twentieth century, and then only after much public and Congressional agitation, would the Court take a more realistic view of the meaning of the Sherman Act and of the problem of industrial monopoly. In short, when the United States achieved the position of the chief industrial power in the world, it had only begun to wrestle with the question of controlling and channeling the new forces and institutions emerging from the Economic Revolution.

The Rise of the Industrial City

The site of the Economic Revolution was the industrial city. Even though cities have been the center of human culture throughout history, never before the nineteenth century have they been the focus of economic life. Theretofore, in all civilizations and at all times, the great majority of people had tilled the soil. Then, about two centuries ago, a momentous change began. Under the impact of industrialization, first thousands, then millions of people in western Europe and in the United States uprooted themselves from the land to move to the cities.

During the 1880s both European and American cities grew rapidly. In Prussia, for example, the population of cities increased by two million, while the rural areas gained a mere 500,000; in England and Wales during the same period the cities added 3.75 million people, while the countryside actually declined by 200,000. In the United States, as we have already seen, the rate of urban growth in that decade was the highest since the Civil War.

At the time of the Civil War, barely one fifth of the population of the nation lived in towns of 2500 people or more, but by the turn into the twentieth century 40 percent of the American people were classified as urban dwellers. In fact, even in 1890 the eight largest cities of the country accounted for one tenth of the total population. Perhaps more significant than the number of people in cities was the concentration in urban areas of the nation's wealth. Whereas in 1880 the value of urban and of rural real estate was estimated to be approximately equal—about $10 billion each—in 1890 the value of nonfarm real estate, $26 billion, was double the value of farms, $13 billion. This change was as good a measure of the shift of social power from country to city as might be found.

Figures that encompass the whole nation, however, obscure the important fact that urban civilization was not evenly spread across the country. In the plains and mountain states and in the South, cities were scarce and widely scattered, for they developed principally where industry was expanding. On the other hand, in areas where industry flourished—such as the Northeast, the states bordering the Great Lakes, and the Pacific coastal states—cities often blended into one another, forming sprawling metropolitan centers that extended the influence of the metropolis far beyond its corporate limits. "Dormitory cities"—suburbs which served as homes for employees of the industry and trade in large neighboring cities—were already emerging in the 1880s. Lake Forest was a "bedroom" for Chicago, as Greenwich, Connecticut, was for New York City and Brookline for Boston.

A large part of the urban growth of these years must be related to the great immigration. After the Civil War the stream of immigrants, especially from eastern and southern Europe, widened, until in the 1880s it became a flood equaled only in the early twentieth century. Most of these millions of immigrants (over five million entered in the 1880s alone) settled in the expanding industrial cities, for there were located the economic opportunities that the newcomers sought in America. The rapid growth of many cities during the 1880s was the result of immigration. The populations of industrial centers such as Fall River, Massachusetts; Paterson, New Jersey; and Rochester, New York; as well as those of big cities—Chicago, San Francisco, Milwaukee, Providence, New York City, and Minneapolis—were from a third to a half foreign born.

Urban Health Hazards. Any city presents problems of organization and social control because of its concentration of people in one place; the spectacular growth of American metropolises in the 1880s compounded the problems. To take one example, as the number of people increased, the disposal of human and industrial wastes changed from an insistent problem to a positive danger. Despite

POPULATION DISTRIBUTION 1870-1900

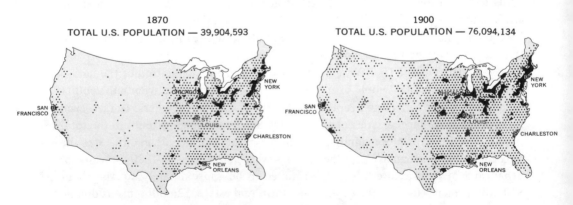

1870
TOTAL U.S. POPULATION — 39,904,593

1900
TOTAL U.S. POPULATION — 76,094,134

each dot represents
20,000 people

PREPARED BY
UNIVERSAL MAP, INC.

During this short period the most striking changes in population distribution include the general westward movement of settlers and the expansion of urban industrial areas, especially in the Middle West and Northeast.

Life on the streets of New York City in the 1880s. The disposal of animal carcasses presented a sanitation problem. *Library of Congress*

the threat to health, nearby rivers and bays were tempting places in which to dump garbage and sewage, and there the wastes were commonly deposited. In Indianapolis, where only 10 percent of the homes in 1880 had indoor toilets, the excrement from the privies was collected periodically to be dumped into the local river. The soil of New Orleans was reported by the Census of 1880 to be saturated "very largely with the oozings of foul privy vaults," while the porous soil in Baltimore (population 332,000) made the 80,000 cesspools a menace to the wells from which the drinking water was drawn.

Such conditions inevitably fostered disease. In fact, death rates in cities were notoriously higher than they were in rural areas. The concentration of people made the spread of infectious diseases painfully easy. During 1869 and 1870, for instance, Philadelphia experienced a scourge of scarlet fever that killed over 1700 people and left many more deaf, crippled, and debilitated.

By the end of the century, however, efforts at improving the sanitary conditions in the cities had begun to pay off. The death rate, which at the time of the Civil War stood at 30 per thousand in New York, Boston, Philadelphia, and New Orleans together, was down to 19 at the turn of the century. After 1900 great epidemics that ravaged whole cities during the middle years of the century were rare. Indicative of the achievements as well as the limitations of the late-nineteenth-century sanitation efforts was the great Chicago drainage project, which diverted sewage from Lake Michigan, where Chicago got its water, to the Mississippi River by way of the Illinois River.

Standing Room Only. Concentrations of people presented new housing problems to which the tenement house was the most obvious response. This multi-family dwelling, usually made of wood, was four or five stories high and had small, often windowless rooms, serving as bedrooms. The interior of a one-room Boston tenement in the 1870s was described in an official report as "unspeakably filthy; the furniture: two or three old chairs and an old table. No fire, and the room, damp, dark and cold. . . . The two oldest children were dirty and ragged and leaning against the window on the side of the room. . . . The youngest was . . . about worn out and apparently half-starved. . . ."

New York introduced the so-called dumbbell tenement in 1879 as an improvement in mass housing, only to see it become the worst of tenements. The structure took its title from the shape of the floor plan; a shallow indentation along the sides formed an air shaft when two such buildings were placed side by side. In practice, the air shaft proved to be much too narrow to offer any air or light to the apartments below the top floor, and the few toilets that were provided were wholly inadequate for the large number of families crowded into the building. Yet the dumbbell plan continued to be used throughout the remainder of the century. The menace to health and to morals that the tenement represented was already biting at the consciences of some people when Jacob Riis, a Danish immigrant, published his book, *How the Other Half Lives,* in 1890. By using the recently developed techniques in photography as well as vivid descriptions of life in the slums, Riis graphically portrayed the depressing and demoralizing conditions of tenement life. Yet in 1900 some 2.4 million people were packed into tenements in New York City alone. Other kinds of housing for the industrial working class were not much better. In Chicago the immigrant poor were often reduced to living in back-lot shanties or in lofts, which one Chicago inspector described as "unfit for habitation by civilized people."

Although buildings occupied more and more of the available land in the cities, urban authorities were slow to compensate for the loss of recreation space or to provide new facilities. It is true that New York City in the late 1850s opened its magnificent Central Park, but some large cities, like Brooklyn (not yet a part of New York), Newark, Pittsburgh, and Cleveland, actually devoted more land to cemeteries in 1890 than they did to public parks. Not until the twentieth century would it be widely recognized that recreation facilities, once readily available and taken for granted in the countryside and the small city, had to be planned and provided for in the new environment of the industrial city.

Breeders of Crime. The wealth and poverty that existed side by side in the city seemed to stimulate crime. At least there was more of it in urban than in country districts. In the 1880s and 1890s urban crime rates rose sharply. Gangs and gang warfare also became more common. In a three-square-mile section of Chicago in

1893, one quarter of the population was arrested at least once in the course of the year for some infraction of the law. Another measure of the social disorganization of the cities was the legislation passed against the homeless and unemployed. Between 1876 and 1893 some twenty-one states passed laws specifically against tramps, imposing such punishments as jail sentences, public whippings, and temporary forced labor.

Since most buildings in the growing industrial cities were of wooden construction, fire was a constant and horrifying menace. The most famous fire of the period occurred in Chicago in 1871. It virtually gutted the central part of the city, leaving thousands homeless and inflicting damage estimated at almost $200 million. Only the next year sixty-five acres of buildings were burned out in Boston; another fire in 1873 caused damage exceeding $1 million. Each year the nation set new records for fire losses. In dealing with deficiencies in recreation, police protection, and sanitation, the cities turned only slowly to meeting the mounting danger. The proper answer was full-time, paid firemen instead of volunteer companies, but as late as 1871 the large metropolis of Philadelphia was still depending on volunteers; St. Paul, Minnesota, did not shift to paid firemen until 1881. As in so many areas of urban development, other aspects of the Economic Revolution supplied some help. New technology—the telegraphic fire-alarm system, the fireboat, the water tower, the sprinkler system in buildings, and fireproof construction materials such as steel, brick, and terra cotta, all of which were introduced in the 1870s and 1880s—helped diminish the loss of life and property from fire.

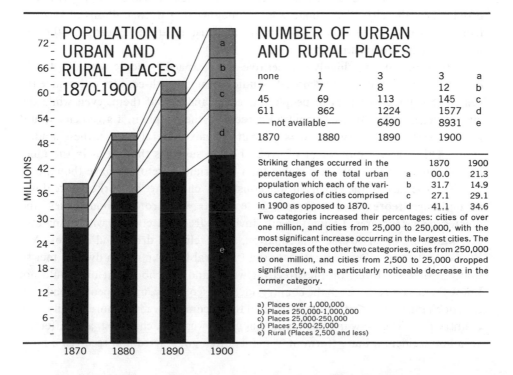

POPULATION IN URBAN AND RURAL PLACES 1870-1900

MILLIONS

72, 66, 60, 54, 48, 42, 36, 30, 24, 18, 12, 6

1870 1880 1890 1900

NUMBER OF URBAN AND RURAL PLACES

none	1	3	3	a
7	7	8	12	b
45	69	113	145	c
611	862	1224	1577	d
— not available —		6490	8931	e
1870	1880	1890	1900	

		1870	1900
Striking changes occurred in the percentages of the total urban	a	00.0	21.3
population which each of the vari-	b	31.7	14.9
ous categories of cities comprised	c	27.1	29.1
in 1900 as opposed to 1870.	d	41.1	34.6

Two categories increased their percentages: cities of over one million, and cities from 25,000 to 250,000, with the most significant increase occurring in the largest cities. The percentages of the other two categories, cities from 250,000 to one million, and cities from 2,500 to 25,000 dropped significantly, with a particularly noticeable decrease in the former category.

a) Places over 1,000,000
b) Places 250,000-1,000,000
c) Places 25,000-250,000
d) Places 2,500-25,000
e) Rural (Places 2,500 and less)

Everyone recognized that the big cities with their overcrowded tenements, dirty streets, and high crime rates were unattractive, but the smaller, more slowly growing cities were not much prettier. Lord Bryce, the English scholar and political commentator, although in general favorably impressed with American institutions, waxed sarcastic over the monotonous appearance of urban America. The cities, he wrote, "differ from one another only herein, that some of them are built more with brick than with wood, and others more with wood than brick. In all else they are alike, both great and small. . . ." Most American cities, he might have added, lacked even paving, except on a minority of their streets. Less than one fifth of the streets of an old and large city like New Orleans were paved in 1880; in the rainy season they were a sea of mud, and in the dry months the dust rose in clouds. Of Chicago's almost 2000 miles of streets in 1890, only 628 miles were paved and less than half of those with asphalt. It was not until the middle eighties that asphalt paving—smooth and long-lived—began to replace the cobblestone or brick paving that was used in the few places where pavement had been introduced.

The Urban Spirit. Although cities responded slowly to the physical problems inherent in rapid urban growth, their real importance lay in their reshaping of human values and attitudes. As one minister said of cities in the 1880s, "The evil of them is not in their size, but in the avarice, luxury, oppression, and vice that haunts them." Although he was mistaken in implying that cities hold a monopoly on vice, he was right in seeing city people as different. They were far more diverse in national background, occupation, standard of living, and education. The source of urban diversity, of course, was the enormous range of economic opportunities provided by the city. That range was the magnet that drew millions of farmers from the American countryside and from the peasant farms of Europe in the last quarter of the nineteenth century.

Life in the city was highly competitive and fastpaced; people were constantly on the move. Indeed, recent scholarly studies of nineteenth-century cities have revealed that large numbers of people moved in and out of them, even while the cities were growing in size. About 50 percent of the people in a given city would not be living in that city ten years later at the next federal census, these studies show. This massive movement of urban people suggests that cities in the nineteenth century were much less stable than historians heretofore have thought.

Even the face of the city itself was constantly changing, as workers tore down its buildings, reorganized its streets, added to its waterfront or boundaries, and erected new structures. Living in a city involved frequent contact with many others, who were often diverse in occupation, race, religion, dress, and outlook. Yet the contacts were often less intimate than in rural life. An urban dweller met so many people in stores, on the street, at work, and in school that one could not know them as directly as in the countryside. Consequently, urban people tended to accept change, to tolerate differences, and to welcome new ideas more readily than country folk. They saw in each day so much that was new, changing, and different. It is not accidental that reform movements often got started and received a more responsive hearing in the cities than in rural regions.

City people paid a price for this greater receptivity to change and novelty. They could not help but feel more insecure and anxious than rural people, who lived among familiar and relatively unchanging surroundings. Urban people were more dependent upon others for jobs, for a place to live, and for their food. Moreover, the weakening of traditional values and morals that occurred in the city attenuated that sense of social cohesion and identification with others, from which security derives.

The Metropolis: Center of Progress. The late-nineteenth-century cities, it should be noted, too, were not simply a source of problems. They were a necessary part of the Economic Revolution. They provided not only markets for agricultural commodities and a labor supply for industry, as we have seen, but also an important fillip to economic growth. As the railroad boom of the eighties subsided, the expanding cities, with their need for new housing, public buildings, street construction, municipal lighting, and intraurban transportation lines, provided one of the principal new sources of demand that kept the economic machine going. Cities, in short, were at once an effect of industrialization and a cause for its further advancement.

The education of millions of newcomers from farms—foreign born and native—should also be recognized as one of the achievements of the late-nineteenth-century cities. Urban schools literally fitted former farm children to the demands of factory and machine production, inculcating precision, punctuality, and order. "A school with an enrollment of fifty, daily attendance of fifty and none tardy," wrote one superintendent in 1882, "is a grand sight to behold in the morning and afternoon." The schools also opened up opportunities for social mobility by teaching literacy and other skills needed in an industrial, urban society. And despite the problems that the rapid growth of cities produced, the educational facilities in cities, even during these years of expansion, were always considerably better than those offered in rural areas. In 1891, for example, the typical elementary-school year in the cities of the United States was 180–200 days as compared with 70–150 in rural areas. Moreover, it was the cities of the 1870s and after that provided secondary education for the masses for the first time; a few even provided college education. In short, the cities of the nineteenth century were centers of cultural as well as social advancement.

Having examined the industrial aspects of the Economic Revolution, we shall turn in the next chapter to the transformation of agriculture and its effects upon the people who carried through the Economic Revolution and felt its impact.

SUGGESTED READING

For a general account of the Economic Revolution there is no better place to begin than with the contemporary David A. Wells, *Recent Economic Changes* (1895). The fullest mod-

*Available in paperback edition.

ern account is Edward C. Kirkland, *Industry Comes of Age: Business, Labor, and Public Policy, 1860 – 1897* (1961). More interpretive and penetrating, and much shorter, is Robert Higgs, *The Transformation of the American Economy, 1865 – 1914* (1971). Douglass C. North, *Growth and Welfare in the American Past: A New Economic History* (2nd ed., 1974), puts these years into broad historical perspective from the standpoint of the new economic history. Social history is mixed with economic history in the old but still useful Ida Tarbell, *The Nationalizing of Business, 1878 – 1898* (1936). Highly provocative in analyzing the meaning and impact of laissez faire thought is the short but incisive study by James Willard Hurst, *Law and the Conditions of Freedom in the Nineteenth-Century United States* (1956). For the role of the Civil War in economic growth an excellent introduction is provided in the collection of essays edited by Ralph Andreano, *The Economic Impact of the American Civil War* (rev. ed., 1967), which includes the justly famous essay by Thomas Cochran, "Did the Civil War Retard Industrialization?" from *Mississippi Valley Historical Review*, XLVIII (1961).

The literature on railroads is voluminous. John Moody, *The Railroad Builders* (1919), is old but still the only synthesis. Also published many years ago but still readable is Robert Riegel, *The Story of the Western Railroads* (1926). A brief yet important study is George R. Taylor and Irene Neu, *The American Railroad Network, 1861 – 1890* (1956). The pioneer article on the evaluation of the land grants to railroads is Robert S. Henry, "The Railroad Land Grant Legend in American History Texts," *Mississippi Valley Historical Review*, XXXII (1945). A more recent and more technical study of the subject reaching a similar conclusion is Lloyd Mercer, "Land Grants to American Railroads: Social Costs or Social Benefit?" *Business History Review*, XLIII (1969). For railroad men's conception of themselves see Thomas C. Cochran, *Railroad Leaders, 1845 – 1890* (1953). Oscar Lewis, *The Big Four* (1938), is an interesting account of the men who built the Central Pacific and Southern Pacific railroads. A knowing summary statement on aid to railroads can be found in Carter Goodrich, *Government Promotion of American Canals and Railroads, 1880 – 1890* (1960). Robert Fogel, *The Union Pacific Railroad: A Case in Premature Enterprise* (1960), measures the gain to the economy from the early building of the Union Pacific. In his *Railroads and American Economic Growth* (1964), Fogel denies the indispensability of railroads in economic growth. Less contentious or "counterfactual" in approach, but also downplaying the indispensability of the railroad is Albert Fishlow, *American Railroads and the Transformation of the Ante-Bellum Economy* (1965). A valuable study that reevaluates the origins of demands for regulation of railroads is Lee Benson, *Merchants, Farmers, and Railroads* (1955). Gabriel Kolko, *Railroads and Regulation, 1877 – 1916* (1965), argues that railroads generally preferred regulation, a position seriously qualified in Edward A. Purcell, Jr., "Ideas and Interests: Businessmen and the Interstate Commerce Act," *Journal of American History*, LIV (1967). Broader and well informed is the important article by Albro Martin, "The Troubled Subject of Railroad Regulation in the Gilded Age—a Reappraisal," *Journal of American History*, LXI (1974).

Virtually the only general study of the relationship between technology and American society in this period is the popular Roger Burlingame, *Engines of Democracy* (1940). Siegfried Giedion, *Mechanization Takes Command* (1948), is broader both in conception and execution and goes beyond the United States. Valuable, but narrower than either, is W.

Paul Strassmann, *Risk and Technological Innovation: American Manufacturing Methods During the 19th Century* (1959); he concludes that not much risk was assumed. A very important though somewhat technical study is H. J. Habakkuk, *American and British Technology in the Nineteenth Century: Search for Labour-Saving Inventions* (1962). A monumental study of an important practitioner of technological innovation is Matthew Josephson, *Edison* (1959).

The many works on the individual entrepreneurs and business enterprises are too numerous to cite here, though Joseph F. Wall, *Andrew Carnegie* (1970), cannot be left out. Among the most important of the general studies is Matthew Josephson's readable though biased, *The Robber Barons* (1934). Equally readable but more sympathetic are the portraits of Ford, Edison, Carnegie, Harriman, and J. P. Morgan by economist J. R. Hughes, *The Vital Few* (1966). Of the several studies on the social origins of business leaders, perhaps the most convincing is F. W. Gregory and I. D. Neu, "Industrial Elite in the 1870s," in *Men in Business,* ed. William Miller (1952). Edward Chase Kirkland, *Dream and Thought in the Business Community, 1860–1900* (1956), does justice to the various aspirations and limitations of the so-called robber barons.

An indispensable article is Alfred D. Chandler, Jr., "The Beginnings of 'Big Business' in American Industry," *Business History Review,* XXXIII (1959). A good study of the movement to limit business is Hans B. Thorelli, *The Federal Antitrust Policy* (1955); it has been largely superseded by William Letwin, *Law and Economic Policy in America: The Evolution of the Sherman Anti-Trust Act* (1965).

The literature on the history of the city has been growing rapidly in the last decade, but all must begin with Adna Weber, *The Growth of Cities in the Nineteenth Century* (1899). A general history of the city in this period is Blake McKelvey, *The Urbanization of America, 1860–1915* (1963). More conceptual and interpretive is Sam Bass Warner, Jr., *The Urban Wilderness* (1972). Arthur M. Schlesinger, *The Rise of the City, 1878–1898* (1933), is old but still good on social history. Gerd Korman, *Industrialization, Immigration, and Americanization* (1967), a study of Milwaukee at the end of the nineteenth century, is excellent as a case study. Equally good on Los Angeles' growth is Robert M. Fogelson, *The Fragmented Metropolis* (1967). David Ward, *Cities and Immigrants* (1971), uses the insights of geography to analyze the nineteenth-century cities of the United States. The role of the city in educating millions is dissected in fascinating detail in David B. Tyack, *The One Best System* (1974). Stephan Thernstrom and Richard Sennett, eds., *Nineteenth-Century Cities* (1969), contains important essays on the new social history of cities.

CHAPTER THREE

THE ECONOMIC REVOLUTION: THE WEST, FARMERS, AND INDUSTRIAL WORKERS

*T*HE DEVELOPMENT OF machines, their application to manufacturing, and the growth of large-scale industrial enterprises constituted only one aspect of the Economic Revolution. Another was the opening up and exploitation of the hitherto untouched far western regions of the country, which contributed new resources to the nation's economic growth. Still a third element was an Agricultural Revolution that raised the production of food and fiber to unbelievable heights in a few years, releasing a flood of American foodstuffs upon the markets of the world. Meanwhile, the expanding manufacturing sector converted millions of native American farmers and European peasants into an industrial labor force, attracted by the new opportunities in the cities and factories of America.

The impact of the Economic Revolution was so profound that both those workers who stayed on the land and those who went into the factories felt impelled to form organizations to help them adjust to the new economic order. The growth of these organizations of protest and adjustment is also a part of the story of the Economic Revolution.

The Challenge of the Far West

When the Civil War began, the continental boundaries of the United States were approximately the same as they are today, but less than half of the area of the country was occupied by white people. White settlements extended just slightly beyond the tier of states west of the Mississippi River. Once westward travelers left those states behind, they came upon virtually no settlements for over a thousand miles except for a few settlers in the Sante Fe region of New Mexico and a cluster of Mormons in Utah. Most of the enormous expanse of land that lay between the great bend of the Missouri River and the Sierra Nevada was given over to the Indian, the buffalo, the prairie dog, and the coyote. The opening and settlement of this vast area—about the size of Europe west of the Soviet Union—was the work of the next thirty years.

A Forbidding Territory. Why was this region the last frontier when California and Oregon, located much farther west, had been settled long before? The primary reason was the difficulty faced by settlers accustomed to the moist, forest frontier of the older regions of the country. What could settlers from the East do with the vast, grassy plains where the sod was so tough that it could snap off the blade of a plow, and where the scarcity of trees deprived them of the wood they had depended upon for fuel, homes, and fencing? Furthermore, although the soil was undoubtedly rich in many places, other portions of the Great Plains and the Great Basin were little more than sandy wastes, on which dust storms had raged long before the first furrow was cut. Early travelers and explorers were so struck by the aridity and treelessness of the plains that maps of the 1840s and 1850s designated large sections of this terrain as the Great American Desert. Though this title was a

Populist party convention at Columbus, Nebraska. *Courtesy of The Nebraska State Historical Society, S. D. Butcher Collection* misnomer, rainfall on the Great Plains, even in the grassy regions, is much scantier than in the East, and west of the 100th meridian, on the so-called High Plains, the average annual precipitation is not enough for farming as customarily practiced in the humid East.

West of the formidable Rockies, the pioneer encountered a landscape that to one nurtured in forested, humid lands was at once breathtakingly beautiful and vaguely forbidding. The Great Basin and Plateau provinces, especially including what are now the states of Nevada, Utah, western Colorado, northern Arizona, and portions of southern Wyoming and Idaho, are the driest regions in the United States. In fact, large sections are literally deserts. Instead of oceans of rippling grasses, as on the plains, these regions have only sparse vegetation, unattractive and useless, consisting largely of cactus, sage brush, and a few short grasses. The most striking characteristic of the southern two thirds of the region is the craggy face of the land. Stark, eroded mesas, wind-carved rock pinnacles of curious and wonderful shapes, deep parched gullies, and broad alkali flats made the area a wonderland to the first explorers and a nightmare to the first farmers. Confronted by such poor economic opportunities, most American pioneers passed over the Great Plains, the Rockies, and the Great Basin, not settling down until they reached the wet and fertile valleys of Oregon and California.

Up to the Civil War, of all the people of European culture and tradition, only the Mormons, after being hounded out of the East, had displayed the industry and imagination necessary to bring to fruit the empty and discouraging lands of the Great Basin. They showed that irrigation, carefully planned on a large scale, could bring life from the seemingly dead soil. Although no others attempted such a task, it is probably accurate to say that the Mormons' efforts, though successful in a small area, could not have been applied with equal results to the whole region. Even today, thousands of acres of the Great Basin lie uncultivated because of a dearth of water, despite the fact that the region now boasts a large number of dams and irrigation projects. But the dams have made clear that only a new technology could meet the challenge of the Far West. Hence its settlement and exploitation waited upon industrial and technological developments elsewhere in the nation.

By the 1860s the forces that would open these regions were in motion. The discovery of gold and silver was the first incentive for people to venture into the hitherto neglected reaches between the Missouri River and the Pacific coastal states.

The Mining Impetus: Gold! More than any other commodity, gold has fascinated people and excited their cupidity; the prospect of acquiring it has drawn them from the ends of the earth and the most comfortable lives. Recognizing this power, Johann Sutter, a Swiss immigrant living quietly in California, tried to suppress knowledge of the discovery of gold on his land in 1848. But his effort to preserve his tranquil and almost idyllic life in the Far West failed. Within a year the news of the discovery triggered a worldwide movement of fortune seekers which soon propelled California into statehood and enormous wealth. By the summer of 1850, when California became a state, the taxable property of San Francisco alone was said to be worth $40 million; in 1852 eager miners extracted from the ground over $81 million worth of precious metals.

In the early days gold mining was an individual enterprise. A man staked a claim near some running water, which he used to flush buckets of dirt through a sluice or over a pan. The heavy gold sank to the bottom, while the water washed away the dirt. The work was arduous, monotonous, and time-consuming, for actual nuggets of gold were hard to find. Most miners, if they discovered any gold at all, had to labor countless hours to accumulate a few fine particles. Despite these drawbacks, placer mining, as this process was called, attracted many because it demanded little capital and virtually no skill; moreover, the miner, if he was lucky enough, did not have to share his good fortune with anyone. Placer mining, however, was only a passing phase of the industry, for gold occurs naturally in rock formations, not in a free state. The loose gold found in streambeds and in the soil was the result of earlier erosion and might be recovered by a single prospector working alone. But no individual miner could extract the large sources of gold imbedded in rock formations; working such deposits required many men, elaborate rock-crushing equipment, and substantial capital.

As early as 1855 gold seekers from California were fanning out eastward into the Great Basin and Rocky Mountains. These prospectors and the people who followed when word of new strikes spread were the first settlers in the vast expanse of land between the Great Plains and California. Many of the present-day towns and cities of the Far West are as truly their creation as are the ghost towns for which the miners are more often remembered.

The push of the miners into the region began before the Civil War and continued right through it. The two earliest thrusts extended into what is now Nevada and Colorado. In the Washoe district of western Nevada, Henry Comstock in 1858 stumbled upon the great gold and silver lode that still bears his name; within twenty years the mine yielded $300 million worth of precious metals. Almost at the same time gold was discovered in eastern Colorado near Pike's Peak. Thousands of fortune seekers flocked to the region in 1859; many came from great distances, as attested by the signs on the sides of their wagons, "Pike's Peak or Bust." Since gold-seeking was a speculative business, many of them did go broke and had to return as best they could. Gold and silver continued to be discovered at various Colorado sites through the early 1890s, thus gradually opening the whole region to settlement.

The ceaseless search for quick wealth drove miners and settlers into both the Northwest and the Southwest. Gold discoveries in 1862 along the Colorado River in what is now Arizona laid the foundation for the town of Tucson. In the North, on the banks of the Columbia and Snake rivers, other prospectors discovered "pay dirt" in the present-day states of Montana, Idaho, and Washington. Idaho's first permanent settlements grew out of the mining activities along the Snake River between 1861 and 1865. Gold also opened up Montana, for one of the biggest strikes of the 1860s was at Alder Gulch, later Virginia City. In 1864 another strike, this time on the upper Missouri River in Montana, started the city of Helena; when mining died out, it remained a commercial center and later became the state capital. The last new area of the West to be settled as a result of the miners' roving and unceasing quest for wealth was the Black Hills, in the southwestern corner of South Dakota; in 1876 perhaps as many as fifteen thousand gold-hungry men flooded into the region. Almost overnight they founded notorious Deadwood City, where Calamity Jane and Wild Bill Hickok were real people, and the robbing of the stage and even murder in the streets at high noon were common events.

What the rough and transient miners began, others finished. Soon after the miners arrived, merchants, craftsmen, cattlemen, and farmers moved in as permanent residents. Indeed, as the first placer sites became exhausted, mining itself rapidly changed. To replace the miner's pan and shovel came crushing machinery, drills, hoists, and large crews of men. Such equipment and labor demanded capital, knowledgeable entrepreneurs, and engineering skills. As a consequence the mining corporation, which was financed by interests in the East or abroad, rapidly supplanted the individual miner in the same way (and for the same reasons) that the individual craftsman or small businessman was superseded in manufacturing. Under the new order of things the miners became wageworkers, paid by the hour and subject to the control of clock and foreman. Many were now family men, living a settled, if dangerous, life similar to that of any factory worker in a large manufacturing center.

Although the development of large-scale mining enterprises indicated that a stable society was growing in the Far West, the population increased slowly. Most of the mining districts achieved territorial status soon after the first strikes, but none of the mountain and Great Basin territories, with the exception of Nevada (1864) and Colorado (1876), acquired statehood until 1889 or after.

The exploitation of precious metals was only the first way in which mining stimulated the population growth of these areas. Industrial ores, which were often found in association with gold and silver deposits, provided another reason for capital and people to flow into these barren and once-scorned regions. In northern Idaho, at Coeur d'Alene, the search for gold uncovered enormous lead deposits, which in the 1880s yielded millions of dollars. Copper mining in Utah and Montana also attracted capital and people. At Marcus Daly's Anaconda Silver Mine, purchased in 1881, miners uncovered a gigantic seam of copper that provided the foundation for the later, very successful Anaconda Copper Company. The production of lead, copper, and zinc, along with gold and silver, from these and other western sites gave an additional thrust to the Economic Revolution that was transforming the United States.

Conquest of the Great Plains. Just as mining was the prime impetus for the settling of the mountain and Great Basin regions, so the cattle industry provided the incentive for the exploitation of the Great Plains. The true Great Plains begin along the line of the 98th meridian and continue to the Rockies. With only the interruption of the Black Hills, they stretch from Canada to the Rio Grande. For a generation, the topographical and climatic conditions of these plains had discouraged settlers; but what was forbidding to farmers was paradise for cattle and

PHYSICAL REGIONS OF THE UNITED STATES
WITH CATTLE TRAILS AND MINING AREAS 1870-1900

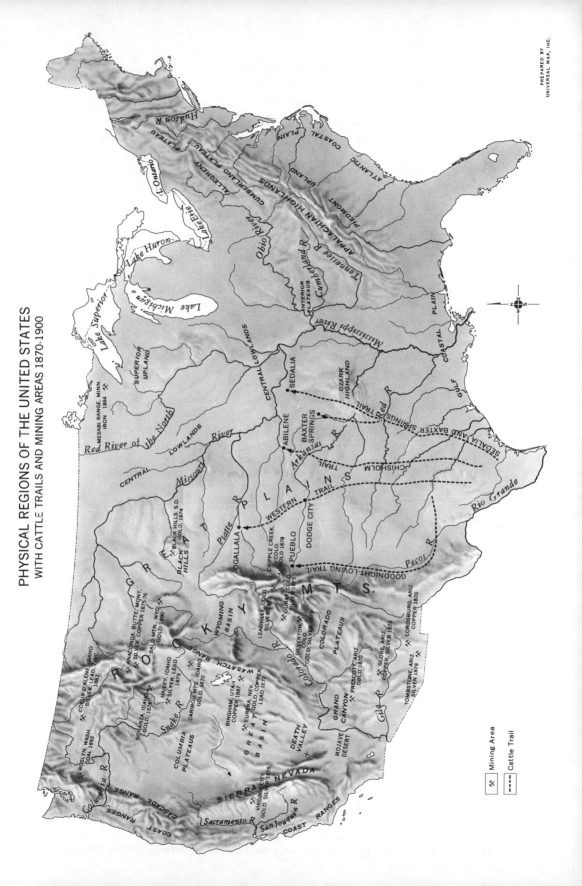

PREPARED BY
UNIVERSAL MAP, INC.

Mining Area

Cattle Trail

sheep. More important, by the 1860s the growing industrial society of the East was ready to sustain a cattle industry. The railroad, which was then just entering the plains, provided the necessary transportation, and a growing urban population's demand for meat supplied the necessary markets.

The Long Drive. The cattle industry began in southern Texas. As a result of the Spaniards' introduction of cattle to the New World, a tough breed of wild cattle, the so-called Texas longhorns, roamed the southern plains in great herds, waiting for equally tough men to round them up. As early as the 1840s some Texas cattle had been driven to markets in Ohio and elsewhere, but their numbers remained small. Although the Civil War temporarily disrupted the moving of cattle, in 1865 and 1866 the northbound herds became so large that farmers in Missouri and Arkansas, who did not want great numbers of transient cattle trampling their crops or transmitting cattle diseases, interfered with the drives. But the measure of success that attended the "long drive" clearly indicated that a route farther west could provide a practical means for bringing together Texas cattle and the growing appetite for beef in the eastern cities.

The enterprising cattleman who worked out this connection was Joseph McCoy. In 1867 he arranged with the Kansas and Pacific Railroad to make the little town of Abilene, Kansas, into a loading depot for cattle driven up from Texas. A cattle trail (Chisholm's) located far to the west of any settlements led straight from southern Texas to Abilene; from there the railroads transported the cattle to the slaughterhouses in Chicago and elsewhere. It has been estimated that between 1867 and 1880 alone some four million Texas steers had been driven the long distance to Abilene or other railheads.

The job of herding cattle on the drive was done by a worker who was neither a boy nor a driver of cows. Nor was he always white, as the movies depict him. Scores of former slaves and free blacks also were cowboys in the early days of the open range, working side by side with white cowboys. Like so much else in the new environment of the plains, the cowboy displayed the marks of adaptation. His wide-brimmed hat protected his eyes and head from the merciless heat and glare of the sun; in rain it served as an umbrella; at a waterhole it substituted for a bucket. The bandanna around his neck was really a mask to shield his mouth and nose from the clouds of dust kicked up by cattle on the move; the "chaps" *(chaparajos)* or leather leggings protected him against the stings and thorns of the sagebrush and cactus; high-heeled boots enabled him to cling to the stirrups or to dig his heels into the ground when a vigorous thousand-pound steer romped on the other end of his lasso. Despite the romanticizing of the cowboy's life, it was in fact a hard one. A migratory worker without a home or family, he worked long hours, frequently encountered danger from stampeding cattle or wild animals, and suffered the monotony and loneliness of the long drive. Hence, upon arrival at Abilene, Dodge City, or Wichita, at the end of the drive, it was not surprising that he indulged in a little aimless shooting and some drinking, gambling, and carousing to let off steam.

When the necessity for the long drive ended in the late 1880s the cowboy's specialized function also ceased; he became a mere cowhand, who lived on a ranch, patrolled the fences, mended the breaks, and sorted the cattle for shipment to market by railroad. Yet despite the limited time span during which the true cowboy flourished—no more than a generation—he has remained, in television shows, movies, magazine serials, children's games, and books (in the United States, Europe, and even parts of Asia), the most distinctive of American figures.

The long drive provided not only a way to get the cattle to the railroad but also a means to stock the ranches of the northern plains. Just before the Civil War, it was discovered that the grass, ostensibly frozen and killed by the severe winters, was actually excellent year-round fodder for cattle and could enable them to subsist even through the winter. Inasmuch as the whole region was virtually unsettled and the amount of grass seemed unlimited, enterprising cattlemen recognized an unparalleled opportunity for gain. Like gold mining, early cattle raising required only a small amount of capital; it, too, encouraged individual enterprise and attracted large numbers of people in a short time. The usual procedure was to obtain 160 acres through the Homestead Act (1862) or to buy a similar amount from the government for $200. On this piece of land, the enterpriser built a crude ranch house and a corral. Usually the ranch included a water hole or some good source of water. The cattle were then brought up from Texas, put out to feed and fatten on the unfenced government lands, and a new cattleman was in business.

Cattle and Sheep Raising: Profits and Risks. Making a profit in cattle raising was deceptively easy. Cattle bought for $5 or $10 a head in Texas and raised on the northern plains could later be sold for at least $25 and sometimes for as much as $50. The sole expense, driving them from Texas to the northern plains, cost less than a cent per mile. In the words of one old cowhand: "It figured good on paper. Borrow money at 10 percent, buy a few cows, and the herd will double every three years." How could a man fail to make money?

And for a while many people did in fact get rich. The Texas longhorns spread into all the plains and mountain territories and states. As early as 1869 Colorado counted a million head, and by 1880 Kansas and Nebraska between them supported over 2.5 million. Cattle raising was so profitable that eastern and even English and Scottish capitalists invested in the flourishing industry. Theodore Roosevelt, with his ranch in the Black Hills in the 1880s, was only one of a number of Easterners who showed a lively financial interest in the booming cattle business. To the optimistic eye there seemed to be no discernible end to the bonanza; to the shrewd and thoughtful, however, it was evident that even the seemingly endless plains of America could support only a limited number of cattle.

Actually, raising cattle was not as devoid of expense and risk as it appeared. Storms, drought, animal diseases, and misadventures often seriously reduced a costly herd or even wiped it out. Moreover, by the 1880s prudent ranchers were stiffening the competition. In order to meet the eastern demand for better beef and to obtain higher prices for their meat, some cattlemen were already improving upon the lean and often rangy longhorns by introducing Herefords and other less "wild" strains. New breeds and the fencing necessary to keep them true also added to expenses. While the investment costs of the industry were rising, the winters of 1885–1887 brought blizzards which left the snow so deep on the plains that thousands of cattle starved to death because they could not get through to the grass. And the disastrous effects of the two winters were compounded by the intervening summer, which was uncommonly dry, thereby reducing the usable grazing lands. These calamities almost wiped out the investments of many ranchers. Hundreds of marginal producers sold out to large ranchers, many of whom were fencing in their lands rather than depending upon the open range.

Thus, even faster than it shot into prominence, the open-range cattle industry contracted to the dimensions of a stable, conservative business, shorn of its romance and potentiality for sudden wealth. To succeed at it now required the same ingredients as other businesses: determination, capital, and entrepreneurial ability. As a result, the corporation came to cattle raising for the same reasons it had come to mining—the need for capital and entrepreneurial skill.

Paradoxically, the growing industrial society which had fostered the devel-

A shepherd and flock in South Dakota, 1891. *Library of Congress*

opment of the cattle industry also caused the elimination of its two early characteristics, the open range and the long drive. The mass production of barbed wire in
the 1870s and 1880s permitted fencing in the treeless plains at a reasonable cost
and terminated grazing on the open range. Railroads during this period gradually
penetrated all sectors of the plains. As they did so, they rang the death knell for
the long drive by offering an economical means of transporting cattle that didn't
wear off pounds of salable meat.

Sheep raising on the Great Plains and in the mountain regions also helped
open the Far West. Like the cattlemen, the sheepherders freely used the government lands as pastures. Because sheep are more tractable than cattle, a single
herder with a dog or two could watch over hundreds as they munched their way
over the plains and through the valleys of the Rockies. The shepherds followed
their animals in a kind of covered wagon which provided crude living quarters.
By 1900 there were more sheep than cattle grazing on the Great Plains, though
the comparison is misleading since the cattle were systematically slaughtered
while the sheep were kept alive to bear wool. In general, by the close of the century the cattle industry dominated the plains, and sheep raising dominated the
mountain states. In Montana, for instance, sheep outnumbered cattle six or
seven to one.

Farming the Plains. As sheep- and cattlemen began to settle on ranches in the
1880s the sedentary farmer, last in the procession of frontiersmen, made his entrance onto the western plains. Some farmers had moved into western Kansas and
Nebraska in the late seventies, but not until the early 1880s did they reach sizable
numbers, and it was even later before there were many in the Dakotas. (Both
North and South Dakota became states in 1889.) Like the ranchers before them,
the farmers fenced in their lands, thus making their contribution to the closing of
the range.

Unlike the ranchers, however, the farmers found the scanty rainfall of the
Great Plains a constant threat to their existence. For a few years in the late 1870s
and early 1880s rainfall in the western plains was more plentiful than normal, lur-
ing farmers into the region. Then in the middle 1880s the more usual dry conditions returned, forcing thousands of farmers in western Kansas and Nebraska to
abandon their farms and flee eastward again. Indeed, part of the discontent of the
early nineties that became known as Populism was rooted in the economic difficulties encountered by farmers in trying to adjust to the unfavorable environment
of the Great Plains.

In time, new techniques and devices from the industrial East would help the
farmers make the Great Plains the breadbasket of the United States. The barbed
wire that permitted the cattlemen to fence in their breeding herds also could be
used to keep wandering cattle out of the farmers' crops. Improved seeds that could
survive the climate of the plains also aided agriculture, as did "dry farming," a
new technique of conserving water through quick and shallow cultivation of the
soil after a rain. Inexpensive windmills, which were activated by the steady winds
of the plains, pumped water from deep wells to fill the cattle and horse troughs.

Nevertheless, even to the present, drought and dust storms have recurrently plagued the farmers of the western plains.

Far Western Frontiers: Molders of a New Breed

In a sense, the history of the United States is the story of the frontier, but for most of American history prior to the Civil War, the frontier was the farmers' domain. The trappers and herdsmen who preceded the farmers into the wilderness were transitory figures, leaving few marks of their passage upon the civilization that followed. Not so with the frontiers of the Far West. There the farmers came late; to some of the regions of the Great Basin they never came at all, and even where they did settle, as we have seen, their tenure was precarious. Largely because the mining and cattle frontiers were so different, they contributed unique and colorful elements to American culture, leaving in folklore and literature monuments to their short history.

The mining and cattle frontiers provided many sharp contrasts to the traditional frontier of the East. For one thing, unlike the Atlantic frontier, the mining frontier moved from west to east, since the pioneers in the opening of the Rocky Mountain and Great Basin country were miners and other migrants from the Pacific coastal settlements. Furthermore, compared with even the most primitive farmstead communities of the forest regions, the mining frontier fostered an unstable society, of which the ghost town is a dramatic reminder. Basically, of course, this instability stemmed from the nature of mining—that is, the town usually lasted only so long as did the ore. But there were other factors that made life in the mining town unstable, rough, often violent, and frequently lawless. Because of the remote places in which gold was frequently found, and because most miners hoped to make a quick strike and return to civilization with their new wealth, few brought their families with them. Indeed, the world of the miner, like the world of the cowboy and cattleman in the days of the open range, was without women, except for the dance-hall singer, the barmaid, and the prostitute. It lacked, therefore, the stabilizing influences of home and family. Furthermore, the prospect of quick wealth attracted all kinds of men to the diggings and to the towns of the mining regions. Farmers, college boys, and physicians came; but so did gamblers, speculators, thieves, army deserters, and other undesirable persons who, drawn by the easy money of the mines, brought instability and violence.

Because of the great diversity of social types and the essentially transitory character of mining, local government consisted of only a few, primitive institutions. In the first few years of the mining frontier, justice was meted out by a "folk court" composed of all the miners of a given region; of necessity it tended to be rough (there were no judges), quick (the men wanted to get back to the diggings), and simple (there were few lawyers). Punishments, in the absence of jails, were limited to death, flogging, fines, or banishment, depending on the seriousness of the crime. The absence of formal institutions of government and justice attracted thieves and thugs who further aggravated the problems of law and order. Indeed, the lawlessness of the new western frontier became legendary.

Violence as a Way of Life. In almost all periods of their history, Americans have displayed a taste for violence that belies their belief in law and political stability. Many examples of such violence can be found in the thirty years before the Civil War in the riots of nativists and in the mobbings of antislavery agitators by Northerners as well as Southerners. But considering the sparseness of settlements in the trans-Missouri West, the law was probably broken more frequently on a per capita basis in that region than in any other. For example, in the West between 1882 and 1903 the number of white people lynched in proportion to the population far exceeded that of either the South or the East. During that period some eighty people were lynched in Montana, though the population of the whole state was only 143,000 in 1890; in the three states of Indiana, Ohio, and Illinois, sixty-two white people out of a population of 9.7 million were killed by mobs during those twenty-three years.

A form of lawlessness more significant than lynching, which the West inherited from the eastern frontier, occurred in the form of the vigilante, who if he did not originate in the West, was certainly characteristic of it. Some vigilante groups, such as the San Francisco committee of 1851, actually improved the administration of justice, since the established authorities were corrupt. But many other vigilantes hanged alleged murderers after only a pretense of a fair trial, and some, in their haste and ignorance, clearly killed innocent men. On occasion, vigilantes interfered with the process of established justice, not because it was weak but because they believed it was too lenient. In such cases, vigilante justice sank to the level of a lynch mob.

Like the cowboy, the vigilante is a uniquely American figure in history; Canadians and Australians moved into unsettled land at about the same time as Americans, but the vigilance committee did not appear among them. Although violence was common on both the Canadian and the Australian frontiers, justice there was meted out by the constituted authorities without the interference of people's courts or extralegal tribunals. The contrast can be explained by the different processes of settlement. In both Australia and Canada, a strong executive authority moved into the unsettled areas ahead of the pioneers, establishing the rule of law and the maintenance of order from the beginning of settlement. The circumstances were exactly the reverse in the United States, where the local communities made their own laws and provided their own officials without much assistance from the central government. Simply because authority on the American western frontier was local, it was susceptible to popular pressures and whims. In Canada, on the other hand, the Royal Mounted Police (founded in 1874), as agents of the central government, were independent of local pressures and armed with more than adequate powers to discipline and control unruly frontiersmen.

"Century of Dishonor." The story of the relations between the western Indians and the invading white men also differed strikingly in the United States and Canada. As we have seen, the subjugation of the Indian and the securing of the

West took a great toll in money, lives, and self-esteem. The Canadian West was settled at less cost, though the Indian tribes and even the topography were very much the same. Canada experienced only one Indian war of short duration (the Riel uprising); no more than three hundred Northwest Mounted Police maintained order in the West even after the settlers came. Even when Sitting Bull and hundreds of his followers fled from the United States into Canada after the massacre of Custer's force in 1876, there was no war; the Sioux kept the peace during their five years in Canada.

A good part of the difference stems from the meticulous fairness of the Canadian officials in working out and honoring agreements with the Indians for their lands. The record of the United States stood in unhappy contrast. But of equal importance in accounting for the difference in Indian and white relations was the dissimilarity in processes of settlement, already described. Government arrived in the western United States only with the settlers and on a local basis. Thus the same men who threatened the Indians' lands constituted the government that was responsible for bringing to justice those white men who violated the Indians' rights. Only considerably later did the more disinterested authority of the central government arrive with a measure of justice. By then, the relations between the cultures were suffused with memories of conflict, treachery, and distrust. In Canada, on the other hand, the Mounties, as the representatives of the central government, preceded the settlers. Furthermore, the Mounties' license to both apprehend and judge lawbreakers in the West, powers which certainly assisted them in keeping order, constituted a degree of government authority that no United States official possessed and which Americans with their firm belief in local home rule would not grant. For that reason the "century of dishonor" is a failure of American frontier institutions as well as a failure of morality.

The Agricultural Revolution

During the long history of farming there have been only a few great improvements. The first was the beginning of agriculture itself, sometime around 6000 B.C., when women found that they could grow their own crops instead of gathering wild plants. Another was the great revolution in techniques in the late eighteenth century, which, by greatly increasing production, for the first time in history freed the majority of the population from the necessity of tilling the soil. It was this Agricultural Revolution that permitted the development of an urban, industrial society. In the years between 1870 and 1900 agriculture in the United States passed through another revolution that is still going on, one that has enabled a very small proportion of the population to feed the rest. In the late nineteenth century this agricultural achievement made possible the industrialization of the economy.

Land of Plenty. There were two important elements in the Agricultural Revolution of 1870–1900. The first was the enormous increase in total farm output. During those thirty years the production of major crops—corn, wheat, cotton, and livestock—increased between 130 and 150 percent. The second part of the revolution was that this increase in production was achieved without a comparable increase in the number of farmers. During the period the agricultural working force rose only 69 percent.

The long-term cause for this increase in both production and productivity was, of course, the enormous demand from the world market newly created by the Communications Revolution. The immediate increase in production was made possible by the conquest of the Great Plains and by the growth of an industrial society with improved technology.

One way in which farmers were able to meet the new demand for foodstuffs and fiber was by cultivating virgin lands. Between the establishment of Jamestown in 1607 and the year 1870 American farmers brought 408 million acres under cultivation; in the thirty years after 1870 an additional 431 million acres were put to the plow, approximately 23 million more than in the preceding 263 years! One result was that during these thirty years American agricultural exports increased enormously. For instance, in the 1860s the annual export of wheat was about 35 million bushels; by the 1880s it was up to 120 million, and at the turn of the century 200 million bushels were exported. Pork exports shot up from 128 million pounds in the 1860s to 500 million in 1900. Immediately after the Civil War cotton exports amounted to a billion pounds a year; in 1901 they reached almost 3.5 billion. The United States was feeding not only its own burgeoning industrial population but the industrial workers of Europe as well. Much of the new farmland opened up in those years was in the Great Plains, for that was an untouched frontier, but old sections as well saw great increases in land under cultivation.

Once the incentive of a world market and a new technology existed, opening untilled land to cultivation and exploitation was fairly easy to accomplish under the liberal land laws of the United States. Contrary to popular impression, the Homestead Act of 1862 did little to help the landless settlers for whom it was intended, but it did bring new acreage under cultivation. The principal reason the Homestead Act failed to do much for the small farmer was that the best land in the West already had been excluded from the operation of the act by previous legislation. Moreover, the provisions of the act were easy to evade; through fraud and deception, thousands of acres of homestead land fell into the hands of large holders, cattlemen, and speculators. Hence the Homestead Act assisted in the transfer of government lands to private hands, even if not in a manner intended by its sponsors. The spirit of the times in agriculture, as in industry, was to expand production under private auspices as quickly as possible, and the Homestead Act, like other land acts of the period, helped achieve that goal. In all, the government gave away 500 million acres, most of it during the last forty years of the nineteenth century. The extensive land grants to railroads also encouraged agricultural settlements, since the companies, especially the Burlington Lines and the Northern Pacific, carried on advertising campaigns in the United States and Europe to entice both Americans and immigrants to buy railroad lands in the West.

The Homestead Act was but one of several acts that facilitated the rapid opening of the Far West. The Timber Culture Act of 1873, for example, awarded 160 acres to anyone who would plant a quarter of his land with trees in ten years. A later amendment, which further modified the requirements, was of little significance, since few grantees bothered to plant trees in any case, though they obtained the land. The Desert Land Act of 1877 granted 640 acres of land at 25 cents an acre to anyone who would try to irrigate a portion of it within three years. When the plot was deemed watered, the payment of a dollar an acre completed the transaction. In this case, as well, few took the trouble to irrigate their new lands, complying with the provisions of the act only enough to obtain cheap acreage for the expansion of their cattle ranches or timber sites.

Both these acts of the 1870s were attempts by men familiar with the humid and forested East to deal with the alien environment of the Great Plains. The purpose of the Timber Culture Act was to grow trees where none grew naturally, and the aim of the Desert Land Act was to make up for the small amount of water on the Great Plains and in the Great Basin. As efforts to transplant the agriculture of the East to the Far West, they were notably unsuccessful.

A third piece of legislation, the Timber and Stone Act of 1878, provided that if a buyer would swear there were no valuable minerals in the land, he could purchase as much as a quarter section (160 acres) at $2.50 an acre for the timber and stone to be obtained from it. Through this invitation, several million acres of timberland passed into private hands.

Increasing Productivity. As the opening of new lands was the principal way in which farm production was increased, so the increasing use of farm machinery and the development of new farming techniques explains the improvement in agricultural productivity. This increase in production per farmer was of prime importance, for it permitted a transfer of labor to industry without reducing the nation's supply of raw materials and food. The best-known example of the new laborsaving machinery is the McCormick reaper, which came into prominence during the Civil War. Later the combine, as the name suggests, made it possible for one machine to perform uninterruptedly several operations of harvesting grain. A government witness told the United States Industrial Commission in 1901 that to reap, bind, and thresh a bushel of wheat by hand consumed almost three hours; with a combine the three operations could be completed with four minutes of human labor. By 1880 as much as 80 percent of American wheat was being harvested by machine. Before the turn of the century, spring-tooth and disc harrows, fertilizer spreaders, and corn harvesters contributed further to the mechanization of agriculture. This mounting use of agricultural implements was reflected in the census figures. In 1850 the value of farm implements and machinery was $6.8 million; by 1870 the figure was up to $42.7 million; and by the close of the century it was over $100 million. Improved seeds, better fertilizers, and new knowledge gained through experiments by the Department of Agriculture, which was established in 1862, also helped increase productivity.

Farm machinery was usually powered by animals, principally horses, but now steam was introduced for exceptionally large pieces of equipment like threshers,

A combine in the wheat fields of the central plains. *Courtesy of the Caterpillar Tractor Company, Peoria*

combines, and corn shellers. A steam-operated corn sheller, for instance, could handle a bushel in one and a half minutes as compared with a hundred minutes required by hand work. Steam tractors the size and weight of railroad locomotives were used for a while on some of the large farms of the Dakotas and the flat valley lands of California; but their excessive weight and the sparks that flew from their chimneys, threatening fire to the dry grain, doomed them to only limited use and early abandonment.

Another source of agricultural efficiency was crop specialization. As the transportation and distribution network of the nation improved, those regions best suited to growing a particular crop could supply the nation with increased quantities of better quality at lower prices. The concentration of cattle and sheep raising in the plains and mountain states, respectively, was one example. Others were the development of corn and hog production in the Middle West and the cheese industry in Wisconsin.

Changing the World Market. As already stated, the enormous increase in American production was a response to demands from foreign markets that were

EXPORTS AND IMPORTS, 1870-1900

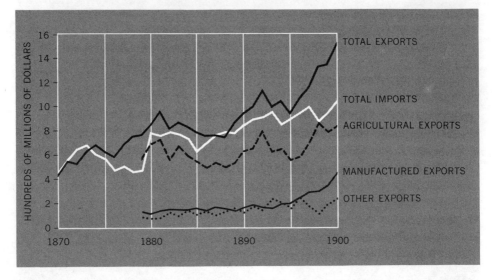

Agricultural exports played the major role in maintaining America's almost continuously favorable balance of trade between 1870 and 1900. Despite industrialization, not until 1900 did manufactured exports rise appreciably.

brought within reach by the new technology of the Communications Revolution. American production profoundly affected Europe. The fall in world farm prices in the 1870s and 1880s was followed by a fall in land values in the agricultural countries of Europe, causing a migration to European cities and the United States. The decline in food prices facilitated industrialization on both sides of the Atlantic, for cheaper food meant workers could survive on lower wages.

The United States benefited from the Agricultural Revolution in another way. In an economy only in the process of industrializing, machinery and other equipment must be imported and paid for by exports of equal value. In all but two years between 1873 and 1900, the United States was able to maintain a favorable balance of trade, thanks in large measure to the farmers, whose products each year constituted three quarters of total United States exports. Without those exports the United States would have had to curtail its imports and thereby reduce its rate of industrialization.

Cash Crops: Development of Commercial Farming

New Commercial Farmer. The Agricultural Revolution was gradually transforming many farmers into businessmen who devoted all their time, resources, and energy to the raising of a commodity for profit. Admittedly, farmers had long been selling some of their produce, but to a much greater extent they had farmed "for a living"—that is, for subsistence. Although they had sold some of their crops for money, they had relied primarily on growing their own food, canning or preserving their own vegetables, baking their own bread, and making their own clothes, as well as, perhaps, their own shoes and agricultural implements. But when agriculture became commercial, many of these items could be purchased from stores and traveling merchants with the cash earned from the sale of one or two staple crops to which the farmers devoted their full time and skill. Moreover, with cash, the commercial farmers could partake of the amenities of life: They could buy books, medicines, better tools, finer clothes, trips to distant places, and a host of other benefits. The considerably higher standard of living to be gained from commercialization easily outweighed whatever objection farmers might have had to involvement in the market.

But there was another side to the lot of commercial farmers. By committing themselves almost entirely to production for the market, they became vulnerable to all the downswings in the price curve. Unfortunately, after the middle 1870s falling farm prices were characteristic of the American and the world economy. Wheat that sold for $1.19 a bushel in 1881 brought only 49 cents in 1894; corn priced at 63 cents a bushel in 1881 fell to 28 cents in 1890. At such prices, farmers grimly pointed out, it was cheaper to burn corn for fuel than to buy coal. It is true that prices in general fell during the same period, but the prices of agricultural commodities always fell faster than the others, leaving the farmer in the position of Alice in Wonderland, producing "faster and faster" just to maintain the same economic position. The more successful he was in increasing production, the more supply outran demand and the lower farm prices fell.

The productiveness of the American farmer was but one of several causes of the increasing supply of farm products. The Communications Revolution was bringing into the world market produce of other lands, old and new. Canadian and Russian wheat, Argentine beef, Indian and Egyptian cotton, and Australian beef and wool now competed with American products.

Growth of Tenant Farming. Falling prices constituted one measure of the farmers' worsening condition; another was the report by the 1880 Census of widespread farm tenancy. Throughout most of their previous history, Americans had been proud of the broad distribution of landownership and the merely temporary role tenancy played in the life of the vast majority of farmers. The Census of 1880, however, reported that a quarter of America's farmers did not own the land on which they labored. And while a large proportion of the tenancy in the South stemmed from the presence of former slaves who had never owned land, the high level of tenancy in the northern states, where there were few blacks in agriculture, showed that the heritage of slavery was not the whole explanation. Because of falling prices, many farmers had obviously lost their land or were unable to purchase it. In Indiana, Illinois, Iowa, and Nebraska, for example, between 17 and 24 percent of the farmers were tenants. As the century wore on, the situation only worsened; in 1900 a third of America's farmers were tenants.

Organization and Protest. Ordinarily in a free-enterprise economy, when an excess of production causes prices to fall disastrously, producers withdraw until the relationship between supply and demand is more favorable to them. That is what usually happens when there is a surplus of a manufactured commodity. But whereas a manufacturer might raise the price of his commodity by cutting production, the only action a farmer could take to influence prices was to abandon his occupation. And this he was reluctant to do. Many farmers during this period of stress migrated to the cities, but not nearly as many as the low economic state of agriculture would have seemed to warrant.

Instead, most farmers sought ways that would enable them to stay on the land. During the last thirty years of the nineteenth century, farmers held meetings, issued protests, and formed organizations, even though previously they had always been distrustful of organization or collective action. But the falling prices brought about by the Economic Revolution threatened the farmer as nothing had before: Only organization seemed capable of meeting the danger.

There are two broad explanations for the decline of the farmers' income. One was overproduction. The other was a combination of increased costs for credit, transportation, and farm equipment, and a shortage of currency, which led to lower prices for farm goods. (As the value of money increased because of the shortage, the amount of goods a given quantity of money would purchase increased; that is, prices fell.) The farmers based their protests almost entirely upon the second group of explanations and largely ignored the effects of overproduction. Yet subsequent history suggests that overproduction, given the character of the market, was in fact the principal cause for the fall in farm income. The only times that farm income in the United States has risen significantly have been either when demand expanded, as in the first decade of the twentieth century and in the 1970s, or when supply was cut by government action, as under the New Deal. Although there was some validity in farmers' claims that interest rates and shipping costs were too high, these factors were not enough to account for the fall in the farmers' income at the end of the nineteenth century. Indeed, recent research into the level of farm mortgage rates in the plains states suggests that interest rates were not excessive, considering the high risks to the lenders.

Since few farmers would admit that their own prodigious production lay at the root of their troubles, they emphasized the disadvantages that an individual producer faced in an age of corporate enterprise. They quickly grasped that in the marketplace the individual farmer was no match for the railroad companies, grain elevator operators, and agricultural-machinery manufacturers, who were backed by vast resources and sometimes enjoyed a virtual monopoly. Consequently, in the last thirty years of the nineteenth century farmers concentrated not on limiting or controlling their production, which was probably beyond their power anyway, but on controlling and regulating the great business enterprises.

Short of curtailing production, there were only two ways in which the farmer could meet the problem of falling income. One was to try to raise the prices received for goods; the other was to cut costs of production in an effort to offset the fall in prices. Between 1870 and 1900 a variety of organizations were formed among farmers for achieving one or both of these goals.

The Grange Movement. The earliest of the principal farmers' organizations was the Patrons of Husbandry, founded in 1867 by Oliver H. Kelley. In the beginning the Grange, as this organization was popularly known, concentrated on educating farmers in better methods of cultivation. But inasmuch as such efforts to cut costs proved inadequate to meet the steady fall in farm income, the Grange in the early 1870s (with membership at a peak of 500,000) turned to other solutions. In order to reduce the costs of farm machinery, insurance premiums, interest on loans, and other items required by farmers, the Grangers formed cooperatives to supply these needs. None of the cooperative and other efforts proved very successful, but the talk and agitation aroused by the Grange meetings led to other activities by farmers, some of which, like political activity, the Grange would never officially sanction.

It was through political agitation that farmers in several midwestern and western states, including Illinois, Iowa, and Wisconsin, succeeded in the 1870s in getting their legislatures to set up commissions to supervise and regulate railroads and grain elevators, which many farmers thought charged excessively high rates. In 1877 these Granger laws, as they were called, were upheld by the Supreme Court in *Munn* v. *Illinois*. Sometimes the aroused farmers in this early period turned briefly to third-party political activity, such as supporting the Anti-Monopoly party of the 1870s and the Greenback party of the late seventies and early eighties. The latter party, as its name implies, also bespoke the farmers' new interest in cheap money as a means of raising farm prices. But third parties and inflationary schemes, both of which farmers would turn to with enthusiasm in the next decade, were still premature in the 1880s. The bulk of the nation's farmers preferred to stick with strictly economic measures to lower costs of production, as had been advocated by the Grange.

Other Self-Help Schemes. Though its philosophy still dominated farmers' organizations in the 1880s, the Grange was by then being superseded by new and more vigorous groups. The important farm organizations in the South were the Agricultural Wheel and the National Farmers' Alliance; in 1888 they coalesced to form what was popularly known as the Southern Alliance, with over a million members. Black farmers were united in the National Colored Farmers' Alliance, which in 1891 claimed to speak for a million members spread over thirty states. Western farmers, mainly of the plains states, organized themselves into the National or Northern Alliance, founded in 1880 in Chicago.

The several efforts to unite the Southern and Northern Alliances failed, even though their answers to the farmers' plight were very similar. Both demanded close government regulation of the railroads, economy in government (to cut the farmers' taxes), and limitation on public land grants so that government land would be given only to settlers and citizens. Like the Grange before them, the Alliances advocated farmers' cooperatives to eliminate the cost of the middleman and thus permit cheaper purchasing of agricultural supplies and marketing of farm goods. By the close of the 1880s the two Alliances were also advocating cheap money in an effort to raise farm prices and make it easier for the farmer to obtain loans. Indeed, the farmers' unending need for credit to buy such items as machinery, land, fertilizer, and seed made the supply of credit a central concern of all farmers' organizations by that time. Both the Northern and Southern Alliances, for example, opposed the National Banking System because only banks in larger cities could qualify as members, and it severely curtailed the supply of paper money.

The Southern Alliance also sought to satisfy the farmers' perpetual need for credit through a so-called subtreasury plan, the brainchild of a leading Texas Alliance man, Charles W. Macune. The plan provided for government loans to farmers at 1-percent interest against the collateral of crops, which would be stored in government-provided warehouses. The farmer could borrow up to 80 percent of the value of his stored crop, which he was permitted to leave in the government storage facility up to one year. From this scheme the farmer would gain not only an easy and cheap source of credit but also the opportunity to hold his crop off the market if prices were depressed at harvest time. To many people, the grave drawback in the subtreasury plan was that it brought government into economic affairs to a degree hitherto unknown in the United States. However, similar devices to aid the farmer have since been enacted and accepted, suggesting that the plan was practical.

Into Politics: Populism. Inasmuch as the subtreasury plan and other such efforts to improve the farmers' income could be realized only through government action, farmers moved increasingly into direct political action. In 1890, for example, candidates sponsored by farmers' groups in Kansas and Nebraska ran under the label of a newly formed People's party. Southern farmers, who were worried about the effects of a third party upon white supremacy, remained inside their traditional Democratic party but succeeded in getting a hearing for their demands for legislation and reform favorable to agriculture. In the elections of 1890 southern farmers scored notable successes; they controlled eight state legislatures, elected several governors, and sent forty-four representatives to Congress. Western farmers that same year, using the vehicle of their new Populist party, were conspicuously successful in Kansas, Nebraska, and South Dakota, sending ten congressmen and two senators to Washington.

The farmers' victories at the polls in the South and the West encouraged the Northern and Southern Alliances to look sympathetically upon the agitation for creating a new national reform party. On July 4, 1892, just in time for the presidential election of that year, the two farmers' organizations joined with other reform groups in a convention at Omaha to complete the organization of the People's (Populist) party. A platform was approved and candidates were nominated for the forthcoming election. This party was the farmers' last great effort to meet the challenge of the Economic Revolution, the forces and direction of which they feared and only partly understood. Not many years after the Omaha convention, the farmers would learn that a third party was no more the answer to falling prices than cooperatives had been. But that story is more properly a part of the political and economic history of the 1890s than of the farmers' movement, and will be discussed in Chapter Five. In voicing their protests, the farmers had done more than any other social group to focus national attention on the need to control the forces released by the Economic Revolution, if a just and humane society was to prevail. Thus, they had achieved something even if their understanding of the problems and their solutions were inadequate. The farmers' agitation and protests were an important beginning in teaching Americans to cope with a new society of cities and factories.

The Recruitment of an Industrial Labor Force

Surplus Farm Labor. Through most of American history the great majority of people in the labor force had been engaged in agriculture; indeed, as late as 1870 farmers made up 53 percent of the workers in all occupations. Yet that census year was the last in which they constituted a majority, and by 1910 only 37 percent of the nation's workers were farmers. Since 1910 the absolute number as well as the relative proportion of farmers has grown smaller until, in 1974, workers on farms constituted less than 5 percent of the nation's labor force. This steady decline was the consequence of the continuing Agricultural Revolution and the attractiveness of life in a city as compared to the country. "Consider the barrenness of the isolated farmer's life—the dull round of work and sleep in which so much of it passes," wrote Henry George, the reformer. "Even the discomforts and evils of the crowded tenement house are not worse than the discomforts and evils of such a life." Moreover, the declining income of farmers and the promise of greater certainty of higher wages, as well as greater variety of activity in the city, drew a steady stream of families from the farms. Indeed, the principal source of labor in the new industrial cities of the 1880s was the surplus native farm population. The exodus from the rural regions was so great that between 1880 and 1890 almost 40 percent of the nation's townships reported an absolute drop in population. In Indiana the figure was 50 percent, in Illinois 54 percent, and in Ohio 58 percent. Two thirds of the rural townships of New York and New England reported declining populations during the 1880s.

Industrial growth also drew women and children into the labor force, if only because they worked for lower wages than men. The number of women gainfully employed jumped from 1.9 million in 1870 to 5.3 million thirty years later. Most women worked in factories, but many also joined the ranks of clerical workers, which between 1870 and 1900 swelled by 825 percent. The number of working children below the age of fifteen also rose significantly—from 750,000 in 1870 to 1.75 million in 1900. Thereafter the number gradually decreased as laws prescribing higher minimum working ages and stricter compulsory school attendance were enacted by the states. Textile mills, coal mines, and meat-packing houses were among the conspicuous employers of children in the 1880s and 1890s. "In the Southern cotton mills," the Industrial Commission of 1901 reported, "12 appears to be the age at which children are ordinarily expected to begin work; but some of

These boys, aged ten to fifteen, worked long hours for low pay as slate pickers to add to the family income. *Lewis Hine, George Eastman House Collection*

the mills employ children under that age, sometimes as young as 9, 8, and even 7 years. In the sweat shops of Northern cities, also, very young children are often employed."

Immigrant Labor. Second to the native population that came from the farms, the most important source of industrial labor was immigration, principally from Europe. Although immigration had been mounting ever since the 1830s, the last thirty years of the nineteenth century saw more immigrants arrive than in the preceding seventy years. Almost 12 million immigrants entered the United States in those three decades.

Although at various times some Americans had been fearful of the effects of large numbers of aliens flocking into the country, most Americans in the nineteenth century placed great value upon the European—though not the Asian—immigrant. For example, in 1871 an official report of the federal government estimated that "the average worth of each permanent addition to our population . . . was $1000."

Well might native Americans celebrate the immigrants, for, as a class, they performed more of the work of an industrializing economy than did the natives. As one writer pointed out in 1893, although a little over 13 percent of the population in 1880 was foreign born, immigrants constituted almost 32 percent of those engaged in manufacturing and mining. In 1890 immigrants constituted 14.6 percent of the total population but made up 26 percent of the total working force. This disproportionately large role the immigrant played in the labor force can be explained by the special and, from the standpoint of American industrialization, favorable character of the immigrant population. Most immigrant workers who came to the United States were adults, yet with many years of productive labor ahead of them. As John R. Commons, an economist, wrote in 1906, "Over four-fifths of the immigrants are in the prime of life—the ages between fourteen and forty-five." Two fifths of the native population, he pointed out, were below the age of industrial employment. Therefore, Commons concluded, "Immigration brings to us a population of working ages unhampered by unproductive mouths to be fed. Their home countries have borne the expense of rearing them up to the industrial period of their lives, and then America, without [that] heavy expense, reaps whatever profits there are on the investment."

American industry also benefited from the industrial skills which some of the immigrants brought with them, such as the glassmaking of the Belgians and the mechanical crafts of the English. But with the notable exception of Russian Jews, most of whom had been in trade or manufacturing before they emigrated, the great majority of immigrants were peasants who brought few industrial skills to their new country.

Simply because of their peasant background, many of the immigrants, if they had the necessary resources, sought out the new lands of the Far West and helped in settling the Great Plains. The Dakotas, for example, were peopled largely by immigrants from Norway and Russia. As late as 1910 foreign-born adults constituted 27 percent of the population of North Dakota, while their children made up another 43 percent.

But by the last decades of the nineteenth century, good farmland was not as readily available as it had been in the first half of the century; besides, the rising industry in the cities now offered ready jobs for the eager, if impoverished newcomers. As a result, after 1880 the typical immigrant was a worker in a factory or mine. In 1910 only 14 percent of the foreign born were employed in agriculture as compared with 43.5 percent in manufacturing. By the opening years of the twentieth century, immigrants supplied most of the labor in a number of industries basic to American industrialization. People born in foreign lands constituted more than 60 percent of the labor force in iron and steel, coal mining, construction, copper mining, and oil refining. The cotton textile industry, once staffed largely by native New England farm girls, now depended upon a labor force that was 70 percent foreign born.

Some industries counted very few immigrants among their employees, often because of the high degree of skill required but sometimes simply because of ethnic discrimination. The boot and shoe industry is an example of low immigrant

LABOR FORCE DISTRIBUTION, 1870-1900

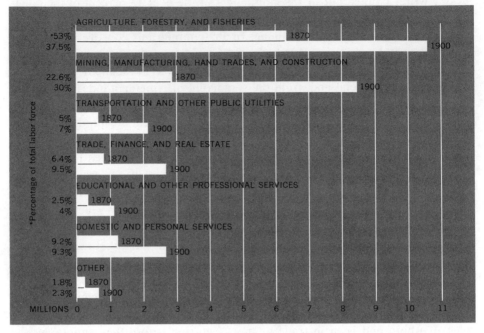

AGRICULTURE, FORESTRY, AND FISHERIES
- •53% 1870
- 37.5% 1900

MINING, MANUFACTURING, HAND TRADES, AND CONSTRUCTION
- 22.6% 1870
- 30% 1900

TRANSPORTATION AND OTHER PUBLIC UTILITIES
- 5% 1870
- 7% 1900

TRADE, FINANCE, AND REAL ESTATE
- 6.4% 1870
- 9.5% 1900

EDUCATIONAL AND OTHER PROFESSIONAL SERVICES
- 2.5% 1870
- 4% 1900

DOMESTIC AND PERSONAL SERVICES
- 9.2% 1870
- 9.3% 1900

OTHER
- 1.8% 1870
- 2.3% 1900

*Percentage of total labor force

MILLIONS 0 1 2 3 4 5 6 7 8 9 10 11

Agricultural employment increased and remained dominant during this period, but its percentage of the total labor force, unlike those of the other categories, decreased. The most significant employment growth occurred in manufacturing and trade, areas likely to expand sharply in an industrial economy, though even then not enough to challenge agriculture's preeminence.

participation; though it was highly mechanized, the foreign born made up only 28 percent of the employees. Because of language differences, immigrants did not share significantly in the great increase in clerical jobs. On the other hand, immigrants dominated the fields of domestic service and day labor; they have always played an important role in filling the unskilled but necessary jobs at the bottom of the economic pyramid. In fact, by moving in at the bottom, the immigrants permitted native workers to move up to more skilled and better-paying jobs.

The Condition of the Industrial Working Class. Even if wages had been high and hours short, the adjustment of erstwhile European peasants and American farmers to industrial labor would have been hard. Work on the farm, to be sure, had been physically demanding, but work in the factory was no less so, and its pace was often faster and more rigorous under the relentless pressure of the clock, the foreman, and the tireless machine. Paid holidays and summer vacations, now commonplace among all workers, were virtually unknown in the nineteenth century. The work week was six full days, so that Sunday was truly a day of rest.

For the newcomers from farms, the world of the factory was not only strange, it was often poorly paying. It is not easy to generalize about the wages and hours of industrial labor, since they varied according to location and occupation, but for many workers the hours were certainly long, the pay low, and the work exhausting. Steelworkers often labored twelve hours, six days a week, in front of blazing furnaces for wages that sometimes barely covered living costs. Silver miners in Nevada worked in such heat in the deep shafts that they had to be splashed with water periodically to enable them to endure the temperatures. In 1902 the annual wage for the highest-paid mine worker in the anthracite coal fields was $560, which was about the yearly cost of maintaining a family. This pay was the highest wage in an industry that was among the most dangerous. Because most wages in coal mining were low, young sons of miners, usually less than twelve years of age, attempted to bolster the inadequate family income by working as slate pickers at 39 cents for a ten-hour day. A study of industrial workers in Massachusetts in 1883 revealed that one third of the families investigated required the earnings of their working women and children, meager as they were, in order to make ends meet. In 1884 factory investigators in Illinois, where the cost of living was reputed to be considerably lower than in Massachusetts, reported that a quarter of the breadwinners did not earn sufficient income to cover household expenses.

Despite the many examples of low wages and long hours that might be cited, the general picture, taking in the whole country, was less grim and suggests that the workers were sharing in the spectacular economic growth. Real wages for industrial workers—that is, the actual buying power of the money the workers earned—rose significantly between 1870 and 1900. Moreover, for the average worker hours declined from sixty-six per week in 1860 to fifty-nine in 1900. And for such occupations as the building trades, the work week, on the average, fell to forty-eight hours—the eight-hour day—by 1900. Leaders of organized labor who appeared before the United States Industrial Commission in 1901 admitted these decided improvements in working hours and wages. While they correctly argued that further improvements were needed, some made the dubious claim that union activity was responsible for gains previously made. To cite one example, the president of the Cigar Makers Union noted that few workingmen in his youth had more than a rag rug in their homes. "Today," he explained, "you can go into the average workingman's house and find several carpets on the floors and a piano. I never saw many pianos in workingmen's homes when I was a boy and I am forty-two years old. I want to say, and I am frank enough to really admit, that we can live better today. . . ."

Even immigrant workers—admittedly less well off on the average than the native workers—must have shared in the benefits of the tremendous production of the Industrial Revolution, for they were able to send back to Europe sizable amounts of money which helped finance further immigration into the United States. A small group like the Greeks remitted over $4.3 million in the single year of 1910; Italians sent back $85 million in 1907. In the fifty years before 1900, one authority has estimated that the Irish in America sent over $250 million to relatives and friends in the old country.

Recently, with the introduction of computers into historical research, historians have been testing the argument that the opportunities of the American economy permitted workers to rise in the occupational, and therefore, the social scale. The picture now emerging is hardly that the industrializing United States was a land of opportunity for all. But it does suggest that during the last half of the nineteenth century in a city like Boston about a quarter of males who were manual workers in their youth achieved a middle-class job in their later years. In Atlanta and Poughkeepsie the proportion was closer to one out of five. Some workers who began as white-collar workers slid down the scale, instead of rising, but their numbers seem to have been significantly smaller than those who rose. These studies have also shown that perhaps a quarter or more of the sons of working fathers, depending on the individual city studied, became skilled workers or white-collar workers.

Studies and figures like those cited cannot in themselves settle the question as to whether social mobility was inadequate or exceptionally good in America during these years. That would require comparisons with rates of mobility in other societies. So far there are only one or two such comparisons. Worker mobility was better in the United States than in Marseilles, France, in the nineteenth century, but one cannot generalize more than that. What we do know is that mobility was not to be expected for all workers or even for most. But as the leading authority on social mobility, Stephan Thernstrom, has recently concluded, if one recognizes that Horatio Alger was saying that in America there was opportunity to go from "rags to respectability" (not riches), then Alger did "not offer wildly misleading estimates of the prospects for mobility open to Americans."

These recent studies also show that immigrants enjoyed opportunities for upward mobility, but not all nationalities fared equally. The Germans and British, for example, were more likely to move up earlier after their arrival and in greater numbers than the Irish. The disabilities of the immigrants seem largely to have been the result of their need to learn English, for wages of immigrants usually rose in proportion to their time in the country. Blacks, however, were not in the same category, regardless of whether they lived in Northern or Southern cities. Neither length of time in the city nor parental occupation gave blacks the same opportunity for mobility that even the Irish enjoyed, much less that of the native whites. Moreover, the wages of urban blacks were generally below those of immigrants and native whites.

The Rise of Organized Labor. If in the long run and for most workers, conditions of industrial labor were improving, in the short run, as the tripling of the number of strikes and other measures of labor dissatisfaction in the 1880s attests, most workers had a number of reasons to be discontented with their lot. Wages might be adequate in a given industry, but long periods of layoffs reduced a good hourly wage to an inadequate annual income. A survey made in Massachusetts in 1885 reported that 30 percent of the state's wage earners lost one third of their potential income because they were unemployed four months of the year. Even if annual income was adequate, working conditions might be intolerable, and there were few government regulations of labor conditions designed to improve them. Workingmen's compensation for injuries on the job was a twentieth-century innovation, and even sanitary inspection and sanitary codes came slowly during the 1880s and 1890s.

Between the pressure from the boss to produce goods and from the invariant tempo of the power-driven machinery, industrial workers often found themselves being fitted to a new way of working. A witness before the Industrial Commission of 1901 reported that in the textile industry the machines were run at a much faster rate than they had been forty years before. Workers in some industries complained that new machines pushed them to greater efforts. Some employers even charged their workers for the machinery on which they worked. To most employers, workers were selling a commodity—their labor—which was to be purchased when needed and dismissed when business declined. This attitude gave employers great power over workers.

Nevertheless, workers did offer resistance to the demands of both employers and machines. Cigar workers and shoemakers often had one of their number read to them to relieve the tedium of work. Religious holidays were often insisted upon by Greek workers, as well as by Polish and other Roman Catholics, thus giving them some respite from labor. In some coal mines Monday was accepted as a slack day so that workers could recover from the celebrations of Sunday. Out of this interaction among workers, employers, and machines an industrial working force was forged. Because employers wanted to minimize worker resistance to the spreading industrial order, a protest committee or a union was usually nipped in the bud by the dismissal of the organizers and then blacklisting them from other jobs in the vicinity. As a consequence, early unions like the Knights of Labor often operated secretly in order to protect their members against reprisals. Unions were a direct response of the workers to the impact of the factory discipline and system. Only by collective action could workers expect to contest the power of the growing business enterprises of the time.

Although there were quite good reasons why workers would join unions to protect their interests, the trade-union movement in the United States developed slowly and fitfully. (Even today, unionization in the United States lags behind that of many European countries. In 1972, for instance, less than 28 percent of those employed in nonagricultural jobs in this country were members of unions as compared with 68 percent in Sweden, 50 percent in Great Britain, or 42 percent in the Netherlands.) Part of this lag in organization undoubtedly stemmed from the hostility of employers to trade unions, but a comparable employer hostility in European countries suggests that repression is not the whole story. At least two other factors were more influential. One was the great diversity of nationalities in the American working class, a characteristic that spawned antagonisms and suspicion within the house of labor that European unions did not have to confront. The second influence was the strong sense of individualism of the American worker, resulting from his or her recent rural background, the opportunities for individual social mobility, and the great amount of geographical mobility. Most American workers simply lacked that sense of identification with their fellow workers that acceptance of a labor union requires. They believed, instead, that social mobility and financial advancement would come more rapidly to them as individuals.

The small size of the unions meant that they were often too weak to withstand downswings in the business cycle. In periods of prosperity workers joined unions, only to leave them during hard times when jobs became scarce. Such had been the case in the panics of 1837 and 1857 and again after the Civil War. In America unionism was so vulnerable to economic crisis that not until the 1890s could organized labor be sure that a majority of its unions would be able to weather a severe depression. When the long depression of 1873 struck, the promising union movement across the country collapsed under the impact. In 1878 labor union membership in the United States was estimated by Samuel Gompers to be 50,000 as against 300,000 in 1872. Throughout the nation during the depression, wages plummeted and hours lengthened as unemployment mounted. In the building trades in New York City, for example, wages fell from a high of $3.00 a day in 1872 to a low of $1.50 in 1875, while the working day jumped from eight to ten hours. Not until the middle eighties was organized labor able to regain the position it had held prior to the depression.

Because employers often refused to deal with a union, workers sometimes resorted to violence to gain recognition or to protest poor working conditions and low pay. The most extreme example of violence in labor relations took place in the anthracite coal fields of Pennsylvania in the late 1860s and early 1870s, when Irish miners organized themselves into a secret labor organization popularly known as

A meeting of the secret labor organization, the Molly Maguires, in the anthracite coal fields of Pennsylvania. *Library of Congress*

the Molly Maguires. Very little has ever been learned about the organization, except that it probably grew out of the Irish fraternal society, the Ancient Order of Hibernians, and that it carried on a fierce struggle against the mine owners. This violence included the extensive burning of mine property and even the murder of company officials. Although the terrorism of the Mollies attracted wide attention at the time and eventually resulted in the hanging of nineteen of the organization's leaders, it brought no substantial gains for the workers. It did, however, leave in the public mind an association between violence and labor organization that was reinforced by the great railroad strike of 1877 and the Haymarket riot of 1886.

The Evolution of an American Philosophy of Labor Organization. The association of unions with violence was essentially unjust because the philosophy of the major labor organizations of the time clearly repudiated violence or lawlessness. Broadly speaking, two philosophies of trade unionism dominated the thought of organized labor. The first type, idealistic, sometimes Utopian, sought through the union to improve not only the worker's position but the condition of society in general. This kind of union advocated a comprehensive membership including all types of workers. It also supported broad social reforms, such as education, temperance, women's rights, and cheap money—not only those beneficial to labor. The second type took the view that unions existed not to improve the lot at all but to gain advantages for their members. Such unions accepted the economic and social system of their time but wanted to increase their own returns from that system. They would have nothing to do with broad programs for social amelioration and confined their membership to skilled workers who could negotiate from strength with employers. The National Labor Union (NLU) and the Knights of Labor represented the first kind, and the American Federation of Labor (AFL), the Railroad Brotherhoods, and the craft unions represented the second.

Utopian Approach to Unionism. The National Labor Union, founded in 1866, was the first truly nationwide organization of labor unions in the United States. Its leading figures, William Sylvis of the Iron Molders Union and Richard A. Trevellick of the Ship Carpenters, were skilled workers who had long been active in labor organization. Just before the depression of 1873 the NLU boasted a membership of 300,000 and some success in gaining better conditions for its members. In 1868 it influenced Congress to repeal the Contract Labor Law of 1864, which, in the opinion of the NLU, had encouraged the importation of cheap, competitive immigrant labor. Like many of the unions before the Civil War, the NLU believed in the use of government action to aid the cause of labor. For example, it advocated cheap paper money (though it is questionable whether a wage earner actually gained anything from inflation). The NLU also agitated, with some success, for a working day limited by law to eight hours. Six states passed laws limiting working hours, and the federal government ordered an eight-hour day for workers at its workshops and arsenals. However, only the federal government's response to the NLU's agitation proved effective, since the state laws were riddled with loopholes. Even before the depression of '73, the reformist interests of the NLU split it asunder. To many workers and to craft union leaders within the organization, general reform was of relatively little interest. The onset of the depression ended the NLU.

One labor organization that did survive the panic of 1873 was the Noble Order of the Knights of Labor, founded in 1869 by a Philadelphia tailor, Uriah Stephens. Destined to be a much more important union than the NLU, the Knights reflected a similar reformist ideology. Stephens' reformist bent was evident in the Knights' practice of opening membership to all gainfully employed workers, including farmers, and excluding only lawyers, stockholders, liquor dealers, and physicians. To emphasize the fraternal, almost mystical unity of all working men, the Knights insisted upon an elaborate ritual and for a time operated as a secret society.

In some respects, the Knights anticipated the modern industrial union in which all workers in a given factory are members of the same union, regardless of their craft or occupation. The basic unit of the Knights was the district, a kind of territorial "local," to which all workers of a given locale belonged, even including members of the traditional craft unions if they wished to join. Unquestionably Stephens wanted to obtain better working conditions for his Knights, but his central purpose was more far-reaching, looking to a renovation of society and the economy. On principle, the Knights opposed "the wage system," which they believed was transforming the independent craftsman into a dependent and degraded proletarian. To Stephens and his followers, the proper course for labor was the formation of workers' cooperatives in which each member could be at once a worker and an employer, sharing in the profits as well as receiving wages. Between 1884 and 1886, when the Knights were at their peak of membership and success, some 135 producers' cooperatives were in operation, a third of them in mining, coopering (making or repairing wooden casks and tubs), and shoemaking.

Certainly in retrospect and even in the light of conditions evident at the time, a cooperative approach to the problems of industrial labor was exceedingly Utopian. Business enterprise, as we have seen, was fast moving in the direction of larger units of production; to have expected the small, weak cooperatives of the Knights to compete successfully with the large corporations already in the field was illusory if not foolhardy. American labor unions took a long time to evolve the bread-and-butter unionism that today is axiomatically considered the purpose of labor oganization.

Exclusive attention to economic issues may well have been the key to success for any labor organization in America, as shown by the history of the Knights in the 1880s. After fifteen years of activity as a Utopian union, the Knights could count no more than 52,000 members throughout the country. But in 1884 and 1885 the Order's energetic organizer, Joseph Buchanan, carried out successful strikes against the Union Pacific and the Wabash railroads, thereby bringing thousands of new members into the ranks. Never before had an industrial giant like Jay Gould, the financier who controlled the Wabash Railroad, been forced to engage in collective bargaining. By 1886 membership in the Knights reached 700,000, making it the largest and strongest national labor organization the

United States was to see during the entire nineteenth century. (It was ironic that the Knights' greatest success should result from strikes, for the Order's Constitution of 1884 condemned strikes as affording "at best . . . only temporary relief" for the difficulties of labor; cooperatives were judged to be the only permanent help.)

The spectacular success of the Knights, however, was only temporary. Most American workers were still not prepared to bear the risks and costs of unionization. A new strike on Gould's southwestern system of railroads in 1886 failed. With the winning streak of the Knights over, many workers left the union as abruptly as they had joined only a few months earlier. Other workers were scared away from the Knights because several of the anarchists hanged for the Haymarket bombing had been members of the Order. But perhaps most important in accounting for the decline in membership was the refusal of the Knights to abandon their strong interest in reform and to confine themselves to issues of direct concern to the ordinary workingman. Skilled workers, for example, discovered that the rising craft or trade unions were much more suited to their needs; even the unskilled workers, who really had nowhere else to go, found the Knights unsatisfactory because the Order was reluctant to support the movement for an eight-hour day. Furthermore, continued support for the producers' cooperatives, which the public did not patronize, drained the resources of the Knights. By 1890 membership in the Order had fallen to 100,000 and was still decreasing.

In 1893 Terence V. Powderly, who had been Grand Master Workman since 1879, resigned his office. In his letter he summed up the Knights' difficulties in the preceding ten years and voiced the Order's continuing Utopian concerns. "Teacher of important and much-needed reforms, she has been obliged to practice differently from her teachings. Advocating arbitration and conciliation as first steps in labor disputes, she has been forced to take upon her shoulders the responsibilities of the aggressor first and, when hope of arbitrating and conciliation failed, to beg of the opposing side to do what we should have applied for in the first instance. Advising against strikes we have been in the midst of them."

The Triumph of Bread-and-Butter Unionism. As the Knights declined, the membership of the trade unions continued to rise steadily. With the trade union, American labor organization had reached its final stage of evolution in meeting the needs and outlook of the ethnically heterogeneous and individualistically minded working class in the United States. The essential character of the trade or craft union was typified by the Cigar Makers Union, reorganized on its modern lines by Samuel Gompers and Adolph Strasser, both of whom would later be active in the formation and leadership of the American Federation of Labor. Gompers and Strasser were immigrants who, though once interested in socialism as an ideology for labor, soon abandoned the idea as impractical for American conditions. Instead, they turned to strong union organization. In accordance with their conception of the trade union, the locals were put under tight control of the national officers; and dues, deliberately set high to permit the accumulation of substantial funds for strikes and organizing activities, were also given over to the national office. Backed by such a structure, labor would have a fighting chance in controversies with employers. As a further inducement to membership, the new craft unions of the 1880s, which followed the Cigar Makers model, usually offered accident, sickness, and death benefits.

In 1886 a group of trade unions formed the American Federation of Labor, which, as the word "federation" in its title implies, was really a loose association of strong unions, free from centralized control. Unlike the NLU or the Knights, the AFL was made up of national unions in which each trade in North America (there were a few locals of some unions in Canada) was represented by a single union only, thereby avoiding conflicts between rival groups, that in the past had often shattered attempts at national organization. For the most part, the constituent unions of the AFL were craft unions composed of skilled workers, though in the 1890s the United Mine Workers, an industrially organized union, also affiliated with it.

At its founding, the AFL, with a mere 140,000 members in its dozen or so national unions and lesser organizations, was distinctly weaker than the Knights, which then had five times as many members. But the newer labor organization was destined to survive and grow in the United States, while the Knights would pass from the scene entirely within a decade. Thus an examination of the differences between the two great rival national organizations reveals something of the institutional requirements for success in labor organization in America.

Aside from the differences in organization that have already been mentioned, there were important differences in membership. The AFL concentrated on organizing the skilled trades, and though professing to recognize no barriers against women and blacks, it in fact mobilized few of these marginal workers. The Knights, on the other hand, included unskilled workers and thousands of women and black workers. Such an approach, while democratic, endangered survival, both because marginal workers were easily replaced during a strike and because, as objects of the prejudice of other workers, they created internal dissension. By limiting its membership to the skilled and the "acceptable," the AFL built a strong union for a few rather than a weak union for the many. As practical men, Gompers and his AFL members saw survival as the first test of validity.

It was in their philosophies that the two labor organizations differed most radically. The Federation, for example, would have nothing to do with the kind of long-range social goals that the Knights had long and proudly stood for. Gompers and the AFL even opposed any government interference in the conflicts between capital and labor, simply asking that government treat each side equally. Primarily concerned with preserving the worker's job, the trade unions of the AFL were eminently, if narrowly, practical. That practicality stood in clear contrast with the fraternalism of the Knights, who, by taking in all workers, sacrificed survival to principle. Gompers instinctively recognized what labor historian Selig Perlman later described as the deadliest disease of American labor unions: their fragility, their inability to endure. Only by the elimination of as many divisive elements as possible, Gompers reasoned, could a national labor movement of consequence be created. And it worked.

Gompers' practical approach, in pragmatic and materialistic America, worked better than the idealism of the Knights, but it exacted a price. The resulting labor movement was narrowly based. By failing to organize the unskilled, immigrant workers in the growing mass industries, the AFL ignored the great majority of American industrial workers. Indeed, not even all of organized labor was affiliated with the Federation. As late as 1900 a third of the organized workers of the country had not joined the AFL, and some of these unaffiliated unions were strong and influential, like the Railroad Brotherhoods, the bricklayers, and the plasterers. By the First World War, however, the principal unions and the overwhelming majority of unionized workers were a part of the Federation. Yet only 15 percent of nonagricultural workers in the United States, even in 1914, were members of any union.

Thus by the opening of the new century, the American working class had at last determined the permanent form of its response to the impact of the industrial system. It was a fragile creation, closely fitted to the practical, conservative, and individualistic temper of the working people. Neither the radical Industrial Workers of the World nor the Socialist party, both of which appealed to American workers for support in the early twentieth century, could dislodge the Federation from its favored place. Not until the Great Depression of the 1930s would American workers be prepared to accept a broader and less individualistic conception of labor organization than that which the AFL represented in the late nineteenth century.

SUGGESTED READING

Walter Prescott Webb, *Great Plains* (1931), is still the outstanding study of the relationship between the settlers and their physical environment in the American West. It has been brought up to date and expanded historically in W. Eugene Hollon, *The Great American Desert: Then and Now* (1966). Everett Dick, *The Sod House Frontier, 1854–1890* (1937), tells the social history of the plains settlements. An excellent general history of the far western frontier is Rodman Wilson Paul, *Mining Frontiers of the Far West, 1848–1880* (1963). Duane Smith, *Rocky Mountain Mining Camps: The Urban Frontier* (1967), emphasizes the urban character of the mining frontier. For an informed and readable general history of the frontier see Richard A. Bartlett, *The New Country: A Social History of the American Frontier, 1776–1890* (1974). Paul F. Sharp, *Whoop-Up Country: The Canadian-American West, 1865–1885* (1955), shows that the border was only an imaginary line insofar as migration was concerned. Wayne Gard, *Frontier Justice* (1949), and W. Eugene Hollon, *Frontier Violence: Another Look* (1974), bring together much material on vigilantism in the Far West. The standard study on the original vigilante com-

*Available in paperback edition.

mittee is Mary Floyd Williams, *History of the San Francisco Committee of Vigilance of 1851* (1921). A systematic study of vigilantism in the United States is greatly needed. The emphasis is on the human side of the cattle ranchers in the fine study by Lewis Atherton, *The Cattle Kings* (1961); the focus in Robert Dykstra, *The Cattle Towns* (1968), is on social organization and development. The fullest scholarly investigation of the cowboy is Joe B. Frantz and J. E. Choate, Jr., *The American Cowboy: The Myth and the Reality* (1955). Philip Durham and E. L. Jones, *The Adventures of the Negro Cowboy* (1966), is not to be missed for its revelation of a forgotten West.

An excellent overall account of agriculture and farmers in the last half of the century is Fred Shannon, *The Farmer's Last Frontier* (1945). For the extent of mechanization in agriculture see also Leo Rogin, *The Introduction of Farm Machinery . . . During the Nineteenth Century* (1931). A full, though not the most readable, survey of discontent on the farm is Carl C. Taylor, *The Farmers' Movement, 1620–1920* (1953). John D. Hicks, *The Populist Revolt* (1931), is the best general study; its weakness on the South is compensated for in Theodore Saloutos, *Farmer Movements in the South, 1865–1933* (1960). Allan G. Bogue, *Money at Interest: The Farm Mortgage on the Middle Border* (1955), calls into serious question the oft-heard complaint that the farmer was exploited by moneylenders.

There are many single-volume surveys of American labor history; one of the best is Joseph G. Rayback, *A History of American Labor* (1959). Philip S. Foner, *History of the Labor Movement in the United States*, 4 vols. (1947–1965), is more critical. The story of the Knights of Labor is told well, if unsympathetically, in Norman J. Ware, *The Labor Movement in the United States, 1860–1895* (1929). Philip Taft, *The A.F. of L. in the Time of Gompers* (1957), is the best work on that national union. A more critical approach to Gompers is taken in Bernard Mandel, *Samuel Gompers: A Biography* (1963). The ideological conflict within the nineteenth-century house of labor is effectively analyzed in Gerald N. Grob, *Workers and Utopia* (1961). Seymour Martin Lipset puts American labor into a social context in "Trade Unionism and the American Social Order," in his book *The First New Nation* (1963). Herbert G. Gutman, "The Worker's Search for Power," in *The Gilded Age: A Reappraisal*, ed. Howard Wayne Morgan (1970), qualifies the usual view that small businessmen opposed labor oganization. In another essay Gutman imaginatively portrays the adjustment of workers to the demands of industrialism—"Work, Culture, and Society in Industrializing America, 1815–1919," *American Historical Review*, LXXVIII (1973). The burgeoning literature on social mobility among the working class is best represented in two works by Stephan Thernstrom: *Poverty and Progress* (1964), which deals with Newburyport, Massachusetts, while *The Other Bostonians* (1973), not only treats Boston, but collates all the studies on social mobility in its last chapter.

The literature on immigration is vast, but the most recent and readable, Philip Taylor, *Distant Magnet* (1971), is an excellent introduction. Humbert S. Nelli, *Italians in Chicago, 1880–1930* (1970), and Moses Rischin, *The Promised City: New York's Jews, 1870–1914* (1962), are two good studies of important immigrant groups. Robert Higgs, "Race, Skills, and Earnings: American Immigrants in 1909," *Journal of Economic His-*

tory, XXXI (1971), differentiates among immigrant groups according to their success in the economy. Charlotte Erickson, *American Industry and the European Immigrant, 1860–1885* (1957), is a valuable study of industry's interest in immigrant labor.

On violence in American labor relations see Vernon H. Jensen, *Heritage of Conflict* (1950), which treats the western miners, and Wayne G. Broehl, Jr., *The Molly Maguires* (1965), which reexamines the labor upheavals in the Pennsylvania coal fields in the 1870s. The two great leaders of nineteenth-century labor organizations have also left their edited testimonies: Terence V. Powderly, *The Path I Trod* (1940), and Samuel Gompers, *Seventy Years of Life and Labor,* 2 vols. (1925).

CHAPTER FOUR

NATIONAL POLITICS LAG BEHIND, 1877—1892

EARLY EVERY HISTORIAN arrives at the same judgment when examining American politics from the time of Rutherford B. Hayes' election in 1876 to the close of Benjamin Harrison's term in 1893—that is, politics reached a low point, both in the quality of candidates and Presidents, and in the level of campaigns and issues. In the midst of the Economic Revolution, politics remained untouched: Unresolved issues from the war and Reconstruction still seemed central. The purpose of this chapter is to explain why this was so. Let us look first at the national elections and parties between 1877 and 1892.

The chronology of national political history can be sketched quickly and then we can look at the meaning of that history. In the election of 1876 Rutherford B. Hayes, a Republican from Ohio, achieved the presidency after a disputed election in which he won a bare majority in the Electoral College, but lacked a plurality in the popular vote. Hayes did not seek a second term in 1880; he was succeeded in the White House by James A. Garfield, also a Republican from Ohio. Garfield won a plurality in the popular vote, but only by 10,000 votes. Within a year of his election, Garfield was dead from an assassin's bullet, the second murder of a U.S. President in less than twenty years. His successor was Chester A. Arthur of New York, the Vice-President. Arthur was not strong enough within his party to seek the presidency in 1884; instead, the Republicans nominated James G. Blaine of Maine, a favorite of many Republicans for years. Blaine's opponent was Grover Cleveland of New York, who won the election and became the first Democratic President since Buchanan, before the Civil War. Cleveland's second try in 1888, however, was not successful; he was defeated by Benjamin Harrison of Indiana in the Electoral College even though Cleveland won a larger proportion of the popular vote than Harrison. Indeed, that very good popular showing by Cleveland assured him a second chance to run against Harrison in 1892. In that election Cleveland was once again elected President, winning over Harrison by a large popular and Electoral College vote. With this brief chronology in mind, what conclusions about parties, Presidents, and elections in the early years of the Economic Revolution might we draw? Let us look first at the Presidents.

Candidates and Campaigns

Presidents Without Political Personality. One measure of politics' unresponsiveness to the Economic Revolution was the dependence of the Republicans upon Union generals for success; they still looked to the past for their appeal. Rutherford B. Hayes, James A. Garfield, and Benjamin Harrison all had served as general officers in the Civil War. Even Chester A. Arthur, who merely succeeded to the presidency following the assassination of Garfield, was quartermaster general of the New York State Militia during the war. In the campaign of 1880 the Demo-

Cleveland's admission during the presidential campaign of 1884 that he had fathered an illegitimate child was used against him in partisan newspaper cartoons. *The New York Public Library*

crats also turned to a Union general, Winfield Scott Hancock, for their presidential candidate in an attempt to repeat the Republicans' success. As a hero at the Battle of Gettysburg, Hancock possessed the standard military requirement for President, but he lacked any experience in political office. Yet his contest with Garfield that year was the closest election in the history of the country. Hancock came within ten thousand votes of Garfield's winning plurality.

When the Republican party in 1884 finally abandoned its practice of nominating a Union general, it lost. James G. Blaine was no Union officer, but he was the most popular Republican of his generation and an ardent seeker of the presidential nomination. Prior to 1884 his dubious political morality denied him the nomination; he had been involved in accepting favors from railroads when he was a congressman in the 1870s. Nevertheless, his magnetic, almost flamboyant, personality inspired devotion from a legion of followers. As a newspaperman, congressman, Speaker of the House of Representatives, senator, and Secretary of State in Garfield's Cabinet, Blaine had rich experience in government, but like many of the candidates and Presidents of this era, he had no cause to which he was dedicated. His name is not associated with any important piece of legislation, though later he would serve with distinction as Harrison's Secretary of State, actively promoting business with Latin American countries through reciprocal trade agreements.

The man who defeated Blaine, Grover Cleveland, was the only successful Democratic presidential candidate during the last forty years of the nineteenth century. Like Blaine, Cleveland had not served in the Army, but by 1884 he had made a good, if unexciting, record as an honest, hard-working, and conscientious public servant; he served terms as sheriff of Erie county, as mayor of Buffalo, and as governor of New York State. His principal attributes were humble ones: forthrightness, a willingness to learn, and stolidity. Imagination and flexibility were conspicuously absent from his activities while governor, as they would be later when he was President. At the time of his nomination he was welcomed as a fresh new face on a political stage that was sorely in need of something other than the leaders and issues remaining from the war and Reconstruction. Moreover, he was untainted by any of the scandal of corruption that still clung to Blaine.

Actually, despite the odor of corruption that pervaded politics in these years, none of the Presidents was personally corrupt. In fact, the personal rectitude of some set a high standard for the nation. Although Hayes entered office under the cloud of the disputed election of 1876 and was referred to by hostile newspaper journalists as "His Fraudulency" and "Rutherfraud B. Hayes," he soon made the White House a symbol of simple living and quiet republican dignity. Mrs. Hayes even refused to serve alcoholic beverages at official functions; her temperance may have amused some sophisticated foreign diplomats, but it warmed the hearts of many rural and earnest Americans. Even Chester A. Arthur, who succeeded to the presidency in 1881 upon the death of Garfield, did not disgrace the office, though prior to being nominated for the vice-presidency in 1880 he had been a notorious spoilsman in New York and loyal lieutenant to Senator Roscoe Conkling, the Republican boss of the state. George W. Curtis, known well as a civil-service reformer, told a reporter in 1881 while President Garfield lay dying: "I presume that if Mr. Arthur should become President, in his ignorance and inexperience he would be compelled to rely on some one more capable than himself. Obviously that person would be Mr. Conkling, and he would be the controlling influence of that administration."

Once in office, however, Arthur proved to be independent of both Conkling and his own past. In 1882 he vetoed a rivers and harbors bill that was clearly a pork barrel for spoilsmen, and the following year he supported the first civil-service legislation ever enacted. It also fell to his administration to prosecute the perpetrators of the so-called Star Route frauds in the Post Office, which had been uncovered during Garfield's brief term. The prosecution of the accused Republican leaders by Arthur's Republican administration was commendably vigorous, though no convictions were secured.

The Presidents of this era may have been personally beyond reproach, but none was a true political personality in the manner of Andrew Jackson or Abraham Lincoln. Least personable of all was Benjamin Harrison. His quiet, almost cold manner could not ignite any warmth of feeling even in his friends, as did clearly the hearty, if bluff, ways of a Cleveland. Even the imposing Chester A. Arthur, with his love of company and his impeccable attire, appeared a warmer person than Harrison. One who knew him wrote later, "President Harrison was the only man I ever saw who could do another man a favor in such a way that all the sweetness and appreciation and sense of gratitude was gone from it. . . ." A successful lawyer and politician, Harrison spoke in public with fire and enthusiasm, but the glow quickly dissipated once he finished speaking. His handshake, it was said, chilled the blood of those whose hearts had only recently been warmed by his fiery words.

Campaigns Without Important Issues. The election campaigns of these years lacked substance and meaning; gossip and scandal, rather than large issues, were the staple appeals. Certainly this was true in 1884, when a Buffalo newspaper article revealed that Cleveland, the Democratic candidate, had fathered an illegitimate child many years before. Cleveland's courageous admission of the truth of the accusation probably won as many votes as the revelation originally lost for him, but the hustings rang with the issues for weeks. Meanwhile the Democrats exploited the fact that James G. Blaine had received favors from railroads when he was a congressman in the 1870s. The personal slip that was assumed, then and since, to have determined the outcome of the election was Blaine's failure to repudiate a fellow Republican's intemperate denunciation of the Democrats as the party of "rum, Romanism, and rebellion." The remark was considered a slur on the Irish, who were supposedly about to vote Republican because Blaine was of Irish descent and his mother was a Roman Catholic. (As a result Harrison refused to tour the country in 1888 as Blaine had done in 1884. "I have a great risk of meeting a fool at home," he wrote a friend, "but the candidate who travels cannot escape him.") Actually, there is good reason to believe that the decisive factor for Blaine's defeat in 1884 was not the slur on the Irish. Roscoe Conkling of New York, who had long opposed Blaine within the party, simply refused to support him for President. The record shows that Blaine lost sufficient votes in Conkling's county to throw the state to Cleveland; the decision in New York determined the close election.

Even when personal indiscretions or slips were absent from a campaign, the level of political discourse rose no higher. Garfield, in the campaign of 1880, his biographer has written, "never once referred in public to any political question that might be supposed to be before the American people for solution." Often after making a campaign speech, Garfield would write in his diary, "I think no harm has been done." Indeed, issues were sometimes deliberately manufactured. In 1880, for example, the Democrats produced a forged letter purporting to show that Garfield did not support the Republican plank favoring restriction of Chinese immigration. Similarly in 1888 a Republican party worker posing as a British national asked British minister Sackville-West his preference in the election. When Sackville-West fell into the trap by naming Cleveland as his choice, the Republicans gleefully twisted the British lion's tail, hoping to wring out a few Irish votes.

When all else failed, there was always fraud. Probably no election in the whole nineteenth century was so infamous for the buying of votes and stuffing of ballot boxes as that of 1888. Harrison won the crucial state of Indiana that year only because thousands of campaign dollars were poured into the state and because the Standard Oil Company threw its employees' campaign efforts and votes behind him. In one county in Ohio, admittedly an exception, fully 90 percent of the voters were voluntarily taking bribes at election time in the early 1890s! In fact, the extensive frauds in the elections of 1888 sparked a long-overdue move to introduce the Australian ballot into American elections. This reform replaced the party-supplied "ticket" with the state-provided ballot. The change greatly enhanced secrecy of voting and helped reduce fraud.

It would be misleading, however, to dwell overmuch upon the corruption or trivialities of the campaigns of those years. The important point, rather, is that campaigns then were primarily intended to get out the vote, not to change people's minds or to win new party members. Men—who were then the only voters—proudly and partisanly bore their party labels; rarely were there independents, and rarely did men change their party affiliations. The real test in any campaign was whether or not the party could get out its adherents. Thus scandals, elaborate parades, rallies, and even bribery were relied upon because they might personally involve the voters and thereby bring them in numbers to the polls. As a result, voter turnout was usually very high by modern standards: More than 80 percent of the eligible voters in the northern states came to the polls in the elections of the 1880s. In 1896 in Illinois, Indiana, Iowa, Michigan, and Ohio the turnout went about 95 percent of the eligible voters. The turnout in Wisconsin that year was "low"—only 85 percent—but that was higher than in any state of the Union in any election after 1908. One of the consequences of the Economic Revolution on parties was that voter turnout fell in the twentieth century as the operation and conception of parties and campaigns changed to being concerned with issues.

Parties in Balance. One reason for the emphasis upon turnout rather than issues was that presidential elections were remarkably close during these years. In both 1880 and 1884 the presidency was won by fewer than 25,000 votes in an electorate of some nine million. In 1888, as in 1876, it was won by a man who received fewer popular votes than the man who lost. Nor was there much party continuity in office. Hayes, a Republican, was followed by Garfield, a Republican; but in 1884 Cleveland, a Democrat, won, only to be followed in 1888 by Harrison, a Republican, and he, in turn, was followed by Democrat Cleveland in 1892. Yet in spite of the party instability, the allegiances of the states were remarkably consistent. The shifting of the presidency back and forth between the parties during the 1880s resulted from changes in party allegiance in only five states, and not even all five changed in any one election.

This consistency of allegiance testifies to the continuing influence of the war and the absence of any real response during the 1880s and early nineties to the problems of a society passing through the Economic Revolution. The Democrats could always count on the states of the former Confederacy—the solid South—and usually on the border states. The Republicans were generally sure of most of New England, Pennsylvania, and a majority of the states of the Middle and Far West. In short, it seemed at least on the surface, even as late as the 1880s, that the parties were still divided by the memories of the Civil War and Reconstruction.

Actually, the division between the parties went back farther than that—to the 1840s and 1850s, when the Democratic party was the majority party of the nation. In the 1880s, despite the preponderance of Republican Presidents after the Civil War, the Democrats were still the majority party, having retained much of their old strength in the North. For example, in a Republican stronghold like Pennsylvania, the party's plurality in 1880 was only 37,000 out of 875,000 voters; in rock-ribbed Republican Ohio it was less than 35,000 out of a total of 715,000. At the same time, the Republicans enjoyed no such comparable strength in the Democratic South, even with blacks voting. In Georgia in 1880 the Democratic plurality was almost 50,000 in a total electorate only one fourth the size of Ohio's.

Perhaps the most striking measure of Democratic popular strength was evidenced in the Congressional elections. In the ten Congresses elected between 1874 and 1892, the Democrats won control of the House of Representatives eight times. Moreover, the Democratic majorities averaged forty-seven seats as compared with an average of less than ten for the Republicans.

In substance, the Democratic party, until the 1890s, was still the majority party of the country, just as it had been before the Civil War. The essential continuity had been obscured by the considerable but only temporary advantages the Republicans received from the Civil War and Reconstruction. The Republicans suffered from an additional weakness in the years after Reconstruction in that they tended not to be as attractive to immigrants as were the Democrats. The re-

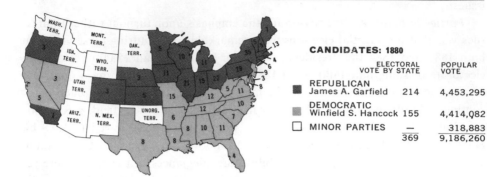

CANDIDATES: 1880

	ELECTORAL VOTE BY STATE	POPULAR VOTE
REPUBLICAN James A. Garfield	214	4,453,295
DEMOCRATIC Winfield S. Hancock	155	4,414,082
☐ MINOR PARTIES	—	318,883
	369	9,186,260

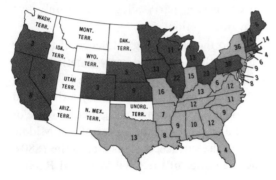

CANDIDATES: 1884

	ELECTORAL VOTE BY STATE	POPULAR VOTE
DEMOCRATIC Grover Cleveland	219	4,879,507
REPUBLICAN James G. Blaine	182	4,850,293
☐ MINOR PARTIES	—	325,739
	401	10,055,539

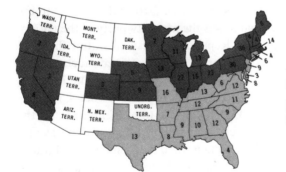

CANDIDATES: 1888

	ELECTORAL VOTE BY STATE	POPULAR VOTE
REPUBLICAN Benjamin Harrison	233	5,447,129
DEMOCRATIC Grover Cleveland	168	5,537,857
☐ MINOR PARTIES	—	396,441
	401	11,381,427

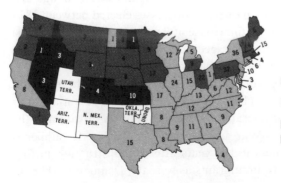

CANDIDATES: 1892

	ELECTORAL VOTE BY STATE	POPULAR VOTE
DEMOCRATIC Grover Cleveland	277	5,555,426
REPUBLICAN Benjamin Harrison	145	5,182,690
PEOPLE'S (Populist) James B. Weaver	22	1,029,846
☐ MINOR PARTIES	—	285,297
	444	12,053,259

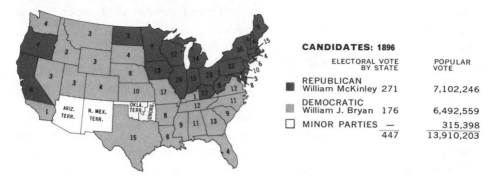

CANDIDATES: 1896

	ELECTORAL VOTE BY STATE	POPULAR VOTE
REPUBLICAN William McKinley	271	7,102,246
DEMOCRATIC William J. Bryan	176	6,492,559
MINOR PARTIES	—	315,398
	447	13,910,203

The voting pattern in presidential elections of this era remained fairly stable. The exceptions were the Populist split of 1892 and the last stand of free silver in 1896. In each case, changes of allegiance were primarily in the West and Midwest; the South remained Democratic throughout.

formist interests of many Republicans often alienated immigrants, especially when that reform took the form of temperance or emphasis upon public schools, and when many immigrants liked their beer or liquor and preferred religious schools to the secular public schools. Historic Republican association with equal opportunity for blacks also aroused immigrant fear of competition for jobs.

Republicans Search for a National Base

Appeal to the South. Republican leaders were so well aware of their weakness that each Republican administration between 1877 and 1892 made some effort to extend the party's popular base. The most obvious place to begin such efforts was the South, where the Republican party had once been sure of the large number of Negro votes. But ever since the failure of Reconstruction, that hope had dimmed. Indeed, the principal political lesson of Reconstruction was that the blacks' vote could be a serious handicap in the South. The Republicans found that the advantage gained by obtaining the support of Negro voters was more than offset by the loss of white voters who were alienated by the acceptance of blacks in the party. In those few states in which blacks constituted a majority, white men used force or fraud to keep the party from power. The Republicans' sole hope, therefore, seemed to lie in making the southern party attractive to whites and minimizing the fact of support by blacks.

Hayes adopted just this approach immediately after his inauguration. As a former Whig himself, he hoped to make the Republican party attractive to his old party associates in the South by abandoning Radicalism and by emphasizing national unity and support for economic growth. Thus in 1877 he withdrew the last federal troops from the South, named a former Confederate officer and Democrat, David M. Key, to his Cabinet, appointed other Democrats to lesser offices in the South, and supported southern demands for federal land grants to the Texas and Pacific Railroad. Much to Hayes' disappointment, however, Southerners in

Congress did not carry out their side of the Compromise of 1877, which had secured Hayes' election. They failed to support a Republican for Speaker of the House. Moreover, in the South at large, very few old Whigs came over to the Republican side. In short, Hayes' efforts to build a Republican party upon appeals to southern conservatives did little to bolster the party's waning strength in the South.

Consequently, it is not surprising that Garfield, and especially Arthur, pursued a different approach when they came into office. Garfield did not live long enough to carry out any legislative program, but he was very much interested in public education as a means of uplifting southern blacks and of building support for the Republican party. In a sense, therefore, the several attempts by Senator Henry Blair of New Hampshire during the 1880s to secure passage of an education bill can be interpreted as an offshoot of Garfield's efforts to build a southern Republican party. The Blair bill—a major social and political issue throughout the 1880s—provided for federal aid to the states in support of the public schools, the funds to be appropriated in proportion to the degree of illiteracy. Because of the large numbers of illiterate blacks and whites in the South, most of the $10-million annual appropriation (ten-year total of $100 million) that was contemplated by the bill would have gone to the southern states. The measure was Republican in origin and support, and was obviously designed to clear up a major piece of unfinished national business left from the Civil War. Four times between 1882 and 1890 the Blair bill was killed in the Democratic House after being passed as many times by the Republican Senate.

President Arthur's response to the Republican puzzle was suggested to him by the rise of independent movements in several southern states in the 1880s. These movements of dissent from the ruling Democratic party all sprang from roughly the same roots. All were protests against the social and economic policies of the "Bourbon" (conservative southern Democratic) state regimes. To keep taxes low and to encourage business, the Bourbons exercised the most stringent economy in government and levied high taxes on land. In some states they even cut back on expenditures for public education.

In the late 1870s and early 1880s these conservative policies aroused much political discontent in Georgia, Mississippi, North Carolina, and Virginia. Some of the new dissident Democratic leaders like former Confederate General William Mahone of Virginia advocated "readjusting" or partly repudiating the state debt in order to save the public schools and reduce land taxes. These dissidents or Independents provided a new opportunity for Republicans to crack the Democratic South. In 1881 and 1882 President Arthur turned over a large number of federal jobs to Mahone and to the Independents in other southern states, hoping that such tangible support would help defeat Democrats, even if new Republicans were not immediately forthcoming. In both years General Mahone's Readjuster party, as his dissident Democrats called themselves, won overwhelmingly in Virginia; in 1882 eight southern Independents replaced regular Democrats in Congress, presumably as a result of Arthur's cooperation with dissident southern Democrats. In

Cartoon attacking Boss Tweed shows him dipping into the public treasury to buy votes from immigrants. *The Bettmann Archive, Inc.*

1884 the Republican presidential ticket captured more votes in the South than in the previous presidential election.

Need for the Black Vote. If the immediate gains were substantial, the long-term ones were disappointing. In 1884, for instance, although the Republican voters in the South increased numerically, they decreased proportionately. Only in Virginia, where Mahone led his Readjusters into the Republican party, did Arthur's policy bring any significant accessions to the party. Republicans, it seemed, could no more base their party in the South upon independent or dissenter support than they could upon support from conservatives. After trying both, it was evident that the essential strength of the party in the South still lay with blacks, if their voting rights could be protected.

Thus in 1890 the Republicans turned again to the policy of federal intervention in the South. President Harrison, for example, supported Congressman Henry

Cabot Lodge's election bill, which would place federal registrars in the South to oversee elections and protect blacks in their exercise of the suffrage. In substance, the bill marked a return to the hitherto repudiated Republican policy of federal intervention in the South, causing Democrats in both the North and South to stigmatize it as the "Force bill." As we have seen, though the bill passed the Republican House, it did not get through the Senate, where the Republican leadership abandoned it in return for southern support of the McKinley Tariff.

The Lodge bill of 1890 was the last effort by a Republican or Democratic administration to protect blacks voting in the South until the passage of the Civil Rights Act of 1957. Two reasons explain why no further efforts were made. The first was that in the 1890s, in the context of the Economic Revolution, the issue of blacks ceased to dominate public attention or interest. The second was that, as a result of that revolution, the Republican party in the 1890s no longer needed blacks or the South; during that decade it emerged as the majority party without the help of either. But that story is properly a part of the next chapter, the history of the 1890s.

Politics and the Economic Revolution

Urban Bosses: Product of the Age. Only in the cities did politics respond appreciably to the social forces of the Economic Revolution. The urban boss, who had appeared in the early 1870s in New York with the Tweed Ring (a group of corrupt Tammany Hall politicians led by William M. Tweed, who pilfered $200 million from the municipal treasury), flourished in many other cities by the 1880s and 1890s. Boss Tweed was overthrown in 1872, but this did not end Tammany's rule even in New York. "Honest John" Kelly in the 1880s and Richard Croker in the 1890s were as much the real powers in Democratic city politics as Tweed had been, though Kelly lacked his predecessor's personal corruption. Nor were all bosses Democrats; Philadelphia and Pittsburgh suffered under Republican rings almost as powerful as New York's Tammany Hall, and the Philadephia Gas Ring was equally corrupt, though on a smaller scale.

The urban boss was one of the many problems presented by the rise of the industrial city. At the end of the 1880s one noted citizen of Minneapolis reflected the growing anxiety of honest citizens in a description of the rise and growth of the political boss' power in his city's government. "There has been for several years past," he wrote, "a very disreputable Ring, which has come into power by capturing the machinery of the Democratic party, through (1) diligent work in the ward caucuses; (2) by its active alliance with the liquor dealers, gamblers and so forth, . . . regardless of national political preferences; (3) by skilful and plausible championship of 'labor' and a capture of the labor vote." To the immigrants and other workers who supplied the votes, however, the boss often appeared quite different. The appeal of the boss lay in his willingness to help the immigrants and the native poor adjust to urban life. He might offer a new job, help if one of the family ran afoul of the law, or send a basket of food at Christmas or a free load of coal during a bitterly cold winter. In return, the immigrant was naturally quite willing to support the boss at the polls. The political boss to many immigrants was similar to the rural landlord in the old country, who might act paternalistically. It was this functional side of the urban machine, as the Progressive movement of the twentieth century was to discover, that accounted for its endurance. The prevalence of the urban boss was one of the first signs of the adjustment of politics to the social realities of the urban-industrial society created by the Economic Revolution.

Federal Inaction. On the national level of politics in the 1880s there was slight recognition of the new problems. The creation of the Interstate Commerce Commission (ICC) in 1887 and the passage of the Sherman Antitrust Act in 1890 were certainly direct responses to the Economic Revolution, but these two measures were virtually the only indications that the federal government and the national parties recognized the new era.

Why didn't the Economic Revolution have a greater impact on political activity? Today, after the Progressive era, and especially after the New Deal of the 1930s, most Americans take government intervention in the economy for granted. It is expected that the political parties, Congress, and the President will be the innovators and the instruments for bringing about that intervention. In the nineteenth century, however, such a concept was incompatible with the prevailing idea of how a republic ought to operate. Only socialists thought of government as a motivating force in society, and while they envisioned government as the proprietor of the economy, they lacked the modern, intermediate view of government as a guiding force, correcting excess and regulating the flow of goods and services, yet leaving the economy principally to nongovernment forces. As we shall see later, some opponents of federal action were willing to grant a larger regulatory role to the state governments, suggesting that these opponents were more concerned with which government should intervene rather than whether any should.

The view that government should keep its hands off the economy not only prevailed among economists, academicians, and publicists but was also reflected in government policy and party platforms. For once, theory and practice were united. Both political parties agreed on the issue. Thus in 1874 Republican James A. Garfield maintained that it was "no part of the functions of the national government to find employment for people—and if we were to appropriate a hundred millions for this purpose, we should be taxing forty millions of people to keep a few thousand employed." Democratic President Cleveland in 1887 vetoed a small appropriation to help drought-stricken Texas farmers, on the grounds that "though the people support the Government, the Government should not support the people." In fact, of the two parties, the Democratic—in contrast with our own time—was the more committed to a concept of limited economic power for the federal government. Extreme philosophers of laissez faire, like William Graham Sumner, were Democrats, not Republicans. Moreover, it had been the Republicans during the Civil War who used the income tax and greenbacks as measures to finance the war. It was also the Republicans who provided the principal support for the Blair education bill in the 1880s. But even if the Republicans had a broader conception of government powers in those years than the Democrats, both parties were, by twentieth-century standards, extremely hostile to government intervention in the economy.

One consequence of such a restricted view of government activity was pointed out in 1884 by a writer in a popular magazine, who noted that the federal government touched the life of the average citizen "very rarely, and only at points of very little importance to him. From his rising up until his lying down, the vast aggregate of his interests and his activities are entirely beyond its scope, and there is hardly any serious interest of his life which is affected by it."

Yet it would be somewhat misleading to ignore the ways in which the federal government did influence the economy, even if its regulatory activities were limited. Both before and after the Civil War, the federal government exercised its powers to encourage economic growth through the tariff, aids to railroad construction, and currency and banking legislation. Although the federal land grants to railroads ended in 1872, other limited aids to economic growth, such as tariffs and currency reform, continued to be advocated and used, even in the so-called age of laissez faire.

Limited Steps Toward Positive Government: Currency and the Tariff. The question of currency reform arose first, stimulated by the effects of the depression of 1873. The fall in prices and the sluggishness of the economy brought demands for an increase in the money supply, especially from farmers who found money difficult to obtain. (In 1875 the Resumption of Specie Act made the amount of paper currency dependent upon the Treasury's supply of silver and gold. From then on, all paper money could be redeemed in gold or silver.) By 1877 and 1878 there were insistent demands for an increase in the currency supply as a means of raising farm prices and of reducing the cost of borrowing. It was then that cheap-money advocates learned about what they called the "Crime of '73"—that is, the demonetization of silver through the Coinage Act. Although free silverites and other inflationists insisted that the removal of silver dollars from the list of authorized coins of the United States was a conspiracy of the gold advocates, the facts seem to have been more complex than a simple conspiracy theory would recognize. In 1873 silver was overvalued; the weight of silver which went into a dollar, as defined by law, was worth more than a dollar as bullion. Hence no silver was being presented for minting. Some congressmen may have realized that a new supply of silver might change this situation; but at the time when minting of silver ceased to be legal, none of the metal was being presented for coinage, and the question seemed to most people an abstraction.

Within a few years, however, the situation had changed. A marked increase in silver production had driven the price of the metal down to a point where the market value of silver was again less than the value it would have had at the mint. But now the minting of silver dollars was no longer authorized by law. Consequently, the silver interests found common cause with inflationists and Greenbackers. Both groups now joined in the cry for "the free and unlimited coinage of silver"—that is, the right to present unlimited amounts of the metal for minting without cost.

The silver question, which first arose in the Hayes administration, neatly epitomizes the limited role of government in the economy of the nineteenth century. The volume of the currency was certainly a vital question, as indicated by the persistent concern with the issue until well into the twentieth century. But in the nineteen century a paper currency could not be expanded directly, because according to the prevailing theory of money, the value of a currency was derived from the precious metals; paper dollars were merely claims or receipts for bullion in the Treasury, used to avoid the inconvenience of carrying and handling heavy metal. Hence, if the volume of the currency was inadequate, the only way to increase it was to augment the amount of precious metal in the money system. Since silver was now plentiful, the inflationists reasoned that to add the yield of American silver mines to the money supply would "cheapen" money—that is, raise prices and lower interest rates.

The issue came before the country in the silver forces' Bland-Allison Act of 1878, which required the government to purchase between two and four million dollars worth of silver each month for issuance as silver certificates—that is, as paper money redeemable in silver or gold. President Hayes, who believed that it was dishonest to cheapen the value of the dollar in that fashion, vetoed the measure despite its support by both parties in Congress. His veto was overridden, but the number of silver dollars injected into the economy by the act was not sufficient to raise prices as its proponents had expected.

Agitation now began for the purchase of still more silver to add to the monetary system, and in 1890 the inflationists and western silver-mine owners finally gained their objective. In return for supporting a high tariff that year, the silverites secured the passage of the Sherman Silver Purchase Act. This act required the federal government to purchase 4.5 million ounces of silver each month, to be paid for in legal-tender notes that were redeemable in gold or silver at the Treasury. The quantity of silver to be purchased was thought to be near the total output of American mines, thereby realizing in practice the goal of unlimited coinage. But once again the inflationists found that success eluded them. Prices did not rise, and the output of American mines far exceeded 4.5 million ounces. Accordingly, the manipulation of the currency as an indirect means of government intervention in the economy continued to be a political issue in the 1890s; yet only in this limited, even ineffectual, way did government venture to exercise responsibility for controlling the monetary system of the country.

The other indirect means of influencing economic development in these years was the tariff. The fostering of economic growth was one of the principal appeals of the Republican party in the 1870s and 1880s. Again and again in election campaigns and from the floor of Congress, party leaders proudly referred to the rapid industrialization of the country, the growth of railroad construction, and high industrial wages as the fruits of the party's policies. "The American people," wrote a journalist reporting for a party newspaper in 1868, "owe a debt of gratitude to the Republican party for constructing a highway to the Pacific, for giving home-steads to the helpless, and freedom to the slave." By the 1880s these particular examples of government support for economic growth were part of the past. The party, however, still regarded itself as the supporter of economic development through the protective tariff, to which both labor's high wages and industry's high profits were attributed. As President Benjamin Harrison told Congress in 1892, "I believe the protective system which has now for something more than thirty years continuously prevailed in our legislation, has been a mighty instrument of the development of our national wealth and a most powerful agency in protecting the homes of our workingmen from the invasion of want. I have felt a most solicitous interest to preserve to our working people rates of wages that would not only give daily bread, but supply a comfortable margin for those home at-tractions and family comforts and enjoyments without which life is neither hope-ful nor sweet."

The Height of Protectionism: The McKinley Tariff. By the 1880s the Republi-can high-tariff policy was producing a formidable surplus in the Treasury. To low-tariff advocates, particularly Democrats, the surplus was a measure of the ex-cessively high rates that the tariff exacted from consumers for the benefit of manufacturers. As a result, in 1882 a newly created Tariff Commission recom-mended a reduction in duties, but Congress, responding to the variety of inter-ests that benefited from the high duties, passed a tariff that made few significant reductions. Consequently the surplus continued to mount at the rate of $63 mil-

The Republican party is warned during the campaign of 1896 to stay away from the free-silver issue on the grounds that it will sink them, as the Democratic donkey in the cartoon. Notice the depiction of Populists in the tree as long-bearded "wild men." The results of the election showed the warning to be accurate since free silver did contribute substantially to Bryant's defeat. *Historical Pictures Service, Chicago*

lion a year. Indeed, in 1885 young Professor Woodrow Wilson wrote, "It has come to be infinitely more trouble to spend our enormous national income than to collect it; the chief embarrassments have arisen, not from deficits, but from surpluses."

To economy-minded men like President Grover Cleveland, the surplus seemed a great temptation to Congress to spend unwisely. As a candidate, Cleveland had shown little interest in either the surplus or the tariff that created it, and soon after taking office he confessed to Carl Schurz, the liberal Republican who supported him in the campaign, "I am ashamed to say it, but the truth is I know nothing about the tariff. . . . Will you tell me how to go about it to learn?" Even when he learned about it, he did not become a strict free trader. Recognizing that many, if not most, Americans believed that the tariff was a protection for high wages and a spur to prosperity, Cleveland was careful not to lay himself open to charges of advocating free trade. And though his forceful presentation of the arguments for lower duties resulted in the Mills Tariff Bill of 1888, in which the Democratic House reduced duties, the Republican-controlled Senate killed the measure by prolonged debate.

Since the tariff was one of the issues of the campaign of 1888, the victory of the high-tariff Republicans that year meant that upward revision was to be expected. The Republican measure, introduced by William McKinley of Ohio, constituted something of a departure from previous tariffs. While undoubtedly protective, it was also designed to reduce revenue in order to eliminate the troublesome surplus. This result was achieved by placing certain raw materials like sugar, coffee, and tea on the free list while raising the duties on certain manufactured goods so high that none at all would come into the country. In that way protection would be high, but revenue would be low. The tariff on woolen dress goods, for example, was placed at 100 percent, and the specific duties on a number of manufactures were scaled in such a way that the rates were almost double what they had been. For the first time, duties were also placed on farm goods, more as a sop to the farmers' discontent than as a practical remedy, since, as exporters, American farmers could not hope to benefit from a tariff.

As a means of expanding markets for American manufactures, the McKinley Tariff Act also included a reciprocity clause, which had been strongly advocated by Secretary of State James G. Blaine. The clause provided that duties on sugar, coffee, and tea, which would be removed under the act, could be restored if the countries from which such imports came placed "unreasonable" tariffs on American imports. This power was used to a limited extent in subsequent years in trade agreements with several Latin American countries.

Although the McKinley Act was one of the highest protective tariffs of the nineteenth century, it was, nevertheless, a clear indication of the limited role the nation thought government should play in the economy. A protective tariff, assuming it did protect wages and support prosperity, still was a feeble means of influencing the economic order. Almost by definition, a tariff is peripheral to the operation of a national economy; it touches only those goods involved in foreign trade and then only in a passive way. But in the late nineteenth century, even a party proud of its aid to economic growth felt it could properly go no further.

The American Pattern Within a Broader Perspective. The practices of European industrial states during these same years demonstrate that the concept of a limited role for the national government in economic affairs was more a characteristic of the era than a uniquely American attitude. Both Germany and France in the 1880s and 1890s used the protective tariff as their principal tool for economic growth and national self-sufficiency. Neither country, it might be added, did anything to interfere with the simultaneous development of large-scale enterprise and monopoly. In fact, the Sherman Antitrust Act of the United States was unique in the western world. No other industrial nation, apparently, found big business either dangerous or undesirable.

In protecting the working class from some of the burdens of the new industrial system, it is true, European countries did more than the United States. For example, under Prince Bismarck, the "Iron Chancellor" of the recently created Empire, Germany in the 1880s provided old-age pensions and workmen's compensation for injuries sustained on the job. It is significant, however, that even the Bismarckian social legislation, which was the most advanced in Europe, lacked any minimum-wage regulations or unemployment insurance. Long before the 1880s, the British government had begun limiting the hours of work for women and children, though men remained unprotected until 1908. The first workmen's compensation act was passed in England in 1881, but only after vehement resistance. The British did not introduce a system of social legislation equivalent to that in Germany until 1908; France did not enact a comparable program of social legislation until 1910, though its first workmen's compensation act had been passed in 1898.

American progress along such lines was partly obscured by the federal character of the national government. In contrast to today, government power in the nineteenth century was not associated with the central government in Washington. The principal agencies of government were the states. Under the Constitution as then construed, they had broader powers, collected more taxes, spent more money, employed more officials, exercised more control, and impinged more on the everyday life of the citizen than the government in Washington. Only in the twentieth century has this division of power and authority been reversed. Hence examples of nineteenth-century concern with the social consequences of the Economic Revolution must be sought in the policies of the individual states, where legislation responsive to the industrial changes can be found. Most of the industrial states, for example, enacted factory inspection and regulatory laws in the last decades of the nineteenth century in emulation of the English factory laws. Many states also restricted the labor of women and children, especially in hazardous or heavy jobs. But no state law limited the hours of work or set wages for private employment on a general basis, though in a few states the workday and occasionally salaries were set by law for railroad and streetcar employees. And though many states held employers liable for injuries to their employees, not a single American state in the whole nineteenth century instituted workmen's compensation laws.

Because of the nearly unanimous belief that the federal government ought to abstain from legislating about such matters, it is somewhat misleading to compare the social legislation of European states in these years with the total absence of such legislation at the federal level in the United States. Yet even when the comparison is properly made, it is evident that the American government's response to the Economic Revolution lagged behind. In order for the national statesmen of the 1880s to have behaved like twentieth-century Progressives or New Dealers, they would have had to transcend the economic and constitutional assumptions of their age. It took time for the forces unleashed by the Economic Revolution to impel the political parties to reassess their basic beliefs about society, the economic order, and government. This rethinking would begin with the Populist party in the 1890s, continue with the Progressives in the new century, but not really be fully developed until the New Deal.

Issues That Could Be Settled: Civil Service and Congressional Reform. Many of the problems brought on by the Economic Revolution could not be dealt with at the national level, and since questions like the nature of the Union and the position of blacks (once the basic topics of disagreement between the parties) were no longer active issues, less weighty concerns claimed the attention of legislators. The most notable example was the growing movement for reform of the federal civil service. Ever since Andrew Jackson had successfully argued for rotation in office, the distribution of political appointments had become a presidential headache of the first magnitude. As government bureaus grew in size, so did the headaches. When President Garfield, for instance, tried to persuade John Hay, Lincoln's former private secretary, to join his administration, Hay declined because the constant importuning by office seekers was more than he could stand. He wrote a friend that the new President was "living in a whirlwind, fighting like a baited bull against the mob, hounded down by politicians from morning till midnight."

An even more important objection to the spoils system blamed it for failing to encourage the use of trained and skilled personnel. As early as 1864 Charles Sumner had introduced a bill into the Senate requiring examinations for those seeking federal civil-service positions. He pointed out even then that "the scale of business . . . and the immense interests involved will require some such system. We cannot transact our great concerns without serious loss unless we have trained men. 'Rotation in office' is proper enough in the political posts where political direction is determined, but absurd in the machinery of administration." The assumption that one citizen could fill a government job as well as another may have been valid in Jackson's day of more restricted government responsibilities, but it was no longer true in Arthur's time. By the 1870s England, France, and Germany enjoyed the substantial benefits to be derived from an established, respected, and professional civil service.

During Reconstruction, civil-service reform attracted to its banner a group of articulate, educated, and well-to-do public figures. Dissatisfied with the low level of American political life, these men hoped to purify politics and increase government efficiency through the elimination of the patronage system. Many of these patrician reformers, like Carl Schurz and E. L. Godkin, editor of the influential weekly, the *Nation,* had been liberal Republicans who, in 1872 and again in 1884, felt strongly enough about this issue to desert their party. In 1884, these "Mugwumps," as they came to be called by the regulars, supported Cleveland in preference to Blaine because the latter was a well-known spoilsman and the candidate of Old Guard Republicans. The Independents were relatively few in number, but their political influence was great, if only because important journals like the *New York Times* and *Harper's Weekly* shared their intense interest in improving administration through civil service reform.

Prior to the 1880s, however, regular party leaders vigorously opposed reform of the civil service, which one of them contemptuously called "snivel service." It was the assassination of President Garfield in 1881 that brought new support to the cause. Since the assassin linked his insane act to his failure to receive a political appointment from the administration, a new popular concern with the inequities of the patronage system was added to the narrowly based interest of the patrician reformers. After some debate, and in response to a recommendation from President Arthur, Congress passed the Pendleton Act in January 1883. This act laid the foundation for the modern civil-service system of the United States.

The new law set up a three-man bipartisan commission to prepare and administer the competitive tests. A very limited list of offices falling within the commission's jurisdiction was established, with the proviso that it could be extended by the President. The jobs placed under civil service regulations could be filled only by applicants who had successfully passed the examinations, thus ensuring competence. To protect appointees from political reprisals, the law provided that appointments were permanent, so long as the work was performed satisfactorily. The act forbade the levying of financial assessments upon officeholders—an old device of the spoilsmen—and provided protection for those who refused to pay such political assessments. The procedures and practices established then have since become the principles of the modern civil service.

Under the original act, only about 12 percent of all federal employees were covered, but the number of jobs within the system gradually increased as each outgoing President found it in his party's interest to protect incumbents by extending the system to more positions. For example, when Cleveland left office in 1889, the number of jobs under civil service regulations was double what it had been when he entered. In fact, he added almost a third of those positions after his defeat in 1888. Arthur had adopted the same tactic even earlier, and Harrison and others would subsequently follow suit.

Another "housekeeping" measure that was only tangentially related to the new demands of an industrial society was the reorganization of the House of Representatives. Like the civil service prior to 1883, the House during the 1880s reflected the easygoing habits of the pre–Civil War farmers' republic. As Professor Leonard White has written, the rules of the House constituted "an unknown jungle" that no representative could penetrate. As a result of alterations and additions over the years, the rules had become so numerous and complicated that business could proceed only by suspending some of them. Since suspension required unanimous consent, the minority held enormous power. Moreover, the Speaker, though ostensibly ruling the House, was actually impotent in the face of the powerful committee chairmen and the complicated rules.

This disgraceful situation in the representative assembly of a major nation was ended in 1890 by the actions of Republican Speaker Thomas B. Reed, steps that quickly earned him the title of "czar." Reed successfully insisted that the Speaker must have the right to rule out of order any attempt by a member to obstruct proceedings or to delay a vote. If Democrats sought to prevent a quorum by refusing to answer the roll call, Reed counted them anyway; if they absented themselves, he had them brought into the chamber by force. The fact that the Democratic House in the next Congress adopted Reed's rules suggests that he was meeting the needs of a modern legislature as well as serving the interests of his party.

An Age of Whiggish Presidents

Congressional Dominance. The striking fact about the political history of these years, as contemporaries and historians alike have noted, is the weak presidential leadership. Woodrow Wilson, later an example of a quite different kind of President, wrote in 1885 that the explanation lay in the great disparity between the power and prestige of Congress and that of the President. As Wilson put it, the United States may have been a presidential form of government in theory, but functionally its form was Congressional. Tested against the administrations after the death of Lincoln, there was much truth in the assertion. Andrew Johnson was crushed by a powerful Congress, and even a popular hero and general like Ulysses S. Grant proved incapable of resisting Congressional domination. In the years after 1877, as in the years under Grant and Johnson, all important legislation—and there was a good deal of it—originated not with the Presidents, but with Congress. The Pendleton Act, the Interstate Commerce Act, the Dawes Act, and the Sherman Antitrust Act simply received presidential assent; the impetus for their enactment came from Congress. The kind of presidential leadership associated with James K. Polk, Andrew Jackson, Woodrow Wilson, Theodore and Franklin Roosevelt, and Lyndon B. Johnson was absent in the years between 1865 and 1900.

Personalities and the Defenses of Presidential Prerogative. Undoubtedly part of this striking contract can be accounted for by differences in personality. Jackson was an irascible, self-willed man; Hayes was quiet and gentle. But that is certainly not the whole explanation. Several of the Presidents of the late nineteenth century showed themselves quite capable of firmly resisting legislative and other pressures. Indeed, most of them were strong- rather than weak-willed men. Both Hayes and Garfield, for example, waged a vigorous and ultimately triumphant fight against Congressional control of patronage and offices.

Very early in his administration, Hayes insisted upon undisputed authority to name his own appointees to important patronage-dispensing offices even though the Senate for the preceding ten years had successfully asserted its right to be consulted on all major appointments, whether the Constitution prescribed senatorial confirmation or not. In the course of his battle with Congress over patronage, Hayes successfully overrode the opposition of even Senator Roscoe Conkling, the powerful Republican boss of New York State. Later, in 1879 and 1880, Hayes foiled attempts by the Democrats to attach "riders" to appropriation bills. Since the President could not veto a part of a bill but had to accept all of it or nothing, a rider was a means of forcing legislation upon him. Congress assumed that the President would not dare veto an appropriation intended to pay judges and the Army, but Hayes firmly vetoed any appropriation bill that contained riders to which he objected. After six such tussles the House gave up and passed the money bills without the objectionable riders.

Hayes also stood resolutely against railroad presidents in the strike of 1877 when they insisted that federal troops be used to break the strike by operating the trains. Hayes permitted the soldiers to be used only to maintain order. Indeed, he was a man of compassion with some true awareness of the novel forces then transforming the farmers' republic in which he had grown up. Immediately after the railroad strike he wrote in his diary, "Can't something be done by education of the strikers, by judicious control of capitalists, by wise general policy to end or diminish the evil? The railroad strikers, as a rule, are good men, sober, intelligent and industrious." After he left the presidency in 1881, Hayes continued to be interested in the problems of labor and was greatly impressed by the social message of Henry George's *Progress and Poverty*. He also devoted a good part of his later years to working for the education of blacks in the South.

Although Garfield was in office only four months before his assassination, he, too, contended with Senator Conkling over appointments. At one point in his fight, Garfield exclaimed, "This brings on the contest at once and will settle the question whether the President is the registering clerk of the Senate or the Executive of the nation." Garfield's firmness won out. He finally maneuvered Conkling into abandoning his Senate seat for good. Cleveland, too, showed his determination to stand up to Congress in defense of the President's prerogatives. In 1887 he compelled the repeal of the Tenure of Office Act, which a powerful Reconstruction Congress had imposed upon Johnson twenty years earlier and had used successfully against Grant.

Cleveland also courageously resisted both Congress and the powerful veterans' lobby on the matter of military pensions. In principle the government's pension program was generous, and in practice it was lenient. Nevertheless, the Pension Bureau rejected thousands of dubious and often fraudulent claims each year. Any claimant who was denied a pension by the Bureau could ask a member of Congress to present his claim as a special private act of legislation. If successful, the claimant could thus secure through Congress what the general pension laws and the Pension Bureau would not allow. Under the prodding of professional pension agents, hundreds of claimants did just that. In fact, the number of pension bills was so great that both houses of Congress regularly interrupted their normal business for specified periods simply to vote on private pension bills, which passed without debate or protest and usually with only a few members in attendance.

No President before Cleveland ever vetoed such legislation. Beginning in 1886 Cleveland began to return scores of these private bills without his signature and often with messages succinctly exposing the fraudulence or inadequacy of the claims. One claimant, for instance, said that he was on his way to join his regiment when his horse fell on his ankle, thereby entitling him to a military pension. Another old soldier contended that a disease of the eyes from which he suffered was the result of a case of diarrhea he had contracted while in the Army years before. Cleveland signed the vast majority of the 2042 pension bills passed during his first administration, but he killed some 400 others with his vetoes. Furthermore, in 1887 he vetoed a general pensions bill for dependents of veterans on the ground that it was extravagant. For these actions in behalf of economy President Cleveland earned the undying enmity of the politically powerful Grand Army of the Republic, the organization of Union Army veterans.

Similarly, Cleveland's willingness to strike out against the surplus and the tariff in his message of December 1887 revealed his backbone as a President. "They

Public concern about the influence of the trusts is depicted in this cartoon, which led up to enactment of the Sherman Antitrust Act. *Library of Congress*

told me it would hurt the party," he wrote later after his defeat in 1888, "that without it I was sure to be reelected, but that if I sent that message to Congress it would, in all probability, defeat me. . . . The situation as it existed was, to my mind, intolerable, and immediate action was necessary. Besides I did not wish to be reelected without having the people understand where I stood on the tariff question and then spring the question on them after my reelection. Perhaps I made a mistake from a party standpoint: but damn it, it was right. I had at least that satisfaction. . . ."

Lack of firmness and courage in facing Congress or public opinion is not the true reason for the poor reputation of these Presidents. When it was a question of upholding the office of President against Congressional encroachment, Cleveland, Garfield, and Hayes certainly did all that could be expected of them. Indeed, it is to them that the office owes its modern independence after the ineffectiveness of Grant and Johnson. Yet there was something missing from these men, something that made a Polk, a Jackson, a Lincoln, or a Wilson a great presidential leader of party and nation.

The Whig View of the Presidency Persists. One of the missing ingredients was a vigorous conception of the office. All of the Presidents of the 1880s and early nineties, whether actually old Whigs or not, subscribed to the Whig interpretation of the presidency. The Whig philosophy of presidential restraint had been a reaction against the vigorous leadership of Andrew Jackson. Hayes, who was, in fact, an old Whig, firmly believed that Congress should lead in matters of legislation and the President should simply carry out its will. Even Grover Cleveland, though a member of Andrew Jackson's party, subscribed to a view that was very close to that of the old Whigs. He saw the President as the executive in the literal sense—that is, as the head of the branch of government that carried out the will of Congress and that did no more than resist unjust or extravagant measures. One valuable result of such an attitude, incidentally, was that Cleveland's administration recovered some 80 million acres of public lands, illegally acquired by railroads, cattlemen, and timber interests. It is this efficient and rigidly honest application of the laws that he must have had in mind when, in 1884, in his acceptance letter, he described the office of President as "essentially executive in nature." At the end of his first year in office, it was characteristic of Cleveland's approach to observe that a rigorous adherence to the separation of powers was perhaps his principal contribution as President.

Harrison, probably more than any other, fitted the Whig view of a President. In the single year of 1890 a number of important pieces of legislation passed Congress: the Sherman Antitrust Act, the Sherman Silver Purchase Act, a new pensions bill, and the McKinley Tariff. But Harrison had no part in any of them except to sign them.

To see these Presidents as lacking a forceful conception of the presidency is but another way of saying that, for all their courage in dealing with Congress, they had no cause of their own. Hayes and Cleveland seem weak compared to Lincoln or Polk because their defenses of presidential power were undertaken in a political vacuum. Lincoln and Jackson, who also fought for an independent executive, were concerned primarily with a larger program or policy. Hayes, on the other hand, strove simply for freedom from Congressional encroachment upon his presidential prerogatives. He was contending for an abstract, if important, constitutional principle. The same conclusion applies to Garfield and Cleveland. Indeed, in the politics of this whole period, and to a certain degree in that of the nineties as well, the presidential emphasis was on the location of power, not on its exercise. In earlier administrations, when the presidential power had been expanded, it had been as a by-product of the drive to deal with a national issue of large importance. (Cleveland's efforts to lower the tariff and end the surplus in 1887 might seem to fit that pattern, but even on that issue he lacked the backing of a united party, and the country proved to be indifferent to his reform.) The rise of the West and the Mexican and Civil wars presented issues that in previous years had forced the expansion of the presidential office.

In the years after 1877, however, the great source of national problems was neither military nor sectional but economic. As Lord Bryce wrote in *The American Commonwealth* in 1888, "Questions of foreign policy and of domestic constitutional change are generally happily absent" in America. Moreover, even the bases of political contest common in Europe were absent in the United States. "There are no class privileges or religious inequalities to be abolished," Bryce pointed out. "Religion, so powerful a political force in Europe, is outside politics altogether." Nor were there any social questions analogous to those which agitated European politics, pushing great men and issues to the fore. The "great political issues" in America, he asserted, "have not hitherto been class issues." And in the field of economic affairs, orthodox thought decreed that the federal government was incompetent and should, therefore, exercise little if any power.

With no issues over which to exercise power, none of the Presidents of these years, Democrat or Republican, was driven to enlarge the authority of his office. In a real sense, aside from the personalities of the incumbents, the diminished presidency of these years was yet another measure of the limited role assigned to government. It was also a manifestation of the way in which politics lagged behind the Economic Revolution, which was changing society.

In the nineties, however, even national politics would begin to feel the transforming effects of the revolution in the economic order.

SUGGESTED READING

Despite the relative lack of excitement about the politics of these years, the literature is rich and growing. Provocative, though bordering on the cynical, is the ever popular Matthew Josephson, *The Politicos, 1865–1896* (1938, 1963), which emphasizes the influence of big business on the politicians. More recent and more understanding of the Republican party is the important revisionist study by Robert D. Marcus, *Grand Old Party: Political*

*Available in paperback edition.

Structure in the Gilded Age, 1880–1896 (1971). Indispensable for all the presidential elections of these years is the compilation of essays by A. M. Schlesinger, Jr., and F. L. Israel, eds., *History of American Presidential Elections, 1789–1968,* II (1971). On the cultural interpretation of politics the following are most rewarding: Richard J. Jensen, *The Winning of the Midwest* (1971); Paul Kleppner, *The Cross of Culture* (1970); and Frederick C. Luebke, *Immigrants and Politics: The Germans of Nebraska, 1880–1890* (1970). Less cultural in its interpretation and less quantified in its method, but no less appreciative of the politics of the time, is the very thorough H. Wayne Morgan, *From Hayes to McKinley: National Party Politics, 1877–1896* (1969). For a path-breaking and informative study of the way the federal government functioned see Leonard D. White, **The Republican Era: 1869–1901* (1958).

The biographical literature is large. One of the best biographies of the era is Harry Barnard, *Rutherford B. Hayes and His America* (1954), which rescues Hayes from an undeserved reputation as a nonentity. The same has not been done for Garfield; Robert Granville Caldwell, *James A. Garfield, Party Chieftain* (1931), is a critical study. A recent study is John M. Taylor, *Garfield of Ohio* (1970). Donald Barr Chidsey, *The Gentleman from New York: A Life of Roscoe Conkling* (1935), manages to make the New York boss understandable and likable. The standard, if rather uncritical, biography of Cleveland is Allan Nevins, *Grover Cleveland, a Study in Courage* (1932). Much less favorably disposed toward his subject is Horace Samuel Merrill, **Bourbon Leader: Grover Cleveland and the Democratic Party* (1957). Merrill's *Bourbon Democracy of the Middle West, 1865–1896* (1953), fills an important gap in the history of the Democratic party during this period. See also Geoffrey Blodgett, *The Gentle Reformers: Massachusetts Democrats in the Cleveland Era* (1966).

The book that has reshaped our understanding of the political relationship between Northern Republicans and the South is C. Vann Woodward **Reunion and Reaction: The Compromise of 1877 and the End of Reconstruction* (1951). Studies that have carried forward the story in subsequent years are Vincent P. De Santis, *Republicans Face the Southern Question: The New Departure Years, 1877–1897* (1959), and Stanley P. Hirshson, *Farewell to the Bloody Shirt: Northern Republicans and the Southern Negro, 1877–1893* (1962). Allen Weinstein, *Prelude to Populism* (1970), discusses the rise of the silver issue.

The question of the civil service has been examined from the perspective of those who pushed the reform in Ari Hoogenboom, *Outlawing the Spoils: A History of the Civil Service Reform Movement, 1865–1883* (1961), and from the standpoint of the service itself in Paul R. Van Riper, *History of the United States Civil Service* (1958). Both Josephson, **The Politicos,* and White, **The Republican Era* (mentioned above), have some valuable material on this subject, too. Excellent on the mentality of the reformers of the era is John G. Sproat, **The Best Men: Liberal Reformers in the Gilded Age* (1968).

For the controversies over the tariff see, in addition to the biographies of Cleveland, the old but full treatment of the subject by Edward Stanwood, *American Tariff Controversies in the Nineteenth Century,* 2 vols. (1903), and Frank W. Taussig, **The Tariff History of the United States* (1931), which is authoritative, if hostile to the idea of a protective tariff.

A book that has to be used with care but that is unfailingly interesting is Harry Thurston Peck, *Twenty Years of the Republic, 1885 – 1905* (1932). Woodrow Wilson, **Congressional Government* (1885), is both incisive on the nature of American government and revealing of a future President. Enlightening the politics of the period is James Bryce, **The American Commonwealth,* which was first published in 1888 and has been reprinted in a number of editions. After De Tocqueville, Bryce is the most knowing foreign appraiser of American politics. A fresh and broad study of the Irish in America and Ireland, particularly in politics, is Thomas N. Brown, *Irish-American Nationalism, 1870 – 1890* (1966).

CHAPTER FIVE

THE NINETIES: THE FIRST DECADE OF MODERN AMERICA

THE YEAR WAS 1892. "We meet in the midst of a nation brought to the verge of moral, political, and material ruin," the Populist platform began. The nineties encouraged such cataclysmic pronouncements, for it was a time of widespread anxiety and social unrest. To the mounting discontent of America's farmers, the deep and persistent depression of 1893 added strikes, violence, and other protests of the unemployed in scores of industrial cities. The thousands of workers who marched on Washington demanding jobs brought the country "dangerously near the conditions of things at the time of the French Revolution," announced the *Nation* in 1894. That same year the New York *Herald* justified the use of federal troops to break the Chicago railroad strike on the ground that "the nation is fighting for its own existence just as truly as in suppressing the great rebellion."

Historian Frederick Jackson Turner was not alone in 1893 when he called attention to the recent closing of the frontier. Throughout the nineties, Americans wondered what was in store for the nation now that its source of prosperity and its historic safety valve for social discontent were gone. Even individuals not alarmed by the effects of a closed frontier foresaw deep changes and new turnings in the offing. In 1894 Henry Adams urged his fellow historians to discover the "tendency of history" in an age of new scientific and social developments. Years later Adams wrote that at the Chicago Exposition of 1893 men asked "for the first time whether the American people knew where they were driving." He admitted, "for one, that he did not know."

In the 1890s otherwise sensible people talked darkly of the imminent threat of communism and anarchism. In 1893, when Illinois' governor, John Peter Altgeld, pardoned the anarchists who had been unjustly convicted of the Haymarket bombing, Theodore Roosevelt interpreted the act as a wish to start "a red government of lawlessness and dishonesty as fantastic and vicious as the Paris Commune." Supreme Court Justice Stephen J. Field, in finding a recent income tax law unconstitutional in 1895, justified his conclusion on the grounds of the dangerous times. "The present assault upon capital," he warned, "is but the beginning. It will be but the stepping-stone to others, larger and more sweeping, 'til our political contests will become a war of the poor against the rich; a war constantly growing in intensity and bitterness." The class consciousness and even class hatred that ran through the speeches and literature of the presidential campaign of 1896 came close to making Justice Field a prophet. Never had Americans so nearly approached being divided into "two nations": one of the many poor and one of the few rich.

Before the decade was out, however, the clouds would lift. Old issues like the position of the Negro may have been prematurely pushed aside and new ones like imperialism impetuously taken up, but the uncertainty and anxiety would be gone. Confidence and prosperity would dominate the opening years of the new century

Crowd watching the posting of announcements at the *Tribune* Building, Newspaper Row, during the Spanish-American War. William Randolph Hearst's *New York Journal* Building is in the background. *The Bettmann Archive, Inc.*

once the Economic Revolution had transformed the political parties and helped launch the nation upon a new life as an imperial democracy.

Portents of Change

The Intensification of Labor Violence: Homestead and Coeur d'Alene Strikes. The decade of the nineties does not really begin until 1892; incidents of that year foreshadowed and characterized the remaining years of the decade. The strike of the steelworkers at the Homestead, Pennsylvania, works of the Carnegie Steel Company in July was only the first of a number of ugly clashes between capital and labor that would punctuate the nineties. The conflict began with a dispute over wages that reached a climax in June when the company refused to deal any further with the steelworkers' union. In an effort to destroy the union the plant manager, Henry Clay Frick, announced that he would treat the workers only on an individual basis. Anticipating trouble, Frick closed the Homestead works on July 1. With the shutdown of the plant, the workers organized to resist the importation of strikebreakers. Both sides were preparing for a prolonged and, if necessary, violent confrontation. Frick had secretly engaged some three hundred Pinkertons (private police) to protect the strikebreakers he intended to hire. In order to escape the notice of the strikers, the Pinkerton guards approached the plant

Pinkerton guards, secretly hired in 1892 to protect strikebreakers in the Homestead steelworkers' strike, were met by armed workers who had learned of the plan. *Historical Pictures Service, Chicago*

from the river side on a large barge. The incensed workers learned of the strata-gem and armed with guns, dynamite, rocks, and a small cannon met the guards at the river's edge. Shots exploded and brickbats flew from both sides, but the Pin-kertons could not break through the strikers' barrage. The battle lasted for twelve hours before the Pinkertons were finally permitted to surrender. Probably as many as nine strikers and seven Pinkerton men died; forty strikers and twenty Pin-kertons were shot. The arrival of the state militia the next day brought order and in time helped end the strike in the company's favor.

That editors of labor newspapers should vehemently upbraid the Homestead managers was to be expected, but many law-abiding and otherwise conservative observers were also alarmed by Frick's use of a private army. Even the general press, usually quite sympathetic to management during strikes, found this aspect of the strike hard to justify. All recognized that society itself was threatened when a labor dispute could escalate into a small war between private armies. Yet a sim-ilar incident of armed warfare occurred later in the month between striking miners and strikebreakers at the Coeur d'Alene silver mines in Idaho. There, too, the vio-lence reached such a pitch that troops had to be sent to the scene.

The People's Party. The very same summer that witnessed the upheaval at Homestead and the battle at Coeur d'Alene also saw the founding convention of the People's party at Omaha. Like the occurrence at Homestead, the birth of this reform party pointed a new direction for the decade. Although the People's party was intended to be a coalition of workers and farmers, its principal impetus was a decade of agrarian discontent. To be sure, a few urban labor leaders like Eugene V. Debs of the railroad workers and Terence V. Powderly of the Knights of Labor rallied to the support of the new party, but the platform adopted in 1892 at Omaha amply demonstrated that the interests and problems of farmers dominated. In-deed, the principal demands were concrete responses to the farmers' long-standing complaints. Thus, one plank in the platform—advocating government ownership of the nation's railroad, telegraph, and telephone networks—was intended to rem-edy the high cost of shipping farm products. Two others, the demand for the "free and unlimited coinage of silver" at the ratio of sixteen units of silver to one unit of gold, and the increase in the currency supply until it reached at least $50 per cap-ita, were expected to raise farm prices by inflating the currency. The Southern Alliance's subtreasury plan, by which farmers could procure government loans for stored crops, was included to meet the farmers' need for cheaper credit.

The other planks of the platform were somewhat less directly related to agri-cultural problems. A graduated income tax was expected to redistribute the na-tional income in a more equitable fashion. And another plank demanded that all land held by the railroads and corporations "in excess of their actual needs" and all land owned by aliens should be reclaimed by the government and "held for ac-tual settlers only."

In a series of resolutions not included in the platform, the convention also sup-ported such political reforms as the direct election of senators, the initiative and referendum, and a single term for President and Vice-President. The only resolutions affecting urban labor in any direct fashion were demands for restriction of "undesirable immigration" and for the improvement of laws against foreign contract labor. One resolution also opposed the use of private police in labor disputes, an obvious allusion to the Homestead lockout.

To many conservatives of the times, these economic and political goals seemed radical. The Supreme Court, for example, declared the 2-percent income tax unconstitutional in 1895, and government ownership of transportation and communications was straight out of the lexicons of socialism. Similarly, in the minds of many of the nation's respectable citizens, to advocate the free and unlimited coinage of silver was to threaten established property relations, for the enactment of such a policy would devalue savings and investments.

In retrospect, the Populists represented a break with conventional ideas in more than the details of their program. Their new conception of the role of government in the economy and their goal to end poverty constituted the significance of the movement in the nineties and later. "We believe," the platform read, "that the powers of government—in other words, of the people—should be expanded (as in the case of the postal service) as rapidly and as far as the good sense of an intelligent people and the teachings of experience shall justify, to the end that oppression, injustice, and poverty should eventually cease in the land." It is true that Republicans advocated economic growth and supported a protective tariff, but few Republicans or regular Democrats believed that the federal government should take any more vigorous action to end unemployment or influence the economy. After the Populists, government responsibility for the prosperity of the economy would be a more acceptable tenet of democratic social thought.

Prominent Populists: Emotional Reformers. The presidential candidate of the Populists in 1892 was James B. Weaver of Iowa, who had been a Republican before the Civil War because of his moral concern over slavery. Following the war, he became a Greenbacker, an allegiance that made him a link between the farmer protest movements of the 1870s and the new People's party. His running mate in 1892 was James G. Field, a former Confederate general from Virginia, whose presence symbolized the revival of the prewar alliance between southern and western farmers.

But perhaps the best-known southern Populist was Thomas E. Watson of Georgia. In the South the Populists, as the third party, ran head-on into the race question. Negro Republicans were natural allies for any third party in the Democratic South, but to accept them could frighten off white Democrats who might otherwise join the Populists. Watson, however, firmly grasped the nettle of race, proclaiming to whites and blacks: "You are kept apart that you may be separately fleeced of your earnings. You are made to hate each other because upon that hatred is rested the keystone of the arch of financial despotism which enslaves you both. You are deceived and blinded that you may not see how this race antagonism perpetuates a monetary system which beggars both." At times, such an appeal to class successfully overrode the claims of race, as when two thousand white Georgia dirt farmers defied a mob of white men who threatened to lynch a black

Populist speaker. But generally the Populists were not prepared to challenge the orthodox southern commitment to white supremacy.

While in the South some Populists like Watson dared to challenge the iron rules of white supremacy politics, in the West other Populists defied convention by encouraging women to become involved in political affairs. Undoubtedly the best known of the several women orators of Populism was fiery Mary Elizabeth Lease of Kansas, who made over 150 speeches during the campaign of 1890. Like most Populists, Lease refused to accept overproduction as a cause of the low prices farmers received for their products. How can there be overproduction, she exclaimed, "when 10,000 little children . . . starve to death every year in the United States, and over 100,000 shopgirls in New York are forced to sell their virtue for the bread their niggardly wages deny them!"

As Lease's remarks suggest, the Populists as a group were emotional rather than coldly analytical reformers. Their analyses of and solutions for the farmers' problems were often crude and inadequate. The Populists were also provincial; they usually looked no further than the American past for their guidance. They liked to see themselves as part of the radical tradition that, stretching back to Jefferson and Jackson, was devoted to the interests of "the people."

As self-conscious radicals, the Populists employed extreme language that then frightened conservatives and has since misled historians. It is true that the Populists tended to see issues in sharp black and white and to blame their plight upon conspiracies, such as the famous "Crime of '73." Richard Hofstadter, for example, emphasizes this aspect of their thought in *The Age of Reform* and further accuses them of popularizing anti-Semitic rhetoric. But as C. Vann Woodward has observed, in the 1890s suspicions and apocalyptic forebodings afflicted many groups, some of whom—like scholars and intellectuals—should have been able to rise above such fears more readily than the unsophisticated Populists. Occasionally, it is true, the Populists fell into the clichés of anti-Semitic rhetoric (as when they attacked the "international bankers"), but W. T. K. Nugent's researches into the Kansas Populists indicate that they gave no significant support to the rather widespread nativist agitation and anti-Semitic violence that flared up in the 1890s. In fact, the Populists supported immigrants for public office, and anti-Semitic comments were, at most, occasional in their literature. Moreover, Nugent's conception of the Populists as small businessmen—farmers who organized to secure better prices and more favorable marketing conditions is more convincing than Norman Pollack's portrayal of them in *The Populist Response to Industrial America* as believers in a class-conscious ideology akin to Marxism.

The Election of 1892. If the populists in the summer of 1892 thought they were destined to become a major party, most people in the nation did not. The Republicans, as might have been predicted, nominated the incumbent, Benjamin Harrison. And the name of the Democratic nominee was almost as easily foreseen. By 1892, Grover Cleveland, despite his defeat in 1888, was once again prominent in his party and the nation. Nor could the Democrats forget that he was their only winner in almost forty years. Already he had forthrightly identified himself as opposed to the rising issue of free silver, having denounced in 1891 "the dangerous and reckless experiment of free, unlimited, and independent silver coinage."

It was on the issue of the tariff that the campaign was fought, since neither party took an unambiguous position on silver. Hoping to repeat their success of 1890 the Democrats again attacked the unpopular McKinley Tariff in particular and protectionism in general. At least one prominent Republican attributed his party's defeat to its defense of that tariff. Writing to President Harrison after the election, he concluded that the people "were thoroughly imbued with the feeling that the party did not do right in revising the tariff up instead of down. They beat us for it in '90 and now again."

In comparison with the close elections of the 1880s, Cleveland's margin of 350,000 votes over Harrison in 1892 was overwhelming. Moreover, solid Republican states like Illinois, Wisconsin, and California had shifted to the Democrats; even Ohio, usually a sure thing for the Republicans, barely stayed with the party this time. Furthermore, the Populists captured the electoral votes of Kansas, Colorado, Idaho, and Nevada and nationally received over a million popular votes. It was this very good showing by a new party of dissent that foreshadowed the political developments in the rest of the decade.

Even the dissent of the substantial Populist party did not measure the full extent of the national dissatisfaction. On the surface, the victory of Cleveland seemed a triumph of conservatism. After the election, for example, Henry Clay Frick, the steel manufacturer, wrote his superior, Andrew Carnegie, "I am very sorry for President Harrison, but I cannot see that our interests are going to be affected one way or the other by the change in administration." Yet the triumph of the undoubtedly conservative Cleveland obscured the victories of a number of radical or reform Democrats in the South and West. In South Carolina one-eyed, coarse-spoken Benjamin Tillman, who later would threaten to "tickle old Grover's fat ribs" with his pitchfork, was reelected governor. In Illinois, John Peter Altgeld, a vehement supporter of organized labor, who in the next year would pardon the Haymarket anarchists, was elected governor, while in Nebraska, young, reform-minded William Jennings Bryan won a seat in Congress. Moreover, much of Cleveland's support came in spite of his conservatism. Among his backers were urban reformers and labor leaders, who distrusted Populism and hoped to make the Democratic party the vehicle of reform. Henry George advised his followers to shun Populist candidates and to support Cleveland, while President Samuel Gompers of the American Federation of Labor told organized labor that Populism and workingmen shared no fundamental aims. In essence, Cleveland's victory resulted from an unstable coalition of conservatives and reformers that could hardly be expected to endure even in tranquil times. The depression that struck soon after Cleveland's inauguration in March 1893 provided the death blow for this shaky coalition.

The key to the history of the nineties was the depression, which dominated the thought and shaped the action of the remainder of the decade. The violence and social unrest at Homestead now became simply an introduction; the reformist politics of Populism were only a suggestion of the bigger changes to come.

And the Earth Shook

The Disease of Depression. "There has never been a time in our history," President Harrison reported in his annual message in December 1892, "when work was so abundant, or when wages were so high." But by the following February, with the sudden failure of the Philadelphia and Reading Railroad, informed observers glimpsed the first sign of financial panic. By early April, as other important firms closed their doors, the signs became clear to everyone. The slide had begun. In the middle of April a precipitous drop in the stock market underscored the seriousness of the situation, and by summer the reversal in the state of the economy from the previous winter was complete. "The month of August will long remain memorable . . . in our industrial history," commented the *Commercial and Financial Chronicle.* "Never before has there been such a sudden and striking cessation of industrial activity." Nor was any section of the country exempt from the paralysis. Before the year was out, some 500 banks and nearly 16,000 business firms had sunk into bankruptcy. Samuel Gompers of the American Federation of Labor estimated the number of unemployed in December 1893 at three million. The financial panic was over, but the nation now staggered under the much heavier burdens of a full-scale depression.

The depression reached bottom during 1894. Approximately 20 percent of the labor force was without work during the winter months of 1893 – 1894; in Chicago alone, more than 100,000 men were unemployed and often without homes. In city after city police stations and other public buildings had to be opened at night to the jobless so that they might have some place to sleep. Municipal and private relief agencies strained to provide even the cheapest and simplest kinds of food for the thousands who could no longer afford to buy their own. During that terrible winter, relief expenditures in New York City alone ran as high as $5 million. For the nation as a whole, the real income of the population dropped 18 percent between 1892 and 1894. The large numbers of unemployed wandering from city to city seeking work were novel enough sights to be frightening. Popular magazines began to print anxious articles on the problem of the "tramp." When the police raided a camp of "tramps" outside of Troy, New York, they found most of the men healthy and presumably willing to work but unable to find employment. "In nearly every case," the police reported, "a wife and children had been left in some distant city." A study of the antitramp laws and ordinances that dozens of communities hastily enacted reported, "Nearly all the real tramp laws have a panicky look which suggests a pressing evil, real or imaginary."

For a time in 1895 there were indications that an upswing in business activity and employment was in the making, but in early 1896 the economy took a new tumble. In the following year people once again spoke with confidence of the nation's recovery, but not until the new century opened was the economic machinery

BUSINESS ACTIVITY, 1876-1901

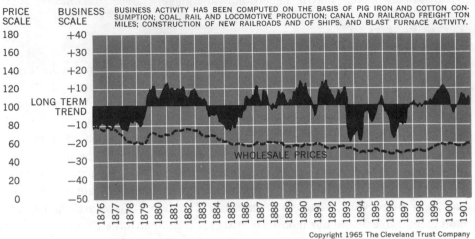

PRICE SCALE | BUSINESS SCALE | BUSINESS ACTIVITY HAS BEEN COMPUTED ON THE BASIS OF PIG IRON AND COTTON CONSUMPTION; COAL, RAIL AND LOCOMOTIVE PRODUCTION; CANAL AND RAILROAD FREIGHT TON MILES; CONSTRUCTION OF NEW RAILROADS AND OF SHIPS, AND BLAST FURNACE ACTIVITY.

The era's principal economic growth occurred during the 1880s, in contrast with the generally depressed levels of the 1870s and 1890s; however, there was some fluctuation throughout. Declining wholesale prices from 1882 to 1898 coincide with the rising farm discontent.

of the United States running smoothly again.

A Policy of Inaction. Nothing illustrates better the pervasive belief in laissez faire than the character of the public action taken to offset the impact of the depression. Businessmen and statesmen alike viewed dips in the business cycle as unfortunate, inexplicable interruptions in prosperity for which there was no government remedy and through which the nation muddled as best it could. (Only the radical Populists suggested any departure from this attitude.) As a result, when President Cleveland called Congress into special session, the only antidepression recommendation he proposed was repeal of the Sherman Silver Purchase Act of 1890. A temporarily compliant Congress quickly acceded to the President's request. The repeal did nothing to counter the depression, but it did much to alienate the many Democrats to whom the Sherman Silver Act was an important reform measure.

Placing the Blame. Several explanations for the panic were offered at the time. As Cleveland's request for repeal of the silver act made clear, each political party blamed the other. Labor ascribed the slump to capitalist greed. Some private citizens agreed with Henry Adams, who attributed it to Wall Street's "dark, mysterious, crafty, wicked, rapacious and tyrannical power . . . to rob and oppress and enslave the people."

In fact, the explanation was at once more obvious and less immediate. The depression had long been in the making; the bankruptcy of a few prominent companies simply acted as the trigger. One of the important causes was the inevitable decline of the railroad construction boom that had been going on since the early

1880s. The subsequent reduction in the number of orders for rails, steel, and other machinery brought about a contraction which soon spread to other industries. The chronically depressed state of agriculture offered no counterweight and may actually have aggravated the fall in demand. Moreover, European investors, hard hit by their own financial panic, that started in 1890, had begun to withdraw capital from the United States. In the single year of 1892, for example, $50 million in gold left the country.

Marches of Protest: The "Industrial Armies." The depression sparked a kind of labor unrest and class antagonism that had been seen only occasionally before, as at Homestead in 1892 and in the violent railroad disputes of 1877. To contemporaries, perhaps the most convincing measure of the discontent in the working class was the several "armies" of unemployed that marched on Washington in 1894, seeking jobs and relief. The idea apparently originated with a self-made Ohio businessman, a former Greenbacker and Populist named Jacob S. Coxey. A radical, Coxey believed that the government bore a responsibility for unemployment and should provide funds to put men to work building roads. When told that his idea could not get a hearing in Washington, he boldly responded, "We will send a petition to Washington with boots on." Coxey's little army of a hundred men left his home town of Massillon, Ohio, at the end of March 1894 bound for

Coxey's army of the unemployed is bound for Washington in 1894 to present a petition for the government to employ the jobless in road construction. *Library of Congress*

the nation's capital. Along the way, several hundred more volunteers joined him, although the trip was certainly no lark; on crossing the Allegheny Mountains, the straggling army was engulfed in a severe snowstorm. When the five hundred marchers arrived in Washington, police were so unnerved by the spectacle that they attacked them with clubs, injuring about fifty people, including some by-standers. Coxey and two other leaders were arrested for illegally carrying banners on the Capitol grounds and for walking on the grass.

The shameful attack upon Coxey's army and the inglorious ending to its march were only the beginning of the industrial army movement. Having struck a hopeful note in the midst of working-class despair, the idea spread. All told, per-haps seventeen industrial armies set out in 1894 from various localities around the country to present petitions "with boots on." Two or three were considerably larger than Coxey's; one on the West Coast mobilized as many as five thousand men. The larger armies were able to commandeer trains and throw scares into the small towns through which they passed. But what conservatives found most surprising about the armies was not the number of marchers nor even their actu-al behavior, reprehensible as it was thought to be. The real revelation was the evident sympathy they received along the way. "I am beginning to feel that the movement has some meaning," wrote journalist Ray Stannard Baker after fol-lowing Coxey's army for a few days, "that it is a manifestation of the prevailing unrest and dissatisfaction among the labor class. When such an ugly and gro-tesque fungus can grow out so prominently on the body politic there must be something wrong."

The Pullman Strike. If the largely peaceful marches of the unemployed did not convince some people that "something was wrong," the violence that accom-panied strikes in 1894 certainly did. Like 1886, the year 1894 witnessed a new high in the number of strikes, some of which attracted national attention. All told, some 1400 industrial strikes were called in that single year, involving over 500,000 workers—the largest number in the entire nineteenth century. Since the workers' right to strike was only reluctantly conceded in those days, violence often erupted in the course of a work stoppage. A strike of 125,000 mineworkers in Illinois, for example, lasting for what was then the relatively short length of time of eight weeks, still required the militia to preserve order.

Born of the depression, the strike on the railroads in 1894 aroused the nation and dramatized, as did no other labor dispute of the century, the new concerns of an industrial society. The Pullman Palace Car Company, against which the strike was first called, maintained the town of Pullman, located just outside Chicago. George Pullman, the company's founder, had built the town as a model of work-ingmen's housing.

The solid brick homes of the workers were commodious; the town itself was well planned, generously supplied with public services, and blessed with one of the lowest death rates in the nation. It represented an investment of $8 million by George Pullman. When the depression hit, Pullman cut the wages of employees several times in order, he claimed, to avoid the alternative of wholesale dismissals.

He did not, however, reduce the rents, though rents in Pullman had always been higher than in surrounding towns. Confronted by the continuing high rents, the workers formed a union to protest the wage cuts. The company refused to consider the rents as a proper matter for discussion and justified the wage cuts on the grounds of bad times. When the strike came, Pullman promptly closed his plant and waited for the workers to capitulate.

But the workers held on, despite increasing destitution and much suffering. Their plight attracted the attention of other workers' organizations in the Chicago area, including the newly formed American Railway Union (ARU). Just that previous spring the ARU had won a spectacular victory against James J. Hill's formidable Great Northern Railroad in a strike lasting only eighteen days. Proud of their quick and substantial victory, the leaders of the ARU—especially its young organizer and president, Eugene V. Debs—hoped to stay free of the Pullman strike, which could only strain their depleted treasury. But the rank and file, sympathizing with the hard-pressed Pullman workers' families, voted not to handle any Pullman sleepers. The other railroads, rather than participate in the boycott of a fellow company, promptly discharged all ARU employees who took part in the boycott. The ARU then, with equal alacrity, called work stoppages against all offending companies. By the end of June 1894 some twenty thousand railroad men were on strike in and around Chicago. Eventually, the economic effects of the strike would be felt in twenty-seven states.

A strike of such magnitude in the most important rail center of the nation could not fail to arouse the concern of the federal government. In fact, men high in the Cleveland administration, such as Attorney General Richard Olney, were very much interested, and federal officers in Chicago were instructed to be alert for any activities which might require federal intervention. The ARU well understood from experience in the Great Northern strike of a few months before that an interruption in the movement of the mails might easily bring in the federal government. For several days the discipline of the strikers averted any incidents; the mails moved unhampered. At the same time, the railroad companies appealed to the federal court, from which they secured an injunction against the strikers on the grounds that the strike constituted just the kind of restraint of trade that the Sherman Antitrust Act forbade. That same day, July 3, by coincidence, rioting broke out along one of the railway lines running to Chicago; cars were overturned and pushed athwart the tracks. One of the derailed trains was carrying United States mail. The federal government now had the incident it needed.

Federal Intervention. On July 4 two thousand federal soldiers arrived in Chicago to break the strike. Their arrival set off an orgy of violence, looting, burning of railway cars, and shooting. More than twenty people were killed and two thousand railway cars destroyed before order was restored. Even after quiet returned, Chicago remained an armed camp, with fourteen thousand state and federal troops stationed in and around the city. Debs and other ARU leaders were arrested, convicted of contempt of court for violating the injunction, and sentenced to between six months and a year in jail.

The consequences of the strike were significant. The case of the convicted ARU leaders, when carried to the Supreme Court of the United States in *U.S.* v. *Debs* (1894), became a landmark in labor history. The high court agreed that an injunction such as was issued against the strikers was a legitimate device for the protection of interstate commerce and the mails. For the next thirty years the court injunction remained a powerful weapon in the hands of employers threatened with a strike. "Government by injunction," friends of labor bitterly called the practice. Not until 1932 was organized labor able to induce Congress to pass the Norris–La Guardia Act, which limited the federal courts' authority to use the injunction in labor disputes.

The crushing of the strike by the federal government also meant the end of the promising American Railway Union and its experiment in industrial unionism. Moreover, the apparent cooperation between industry and government which Debs saw in the breaking of the strike was probably the most influential factor in his conversion to Socialism. For the next quarter of a century he was the best-known Socialist leader in the United States; in 1912 as Socialist candidate for President he received more votes than any other Socialist in the history of the Republic.

Although most Americans who resented the antilabor action of the Cleveland administration did not become Socialists, virtually all of them now declared war on the administration. John Peter Altgeld, the governor of Illinois whom Cleveland had ignored when federal troops were sent into Chicago, was infuriated by the administration's actions. As a friend of labor, Altgeld opposed government intervention which helped the employers; as a governor, he opposed the sending of federal troops, which he had not requested, as a violation of his constitutional prerogative. Despite the fact that he was a businessman of some wealth, Altgeld now became one of the Democratic party's most vociferous and uncompromising critics of the Cleveland administration.

Revolution in Politics: Act I

In the political history of the United States, the nineties are significant because during this decade the political parties caught up with the Economic Revolution. The resulting realignment of parties and voters not only made the Republicans the majority party of the nation for the first time but set the stage for the social and economic reforms of the twentieth century. This transformation in politics occurred in three steps. The first was the repudiation of the conservative leadership of Grover Cleveland.

The depression, climaxing a decade of mounting agrarian discontent, put the new Cleveland administration to tests that its conservative outlook could not meet. Men like Secretary of the Treasury John G. Carlisle and Richard Olney, the Attorney General and later Secretary of State, were competent and experienced, but, like Cleveland, they proved unequal to the demands of the new age of cities, factories, and political dissatisfaction. It was Carlisle, for example, who encouraged the President to uphold the gold standard—that is, to redeem in gold all paper money upon demand. The principle came in for severe testing as the financial panic, first in Europe and then in the United States, caused nervous holders of United States notes to exchange them for gold, a practice that steadily depleted the Treasury's reserves. By January 1894 the gold reserve had fallen to $62 million, though $100 million had long been regarded as the lowest safe figure.

Saving the Gold Standard—At a Price. Cleveland's determination to keep the country on gold was not shared by Congress, which preferred a bimetallic standard of gold and silver. As a result, Congress would not grant the administration the necessary powers to replenish the gold reserves through long-term borrowing or by any other device suggested by the President. In February 1895, after trying several ineffective means of stopping the drain, the administration turned in desperation to the banking houses of J. P. Morgan and August Belmont, which, for a sizable profit to themselves, obtained gold from abroad. Although this unprecedented measure did not immediately halt the drain, the cumulative and persistent efforts of the administration did, and as public confidence in the government's paper money returned, fewer and fewer bills were presented for redemption. By January 1896 it was evident that the gold standard had been saved.

But was it worth the strenuous effort? Although Cleveland never doubted that he had done the right thing, he could not help but recognize that it cost him the support of the majority of his party. To many Democrats and free-silver backers, his policy was nothing less than subservience to the interests of bankers, financiers, and creditors at the expense of the other classes of society. As the free-silver backers pointed out, silver coin could have been used at any time to redeem United States notes (currency), but the Treasury, intent upon adhering to the gold standard, met all demands for redemption of paper currency only with gold. Had silver been paid out along with gold, it is uncertain that the disastrous consequence of runaway inflation, freely predicted by the gold advocates, would have occurred. After all, when the dollar was greatly devalued in the 1930s, there was almost no effect on prices or business activity; a similar devaluation through the introduction of silver into the monetary system in the 1890s—also a time of severe deflation—would probably have been no more disastrous. The real problem in the 1890s was how to maintain the circulation of both gold and silver when the former was overvalued and hence tended to be hoarded. In short, precious metals were not a sufficiently flexible base for a monetary supply in a modern industrial economy.

The policy that the administration followed was the worst possible in a depression. To preserve the gold standard, the Treasury in effect contracted the money supply just when the economy needed an expanding one to lift itself out of the depression. The Treasury's policy permitted domestic hoarding and exportation of gold, thus removing it from circulation. At the same time, paper money went into the Treasury, where, in order to avoid repeated redemptions, it was held as long as possible, thereby further contracting the currency supply. Finally, since gold was being hoarded and exported, bank reserves fell, thus further reducing the money available for loans and circulation. In sum, in saving the gold standard, the expansion of the economy was seriously curtailed and recovery from the depression undoubtedly hampered—just as the free-silver backers had predicted.

The Wilson-Gorman Tariff: A Failure in Presidential Leadership. In the gold crisis, it was triumph that hurt Cleveland; in his efforts to reduce the tariff, it was his failure that would be held against him. That he should suffer in both instances reveals once again how out of touch he and his administration were with the political developments growing out of the Economic Revolution.

During his first term, it will be recalled, Cleveland boldly proclaimed himself an advocate of tariff reduction. The subsequent disaster which the high McKinley Tariff brought upon the Republicans in 1890 gave additional reasons for expecting that the Cleveland administration would do its best to reduce the tariff. A bill to do just that, and add some raw materials to the free list, was promptly introduced on behalf of the administration by Congressman William Wilson. The Democratic House quickly and overwhelmingly passed it, though not before a modest tax on incomes had been tacked on at the insistence of the radicals in the party. The trouble came in the Senate, where the Democratic majority was small and disunited on the issue of downward revision. Several of those who refused to support the President came from the New South (that is, the industrialized South), which was interested in securing some protection for its infant industries. As a result, the Senate added approximately six hundred amendments to the House bill, turning it into the usual tariff, in which all well-organized special interests got some protection. As finally passed, the Wilson-Gorman Tariff reduced the schedules only slightly, to 41 percent from the 49 percent of the McKinley Act. The bill repudiated both the party's campaign pledge for reduction and the President's leadership. Cleveland, recognizing the lack of any practical alternative, let it become law without his signature.

It was evident that in the new age of industry not even the Democratic party could be depended upon to reduce the tariff. Chief responsibility for the high duties, after all, lay with Democratic Senator A. P. Gorman of Maryland, who had led the fight in the Senate to raise the duties and then successfully maneuvered behind the scenes to prevent the House from rejecting them.

Interestingly, the one section of the bill that emerged unscathed from the Senate's surgery was the provision for an income tax of 2 percent on all incomes over $4000. Cleveland had been willing to accept the tax in order to secure the necessary votes in the House from the radicals and reformers, who supported the measure. In 1895, however, the income tax was struck down by the Supreme Court as a violation of the constitutional provision requiring that any direct tax be apportioned among the states according to population. The action of the Court was more a reflection of the anxieties of conservatives in the nineties than a result of pure constitutional principles; as recently as 1881 the very same court, in *Springer v. Illinois,* had upheld the constitutionality of an income tax. Moreover, during the Civil War the Lincoln administration had used such a tax as one of its several wartime fiscal devices. Now the nation would have to wait nearly twenty years longer before a constitutional amendment would make it possible to tap the wealth being amassed by the Economic Revolution.

Revolution in Politics: Act II

Shift to the Republicans. The crowning rebuff to, and the most dramatic failure of, the conservative Democrats came in the Congressional elections of 1894. During the fight over the gold standard Cleveland lost the support of a large segment of his party; in the tariff battle he lost control of his party in Congress; and in the election of 1894 he found that he had lost the support of the nation. The transfer of seats that year from the Democratic to the Republican side of the House was the largest in history; the Republicans now gloried in an unprecedented majority of 132. Prominent Democrats like William Wilson of West Virginia, William Springer of Illinois, and Richard Bland of Missouri lost their seats. In twenty-four states not a single Democrat was elected, and in each of six others only one Democrat was returned. Without the ever faithful and solid South, Democratic strength would have been almost wiped out. As it was, border states such as Delaware, Maryland, West Virginia, and Missouri either went Republican entirely or elected more Republicans than Democrats to the House. Old Democratic strongholds outside the South, like Indiana, Connecticut, and New Jersey, sent to Congress more Republicans than Democrats.

Impressed with the excitement of the presidential election of 1896, historians have underestimated the importance of the Congressional elections two years before. The defeat of the Democrats in 1896 comes as no surprise once the tremendous popular switch to the Republicans in 1894 is recognized. Indeed, as we shall see later, the twin Republican victories in 1894 and 1896 mark one of the great divides in American political history.

The immediate cause for Republican victory in 1894 was the depression. As usual, Americans blamed hard times on the party in power and acted accordingly. Yet it was not simply a victory by default, for the Populists, the third party in the field, did not benefit much from the Democratic losses. Although the total Populist vote increased by almost 400,000 over the 1892 returns, the party managed to send just four senators and four representatives to Congress. Only in Nebraska and North Carolina did the Populists win as much as 48 percent of the vote, and even that degree of success was achieved solely through fusion with the Republicans. Four western states, Kansas, Colorado, North Dakota, and Idaho, all of which had been Populist in 1892, went Republican in 1894. As John Hicks, the historian of Populism, has pointed out, not a single state in 1894 could any longer be called Populist. Thus, rather than accepting any available alternative, the voters seem to have turned deliberately to the Grand Old Party. The reasons for this new support for the Republican party will be discussed later in conjunction with the election of 1896.

By 1895 Cleveland and his administration were almost bereft of support in the country. Ardent "gold bugs" and spokesmen for the old Mugwumps, such as *Harper's Weekly* and E. L. Godkin's *New York Evening Post,* still vigorously supported the President, cherishing him as a champion of clean government and sound money, but the country at large rejected him. His mail, a biographer has noted, shrank to "less than that of an ordinary business man." In February 1895 Cleveland himself expressed his isolation to a close political friend, "Think of it! Not a man in the Senate with whom I can be on terms of absolute confidence. . . . Not one of them comes to me on public business unless sent for and then full of recrimination and doubts." Yet he continued to speak out in favor of the gold standard, the very issue provoking the mounting opposition to his administration.

Free Silver: Key Issue. For Americans living in the second half of the twentieth century, it is hard to fathom the central place the issue of free coinage of silver came to occupy in the politics of the 1890s. Today the gold standard for which Cleveland and afterwards the Republicans battled no longer exists; it was abandoned in the course of the Great Depression of the 1930s without any of the dire consequences predicted by the advocates of gold in the 1890s. On the other hand, it is evident that victory for free silver in the nineties certainly would not have ushered in the millennium foreseen by the silver backers. In short, both sides exaggerated the importance of the currency issue—but that is not to say it was contrived or unimportant.

On one level, the silver problem was symbolic. Western and southern reformers saw reflected in it their hopes for an improved society, based upon government concern for the welfare of the ordinary citizen. This was true even though free silver could not have achieved all that the Populists and silver Democrats wanted. Insofar as it involved government interference in the economy through the manipulation of the currency, it symbolized the drive for broader reforms. Conversely, free silver represented everything abhorrent to the conservatives of the day: It threatened established ways of operating the economy; it promised to isolate the United States from the financial affairs of the principal nations of Europe; and it sought to redefine the proper role of government in the economy. As a symbol, the issue of free silver was important; moreover, free silver was an answer to a problem not clearly recognized by either side.

The issue that lay behind the demand for free silver had engaged political attention since the seventeenth century. In a new country like the United States, overflowing with natural resources and opportunities for economic gain, business expansion required a currency supply that would grow along with it. During the colonial period and down to the Civil War, paper in the form of notes issued by banks under more or less public regulation had answered the need for a large and growing supply of money. The one difficulty with paper money, as the hard-money Jacksonians among others had pointed out, was that it fluctuated in value, depending on the degree to which it was "backed"—that is, convertible into gold or silver. In order to remedy this defect of unstable value, the National Banking Act was passed during the Civil War. Under that act and others, the primary circulating medium became paper money backed by bonds of the federal government. Since the bonds were payable in gold, the act, in effect, made the currency a gold-backed one.

While this strong backing of the banknotes virtually guaranteed that there would be no depreciation, it effectively placed a limit on the quantity of currency because the volume of notes issued was now tied to the dollar value of outstanding government bonds. Hence the amount of money in circulation, instead of being responsive to the needs of the economy as it should have been, was determined by the federal government's need to borrow funds, a factor quite irrelevant to the monetary needs of the economy. During part of the Civil War and immediately thereafter, this restrictive aspect of the National Banking Act was mitigated by the issuance of additional currency without any backing—the well-known greenbacks. Within four years after the Resumption of Specie Act of 1875, however, the greenbacks became both convertible into gold and fixed in amount.

By the decade of the nineties, then, the currency was inflexible in amount and unresponsive to the needs of the economy. Indeed, because the supply of currency could increase only as the amount of government bonds did, the money supply varied in reverse of the ideal. It was during times when business was expanding and the demand for money was greatest that the government would most likely retire some of its debt—that is, pay off some of its bonds. Such a retirement of the debt, however, would compel the National Banks to reduce their issues of paper money, since they had to be backed by bonds. For this reason, among others, the Populists and backers of cheap money in general objected to the National Banks. Fortunately for the well-being of the economy, the constrictive effects of this inverse elasticity of the currency were offset by an increasing use of checks and bank deposits as money.

In Search of a Flexible but Stable Monetary Supply. The cheap-money backers not only complained about the rigidity of the money supply but also blamed it for the decline in prices during the 1880s and 1890s. A decline in prices, by definition, means an *appreciation* in the value of money, for as prices of goods fall, each dollar purchases more goods—hence, it is worth more. Free silverites blamed the fall in prices and subsequent appreciation of the dollar on the scarcity of money, arguing that money, like any other commodity, rose in value when there was not enough of it to satisfy the demand. Greenbackers, free silverites, and inflationists in general all agreed that the low prices on farm products were the result of an insufficient supply of money. (Actually, this reasoning is valid neither in theory nor in fact. An increase in the supply of agricultural commodities, for example, would cause a fall in prices regardless of whether or not the money supply was adequate.)

What really disturbed the inflationists was that a dollar that increased in value in this fashion was inherently as unfair as one that depreciated, though the gold advocates confined their expressions of horror to the dollar that *declined* in purchasing power. Where you stood in the credit relationship determined which you preferred, appreciation or depreciation. A farmer who borrowed—and most did—was severely hurt by an appreciating dollar. If wheat, for example, was selling at $1 a bushel when he borrowed money and then fell to 75 cents at the time he was to repay the loan, the farmer would have to sell an additional third of a bushel for each dollar to be repaid. For this reason William Jennings Bryan referred to the gold standard as establishing a "dishonest dollar."

Despite the acuteness of the problems that the monetary policy of the United States presented to farmers and other debtors, the free coinage of silver was both an inept and inadequate remedy. For one thing, using silver as backing for paper money was little more than a tactical move by those who wanted inflation but were not prepared to go to the extreme of advocating fiat money or greenbacks. Logically, the same arguments of a limited supply that were brought against gold could be laid against silver: It was no more responsive in amount to the needs of business conditions than was gold. In addition, a silver dollar (highly overvalued) as it would have been at the silverites' preferred ratio of sixteen to one with gold) would have driven gold into hoarding, thus reducing the money supply anyway. Finally, the underlying weakness of the free-silver position was that no one, professional economist or Populist dirt farmer, understood what is well known today—namely, that government by its own action can issue money, unrelated to its stock of gold or silver.

Yet there were aspects of the silverites' case that were eminently sound and worthy of consideration. One was their demand for a monetary supply that fluctuated in amount in accordance with the needs of business and yet was stable in value. In fact, events after 1896 generally bore out the silverites' contention by bringing about the kind of monetary system they favored. New discoveries of gold in the late 1890s increased the money supply and helped raise prices. Even more important was the establishment of the Federal Reserve System in 1913, which introduced the kind of flexible and responsive monetary and banking system the farmers and Populists had been demanding for so long. Nor is it an accident that after 1913 the long debate on currency and banking that had persisted throughout previous American history finally came to an end. With the Federal Reserve System, both sides in the historical debate received recognition in law and in the nation's banking institutions: A fairly stable value for the dollar was combined with a banking system that ensured a money supply responsive to changes in business activity.

Because the nature of the money supply affected everyone, the issue of free silver swallowed up all others as the election of 1896 approached. A voter's position on a host of measures, in effect, was represented by his stand on silver. Increasingly, in the eyes of Populists and many anti-Cleveland Democrats, belief in the wonder-working properties of free silver became the test of a true reformer. But this equation between free silver and reform turned out to be disastrous for the success of economic and political reform. As the election was to demonstrate, not all those who were dissatisfied with Cleveland and the status quo accepted free silver; when free-silver advocates succeeded in tying their cause to reform in general, the reform forces split apart. And all went down to defeat at the hands of the Republicans.

From both sides of the debate flowed tracts, articles, books, and speeches in an almost constant stream right down to the election. Perhaps the best known was W. H. Harvey's *Coin's Financial School* (1894), which brought the cause of silver into literally millions of homes, shops, and farmers' clubs across the country. The gold forces were able to draw upon more sophisticated sources of support, principally professional economists and bankers. "Coin" Harvey's clever pamphlet was an effective counterargument. Exchanges between the gold advocates and silverites were usually heated, cutting, and laced with a degree of class consciousness rarely found in American political discourse. In the East, where the gold standard was orthodox, some college professors were dismissed for supporting free silver, while in the western, free-silver states, Populist legislatures took similar action against conservative professors who defended the gold standard. Even friendships and households were known to be disrupted by the money question.

Revolution in Politics: Act III

Free Silver and the Election of 1896. The way in which the silver issue enveloped all other reforms was best illustrated by the behavior of the Populist party in 1896. Populism, as the platform of 1892 made evident, stood for a reform program considerably broader than free silver, but many of the party members and leaders regarded the broad national interest in currency reform as a rare opportunity to unite all radicals and reformers in a common bid for power. Hence, when the Democratic party in the summer of 1896 nominated a fervent western silverite, William Jennings Bryan, as its presidential candidate, many Populists eagerly embraced him as their own.

But not all did so. Some of the more radical or fundamentally reformist Populists, like Thomas Watson of Georgia and Henry D. Lloyd of Illinois, thought that to nominate Bryan would be to sell out the broader Populist program for a mess of silver. But Populist leaders like Senator Marion Butler of North Carolina, who were as dedicated to reform as Lloyd or Watson, thought the party had no practical alternative. By the summer of 1896 the primary symbol of agrarian-sponsored reform was free silver; whether that was a good symbol or not did not matter. If the reform forces were to unite against the Republicans, it would have to be on free silver or nothing. And it was clear that free silver had captured the Democratic party. Certainly a separate Populist candidate would have won no more votes than Bryan did, and there is good reason to believe that he could not have polled as many. The Populists, it is true, did make a gesture of independence by naming Thomas Watson as their vice-presidential candidate while accepting the Democratic Bryan as the leader of their ticket. But with that gesture the Populist party in effect committed suicide, apparently prepared to sacrifice itself for a union of reform forces. The election was between the Democrats and the Republicans, who had already nominated Governor William McKinley of Ohio as their candidate. Although McKinley had never been a strong gold man, under the tutelage of his campaign manager, industrialist

Marcus Hanna, he espoused that cause, thus drawing the lines that shaped the campaign.

No election since 1860 had aroused the enthusiasm and passion of this one. Bryan, probably the finest orator of his day, traveled more than eighteen thousand miles in almost two dozen states to deliver over six hundred speeches. Five million people, it was estimated, heard his powerful and apparently tireless voice, a number that would not be approached again until the advent of radio and television. McKinley, on the other hand, stayed at home in Canton, Ohio, receiving visitors and making speeches from his front porch under the careful arrangements and supervision of Hanna. The immobility of the Republican candidate was well compensated for by the whirlwind campaign of the party machine throughout the country. It kept up a constant barrage of speeches and literature on behalf of the Republican doctrines of a high tariff and a gold standard, which were alleged to be the principal sources of high wages and business prosperity. At the same time, it blamed the Democrats for the depression in 1893 and warned of an even worse disaster with free silver. The Republicans enjoyed an enormous campaign fund, drawn from the treasuries of businessmen fearful of a panic if Bryan was elected. Two large contributors, Standard Oil and J. P. Morgan, for example, gave $500,000 between them, more than the total campaign fund of Bryan. Before the campaign was over, Hanna was returning unneeded contributions.

By the end of October, despite Bryan's herculean speaking efforts and the enormous enthusiasm his oratory almost invariably evoked, especially in rural districts, Mark Hanna was confident of victory. Returning a campaign contribution, he wrote, "It is all over. Reports are satisfactory just where we wanted them most." Some businessmen, however, were not so sanguine or confident. In many factories and shops the word was passed that if Bryan were elected, there would be no work the next day. It is hard to believe that these threats were either widespread or effective enough to have influenced the election results, but they do attest to the intense feelings aroused by the campaign. ("By defeating Mr. Bryan," wrote an editor of *Harper's Weekly* after the event, "the country has escaped an actual experiment in Socialism.")

The high popular interest in the campaign was also measured by the huge vote. Although Bryan lost by 600,000 votes, his total of 6.5 million was larger than that received by any candidate in any previous election. On the other hand, he ran farther behind the winner than any candidate of a major party since Grant's victory over Greeley in 1872. Bryan's energetic campaigning undoubtedly brought out voters who had never bothered to cast a ballot before, but the increase did not necessarily add to his total. The vote for Bryan was smaller than the combined vote for Cleveland and Weaver in 1892; yet in 1896 Bryan was the Populist as well as the Democratic candidate. Bryan's strength was concentrated in the South and the West, but only in the old Populist portions. He lost California and Oregon and proved to be weak in the older agricultural states; he was defeated in Minnesota, Iowa, Wisconsin, and Illinois. In these middle-western states agriculture was less dependent on a single crop than in the plains states; the farmers could balance an adverse world market price for their corn or wheat with dairying and hog raising. In this more secure position, they were less radical than the plains farmers. As one historian has observed, "a high degree of farm ownership" in a state tended to make it Republican; farm tenancy, on the other hand, inclined a state toward Bryan. To see Bryan as the spokesman of farmers everywhere, then, is to exaggerate the social basis of his support; thousands of farmers in the older areas of the East and the West rejected him in 1896 as they had rejected Populism four years before.

Triumph of the City. The really decisive reason for Bryan's defeat should have been apparent from the start: He could not capture the votes of the cities or of industrial labor. It was all very well for farmers and small businessmen to like a little inflation as a stimulus to business, but to workers with a fixed income free silver and inflation meant a rising cost of living. Moreover, insofar as urban white-collar and professional workers were holders of bank accounts and insurance policies, they were creditors, to whom cheap money was anathema. Mark Hanna sensed the limited appeal of free silver early in the campaign. Referring to Bryan, he wrote, "He's talking silver all the time, and that's where we've got him."

And they did! The cities, where the industrial workers were concentrated, voted overwhelmingly Republican. Only twelve of the eighty-two cities with a population of 45,000 or more supported Bryan, and of those twelve, seven were in the Democratic stronghold of the South, and two more were located in the silver-producing states. For the first time the Republicans made substantial gains in the cities of the Middle West. In the industrial East, Bryan's cause was hopeless; he did not carry a single county in all of New England and only one in New York. He even lost usually Democratic New York City. Strong evidence indicates that McKinley successfully appealed to urban immigrants, who responded to the Republican's "full dinner pail" campaign. Nor did urban voters forget that the depression had come under a democratic regime.

Bryan, regardless of his talk about the unity of farmers and workers, was unable to make himself the spokesman of the industrial discontent that permeated the nation's working class. McKinley came closer. Both Hanna and McKinley, for example, had good labor records. Hanna had been conspicuous in urging George Pullman to arbitrate his labor dispute in 1894; McKinley as governor had supported several labor measures and had contributed to relief funds for the unemployed during the depression of 1893. In short, the Republicans, by appealing to immigrants and urban workers in general, were dealing realistically with the new America. The Democrats and Populists were not; by making their principal pleas to the rural population, they misjudged the direction in which the country was moving. By the nineties, political decisions were being made in the cities. In 1896 the decision went to the party that had frankly identified itself with the achievements of the Economic Revolution.

Actually, the shift had been under way for some time. As we have seen, in the 1880s neither party had been the favorite of the voters; hence presidential elections had been close and without continuity for either party. Before the depression of

1893 it appeared that the long-term popularity of the Democrats would swing the nation in the nineties behind the party of Jackson and Jefferson, leaving the Republicans permanently in the minority. The depression, however, changed that, for in 1894 there began a massive swing to the Republicans, which was confirmed in 1896 with the defeat of Bryan.

Recently some historians, notably Paul Kleppner and Richard Jensen, have provided evidence of a cultural explanation for the political shift of the mid-nineties. They point out that particularly in the Middle West the Republican party was strongly supported by native-born, Protestant voters who were of an evangelical and moralistic outlook, such as Methodists, Baptists, and some Lutherans. It was because of this association that Republicans were heavily represented in moralistic reforms like antislavery and temperance. The Democrats in the 1880s, on the other hand, tended to be less moralistic and more ritualistic in religion, being Roman Catholic, Presbyterian, or traditional Lutheran. The Democrats, as a result, were more likely than Republicans to attract immigrant voters, many of whom were Roman Catholic, and who did not like restrictions on drinking liquor or beer.

What happened in the mid-nineties, according to this cultural explanation, was that the Republicans sought to attract immigrant voters by abandoning the moralistic causes and outlook that had cost them votes in local elections during the 1880s. On the other hand, the moralistic, free-silver appeals of a teetotaler like William Jennings Bryan brought many pietistic Protestants into his camp. At the same time many more Democrats, alienated by the moralistic tone assumed by fellow Democrats, voted instead for McKinley. (Although few Irish deserted the Democrats, it is known that many Germans did.) This cultural-ethnic explanation is not sufficient in itself to account for the reversal in 1894–1896, for the depression was probably of central importance. Yet economic considerations were clearly not the only ones; ethnic and cultural divisions helped shape voters' preferences in the 1890s as they continue to do today.

Republican Mandate. What makes the 1894 and 1896 victories significant is that from then on Republican victory became a habit. For the next sixteen years and without interruption, the Republican party captured the House of Representatives by large majorities as well as the Presidency by heavy popular votes. Indeed, one might look upon the election of Woodrow Wilson—with only a minority of the popular vote—and a Democratic Congress in 1912 and 1916 as exceptions, for Republican ascendancy continued until 1932, when another revolution in American politics occurred. For this reason, the elections of 1894 and 1896 constitute a watershed. Not only had the indecisive era of American party politics ended, but a new era of Republican influence had begun. The shift also was a clear sign of the political consequences of the growth of the city and the factory, for the Republican ascendancy then and later was dependent on changes wrought by the Economic Revolution. San Francisco, Columbus, Detroit, St. Paul, and other cities, all regularly Democratic in the 1880s, voted Republican in 1896 and remained Republican until well into the twentieth century. On the other hand, none of the large cities that had been Republican in the 1880s and early 1890s changed party affiliation in 1896 or for many years thereafter. It is not surprising, either, that some of the earliest Progressives of the twentieth century, like Theodore Roosevelt and Robert M. LaFollette, were Republicans. They epitomized the party's recognition that politics and government must come to terms with the new voters and issues raised by the Economic Revolution.

Although the Populist party never recovered from its fusion with the Democrats in 1896, it could take comfort in knowing that a large part of its program of 1892 was enacted in the next decade. In fact, the Populists helped set the goals of the Progressive movement of the early twentieth century. By 1920 the direct election of senators, the income tax, adequate railroad regulation—but not government ownership—the initiative and referendum, postal savings banks, and even a form of the subtreasury plan had all been written into law.

After the defeat of Bryan, agrarian agitation for cheap money was rarely heard again, but the reasons for the silence stemmed from economic change, not political defeat. Agricultural and other prices began to rise in 1897 and 1898, thus forestalling a revival of the farmers' demand for inflation. Several reasons probably account for the improvement in agricultural prices. The growing urban population in the United States and Europe raised the demand for agricultural commodities at the same time that poor wheat crops in India and Europe in 1896 and 1897 reduced the world supply. Another factor was the increase in the world's gold supply. Discoveries of gold in the Klondike region of Alaska, in Australia, and in South Africa, as well as the introduction of the new cyanide process of extraction that permitted lower-grade ores to be used, raised prices by reducing the cost of gold through an increase in its supply. In 1899 the world's annual production of gold was almost two and one half times what it had been in 1891.

Events, in short, proved both sides in the bitter and hard-fought campaign to have been poor prophets. Contrary to the forebodings of Democratic and Populist orators, the triumph of the gold bugs did not result in ruin for the common person. Instead, farmers after 1898 actually entered upon a period of prosperity such as they had not enjoyed in two generations. But the gold advocates also had their false conceptions, for events demonstrated that their favorite monetary metal could inflate the currency as readily as silver.

Removal of Blacks from Southern Politics

A final and significant measure of the degree to which the 1890s marked a new era in the life of the nation was the disfranchisement of blacks in the South. When President Hayes withdrew the last troops from the southern states in 1877, the conservative Democratic regimes that came to power did not insist upon the disfranchisement of blacks, but were determined only to prevent them from challenging the white Democrats' control of the states. As a result, the 1880s and much of the 1890s witnessed large numbers of blacks voting in most southern states, holding minor political offices, and sitting in state legislatures, which usually represented lopsidedly black districts. A few southern states like North Carolina, Mississippi, and South Carolina even sent black congressmen to Washington during these years, the last of whom finished his term in 1901.

This limited participation of blacks in southern politics came to an abrupt end in the 1890s for several reasons. The rivalry between Populists and Democrats in the 1890s suddenly revived the southern whites' old Reconstruction-born fear of Negro domination. When white candidates competed for black votes, as occurred in the 1890s, the Negro held the balance of power. By removing them from politics, it was argued, the fear of black rule would be ended, thus permitting whites to enjoy the benefits of a two-party system. Disfranchisement was defended, too, on the ground that white supremacy deserved to be supported legally, without resort to fraud and violence. There were class as well as racial reasons, for disenfranchisement. As Morgan Kousser has recently shown, the removal of blacks from the voting lists would ensure upper-class domination of the Democratic party in the southern states by making a political alliance between poor white farmers and poor black farmers impossible. Moreover, the disenfranchisement devices removed many white voters as well, for illiteracy and

Blacks serving in the 41st and 42nd Congress during Reconstruction included (l-r): Sen. H. R. Revels, Miss.; Reps. B. S. Turner, Ala.; R. C. DeLarge, S.C.; J. T. Wells, Fla.; J. H. Long, Ga.; J. H. Rainey and R. B. Elliott, S.C. *Library of Congress*.

poverty were not confined to Negroes.

Circumventing the Constitution. Beginning with a constitutional convention in Mississippi in 1890, the southern states, during the next decade and a half, added to their laws devices to circumvent the Fifteenth Amendment (which forbade restricting suffrage on the basis of race). The most effective disenfranchising devices were the literacy test, supplemented by the understanding clause, and the poll tax. Because many whites were illiterate, a number of states, as an alternative to the literacy test, permitted a prospective voter to interpret a passage of the Constitution that was read to him; the assumption was that registrars would automatically pass whites and fail blacks. Another loophole for illiterate whites was the so-called grandfather clause, which was not declared unconstitutional until 1915; it permitted any adult male to register if his father or grandfather had been a voter before 1868—that is, prior to black enfranchisement.

Despite the loopholes, whites as well as blacks were kept from the polls by the new restrictions. Many white citizens either could not pass the tests or were embarrassed to submit to examination. With the removal of most of the Negroes and many whites, the nineties saw the first legal reversal in a century of steady expansion of the suffrage. Moreover, the removal of blacks from politics virtually ended the Republican party in the Deep South for the next half century. With all voters concentrated in a single party, popular participation in elections, and political activity in general, declined precipitously in the South. Voter apathy—always a threat to a democratic polity—settled like a pall over southern politics.

Significantly, the disenfranchisement of the Negro was accepted without serious objection in the North. As recently as the 1880s such blatant moves to undo the results of the Civil War and Reconstruction would have met with outraged protests from northern Republicans and the northern press. But in the 1890s the protests were few and halfhearted. The great interest in equality for blacks that the antislavery crusade, the war, and then Reconstruction had generated subsided; this was a new era in which economic growth and foreign expansion commanded the attention of leaders and led alike. In fact, many Northerners, including reformist Republicans, openly accepted disenfranchisement as "realistic" and justified.

Equal but Separate. Even before the Supreme Court upheld the disenfranchising devices of the southern states in *Williams* v. *Mississippi* (1898), it provided a kind of sanction for them in a decision in 1896 which ruled that blacks and whites could be compelled to accept separate facilities on trains, provided the accommodations were of equal quality. This case, *Plessy* v. *Ferguson,* concerned railroad cars, but the principle of "equal but separate" enunciated in the decision was soon applied in a host of new situations. Long before the Supreme Court decision, the principle had been practiced in schools, hotels, and trains; now it was also applied by law to streetcars, waiting rooms, public toilets, tax offices, restaurants, and, in at least one state, telephone booths. Before the late 1890s, for example, no southern state required segregation of the races on streetcars. Soon after, all did.

Ironically, the sole Supreme Court dissenter in the *Plessy* case was the single southern justice, a former slaveholder, John Marshall Harlan of Kentucky. "The white race deems itself to be the dominant race in this country," Harlan pointed out. "And so it is, in prestige, in achievement, in education, in wealth and in power. . . . But in view of the Constitution, in the eye of the law, there is in this country no superior, ruling class of citizens. There is no caste here. Our Constitution is color blind, and neither knows nor tolerates classes among citizens."

Although, as one historian has written, the last decades of the nineteenth century constituted "the nadir" for blacks in America, it must not be thought that they had not been able to record significant gains on their road from slavery to freedom. Most blacks still lived in the South in 1900, and most of those who remained continued to work the land, usually as sharecroppers or tenants. Nevertheless, some former slaves managed to acquire land; by 1890 over 100,000 farms were owned by blacks, a figure that would almost double by 1910. By 1900, too, more than 2000 black people had obtained a college degree, usually in the newly founded black colleges in the South. Almost 30,000 blacks were teachers in the segregated public schools of the South. Most blacks who did leave agriculture became industrial workers; in 1886, for example, about 60,000 blacks were members of the Knights of Labor. Yet when the Negro Business League was founded in Boston in 1900, over 400 businessmen-delegates attended.

The first president of the newly formed League was Booker T. Washington, a rising young southern black—a former slave, in fact—whose headship of Tuskegee Institute in Alabama in 1881 launched his remarkable career as an advocate of industrial education for blacks. Probably no other single person, black or white, advanced the education of Negroes in the South as much as Washington. Although he has often been scorned in recent years as an accommodationist because of his public acquiescence in segregation and disenfranchisement, any other stance in the South would have prevented Washington from being the impelling force behind gains made by blacks. By the opening years of the twentieth century Booker T. Washington was recognized by blacks and whites as the national spokesman of black people.

The cultural achievement of blacks by the end of the century extended beyond education. Already by that date the novels of Charles W. Chestnutt and William Wells Brown were recognized beyond the black community for their literary merit. Paul Laurence Dunbar's poetry was already being praised by the best-known white critics. Among the black journalists who worked on the 150 black newspapers in 1900, T. Thomas Fortune was the best known. W. E. B. Du Bois, the first black to receive a Ph.D. in history from Harvard, was then just entering upon his post-doctoral career; his efforts would make him not only the critic and rival of Booker T. Washington in the early twentieth century, but the leading black intellectual of his time as well.

If the opportunities for blacks in American society after slavery were still far from equal to those for other Americans, the achievements of blacks were that much more notable, having been gained against obstacles no other minority or newcomer has encountered in America.

The Great Departure

In 1936, when Samuel Flagg Bemis published his influential textbook on American diplomatic history, he referred to the acquisition of the Philippines as "the Great Aberration." The implication was that the movement of the United States into the imperialist race for markets, sources for new investment, and colonies, which then engaged the principal European powers in Asia and Africa, was a sharp and inexplicable departure from previous American practice. In one sense it certainly was. Prior to the 1890s, with the single exception of the joint protectorate over Samoa, established only in 1889, the expansionist energies of the American people had been confined to the North American continent. The efforts of the Grant administration to acquire Santo Domingo had been completely frustrated by a continentally minded Congress, just as pre–Civil War interest in acquiring Cuba had come to nothing. Yet by the close of the nineties, the territory of the United States extended into the Caribbean and, by a series of island stepping-stones, completely across the Pacific to Asia. As President McKinley observed, "And so it has come to pass that in a few short months we have become a world power. . . ."

That the nineties witnessed a turning point in American relations with the rest of the world, there is no doubt. The question is why and how this alteration came about. The word "aberration," which Professor Bemis used, suggests an erratic outburst, without substantial roots in the past or in the broader social developments of the decade. And since the publication of Julius Pratt's *Expansionists of 1898* (1936), this view has been widely accepted. As a result of Pratt's work, most historians have rejected the idea that the Spanish-American War and the colonial expansion that followed were to be explained in classic European terms—that is, as the result of businessmen's drive for markets of profitable investment. Pratt, after an examination of the business press of the nineties, showed quite conclusively that the great majority of businessmen did not want war in 1898, if only because it would disrupt trade. As an alternate explanation, Pratt pointed to the prowar feelings of the people and especially to the activities of a small group of articulate and highly active expansionists.

Voices of Expansion. Among these proponents of expansion were important political figures like Theodore Roosevelt, Henry Cabot Lodge, and John Hay; influential editors like Walter Hines Page of the *Atlantic Monthly* and Albert Shaw of the *Review of Reviews;* and prominent experts like Admiral Alfred T. Mahan, whose book, *The Influence of Sea Power upon History* (1890), along with other writings, became almost sacred writ for the imperialists. These and other like-minded men wanted the United States to assume a larger place in world affairs, to translate America's obvious economic power into military, or, more precisely, naval power. Mahan tirelessly called for a navy that would be commensurate in size and strength with the continental dimensions of the United States. No nation could become great, he argued, until it became a naval power. Since a large navy required coaling stations and bases across the oceans of the world, he advocated the acquisition of territory outside the United States. "Whether they will or no," he prophesied in 1893, "Americans must now begin to look outward." Theodore Roosevelt, who was Assistant Secretary of the Navy in McKinley's first administration and was destined to be a hero of the Spanish-American War, was an expansionist, an ardent booster of naval power, and an avid reader of Mahan. His close friend, John Hay, who wanted the United States to wield influence and power in Asia, had the chance to further his cause through the enunciation of the Open Door Policy in China in 1899, while he was McKinley's Secretary of State.

Yet even an influential group like the expansionists of 1898 cannot account for the popular will that drove the McKinley administration into war with Spain and opened the way to a new colonial empire. The expansionists were more the result of the new interest in the outside world than they were its cause. Broader forces had to prepare the ground before the seeds of militant nationalism sown by the expansionists could take root and flourish. These broader forces are to be found in the social character of the decade itself.

Nationalist Fervor and International Recognition. By the 1890s Americans may have been confused and even bewildered by the new industrial society they had built, but they did not fail to recognize the new economic power of the United States. As a result, the nineties witnessed a high tide of nationalist fervor; Americans of all social classes swelled with a new pride of country. Even Edward Bellamy's brand of socialism took the name "Nationalism," and radical, free-silverite William ("Coin") Harvey founded the "Patriots of America" society in 1895. Indeed, many more patriotic societies were founded in this single decade than in any previous one. It was then that the flag and the ritual of the flag salute were introduced into the schoolrooms of the nation. When in 1893 the United States agreed for the first time to receive and send emissaries with the "monarchical" title of Ambassador instead of the old "republican" title of Minister, President Cleveland justified the change to Congress as "fittingly" appropriate to "the position the United States holds in the family of nations." On all sides, press and pulpits rang with testimonies to American greatness. As one speaker before a group of Civil War veterans said in 1896, "The place of this nation is at the head of the column of civilization. Not that we would put other nations down. . . . Our idea has always been and is now to point to other nations the way to come up higher."

The social unrest of the decade also contributed to the drive to seek recognition among "the family of nations." Organized labor and farmers, dissatisfied with the returns they received from their efforts, were resorting to strikes and joining new political organizations like the Populist and Socialist parties. But they were also discharging some of their dissatisfactions by projecting them upon external targets like the Spanish government, which was then trying to subdue a rebellion of its colony in Cuba. Urban labor, Populists, and Bryan Democrats, it is worth noting, were conspicuous among the supporters of the Cuban rebels and were outspoken advocates of American intervention prior to 1898.

Conservatives, too, looked to outside enemies as an answer to social turmoil in a decade beset by hard times. A newspaper editor in Kansas wrote in October 1895, "While it might be putting it too strong to say that war is needed in this country now, yet who is there who does not believe, and in fact know, that such a thing would clear the atmosphere and stamp out the growth of socialism and anarchy, discontent and sectional prejudice that is gaining a foothold in this nation." In 1896 a member of Cleveland's Cabinet wrote in his diary, "The jingoism in the air is a curious thing, and unaccountable except on account of the unrest of our people, and the willingness to turn from domestic to foreign affairs." Theodore Roosevelt, who always seemed to believe in the social therapy of war, wrote to a friend in late 1897, "In strict confidence . . . I should welcome almost any war, for I think this country needs one."

The Desire for New Overseas Markets. In a more direct fashion the Economic Revolution also helped turn the nation's attention outward. Although Professor Julius Pratt's researches effectively eliminated the business interests as an important force for war, more recent investigations have shown that economic motives were very influential with statesmen and publicists. Their concern was not to secure colonies nor even to garner national prestige but to open up markets for the prodigious amounts of goods that were pouring from the factories of an industrialized America.

The beginnings of this interest go back at least to James G. Blaine, Harrison's first Secretary of State. While in that office, Blaine actively promoted reciprocal trade agreements, particularly with Latin American countries, as a means of obtaining broader markets for American goods. He was acutely aware that in an age of industry the United States might well find itself with surplus production. "Under the beneficent policy of protection," he pointed out in 1890, "we have developed a volume of manufactures, which, in many departments, overruns the demands of the home market." The reciprocity clause written into the McKinley Tariff of 1890 was a further reflection of this concern. Significantly, too, in 1896 the Republican platform contained a strong reciprocity plank.

It was the depression of 1893 that convinced the leaders of both parties that the home market was insufficient to absorb American production. New foreign markets might offer a solution to the hard times. Both President Cleveland and Secretary of the Treasury John Carlisle, neither of whom was an imperialist in the mold of Theodore Roosevelt, talked of foreign markets as a means of halting the outflow of gold that plagued the country. When another Democrat, William L. Wilson, wanted to defend a low tariff, he called attention to its potentialities for expanding American markets. "There is not one of our leading industries," Wilson emphasized, "that can find free and healthful play within the limits of our home markets." Expand American markets abroad, he asserted, and many social problems like strikes and labor unrest would be reduced. "With all our mills running and orders ahead, labor can achieve its own emancipation and treat on equal terms for its own wages." The depression also made those outside of government conscious of the need of outlets for American goods. One prominent writer went so far as to explain the contemporary relocation of New England textile mills in southern states as a means of getting closer to Latin American markets! The National Association of Manufacturers was founded in 1895 as a direct result of business interest in the opening of markets in Latin America.

This emphasis on new foreign markets, it should be observed, was not the colonialist or prestige-seeking variety advocated by navalists or expansionists like Admiral Mahan or Theodore Roosevelt. But whatever the motivation behind the interest, the outward turning of America's people and their leaders was clear.

Protecting Foreign Markets. The distinction in motivation helps account for the apparent contradiction between Grover Cleveland's action on the issue of Hawaiian annexation in 1893 and his stand on Venezuela two years later. When Cleveland entered the White House for the second time in March 1893, the Senate was considering a treaty that would annex Hawaii to the United States. Annexation of the islands had been a goal of expansionists and American sugar growers on the islands for some years. In January 1893 a group of American sugar planters, with the support of the American minister in Honolulu, had overthrown the native government and then asked the favorably disposed Harrison administration for annexation of the islands to the United States. Cleveland, however, recognized that neither the revolution nor annexation to the United States was desired by Hawaiians and promptly withdrew the treaty from Senate consideration. Later, he explained his action on the ground that "The mission of our nation is to build up and make a greater country of what we have instead of annexing islands." In the jingoist nineties Cleveland appeared an anomaly. Two years later, however, he did not seem so out of fashion in dealing with England over a boundary dispute between Venezuela and British Guiana.

When Great Britain threatened to settle the dispute militarily, Secretary of State Richard Olney, in July 1895, wrote a sharp note of protest. He invoked the Monroe Doctrine as the American justification for intervening in what appeared to be a dispute between Venezuela and Great Britain only. The language of his message was quite in keeping with the fervent nationalism of the decade. "The states of America, South as well as North, by geographical proximity, by natural sympathy, by similarity of governmental constitutions, are friends and allies, commercially and politically, of the United States," Olney wrote. "To allow the subjugation of any of them by an European power is, of course, to completely reverse that situation and signifies the loss of all the advantages incident to their natural relations to us. . . . Today the United States is practically sovereign on this continent, and its fiat is law upon the subjects to which it confines its interposition." Olney insisted that Britain submit the dispute to arbitration. The British government's cool silence of four months so irritated Cleveland that he asked Congress for money to set up a commission to decide the issue and for the authority to settle the matter by force if necessary. In short, the United States was prepared to go to war to assert a highly nationalistic interpretation of the Monroe Doctrine. Fortunately, the British government yielded.

At first glance the chauvinism of Cleveland in 1895 seems in marked conflict with his refusal to support the annexation of Hawaii in 1893. Actually, there is less contradiction than first appears. Olney and Cleveland, for all their nationalism, were certainly not colonialists or expansionists. Both of them, for example, later opposed the acquisition of the Philippines. But anti-imperialism did not preclude a strong sense of American nationalism and power. Nor did it prevent recognizing that surplus American manufactures needed markets, especially when the country was deep in a depression. To have failed to assert the Monroe Doctrine vigorously in the Venezuelan issue of 1895 would have been to deny the new feeling of nationalism which was so characteristic of the nineties; and it would have given Britain an advantage in the commercial competition in Latin America that might well have hurt American trade. An interest in keeping foreign markets open to American goods also seems to have been an important reason behind the Cleveland administration's support of the legitimate government during the abortive Brazilian revolution of 1894–1895 (when American trade was threatened with an embargo). Several years later Olney cited the year 1895 as the real turning point in American foreign relations. Significantly, he related that shift to the Economic Revolution. "This country was once a pioneer and is now the millionaire," he wrote. Home markets were no longer sufficient to absorb the products of "the inventive genius of the American people."

Nationalism, social unrest, and the common interest of imperialists and anti-imperialists in foreign markets all helped explain the new American interest in the outside world. But they only provided the background for the coming of the Spanish-American War and the triumph of the imperialist point of view. A complete explanation for that momentous step into the orbit of the great powers requires a recognition of the additional and precipitating factor of Cuba.

Whipping Up the War Spirit. Many Americans had long been casting covetous eyes upon the Spanish colony off their southern coast. In the 1850s there had been talk of buying Cuba, and after the Civil War the Grant administration toyed with the idea of deliberately encouraging the rebellion that broke out in 1868. When a second revolt erupted in 1895 as a result of a sharp decline in sugar prices, Americans found themselves very directly involved. The rebellion, which was financed by Cuban exiles in New York, seriously interrupted the $100 million trade between the United States and Cuba and threatened to destroy the $50 million investments of Americans in Cuban sugar plantations and iron mines. The economic interests of Americans in Cuba drew the attention of the Cleveland administration, though not to any great extent.

It was the public that became exercised because of the reports of cruelties and suffering resulting from Spain's efforts to suppress the rebellion. The *reconcentrado* policy of Spanish Governor Valeriano Weyler worked severe hardships. Under that policy Cubans who were loyal to the regime or lived in government territory were herded into camps to protect them from the guerrillas or to prevent their giving aid to the rebels. The hardships resulted not so much from Spanish intention but from the lack of adequate facilities for the large number of people involved. More significant than the policy itself was its treatment by the American press, in which the Spanish Governor became known as "Butcher" Weyler. The Cuban rebellion was ready-made for scare headlines. True, any war

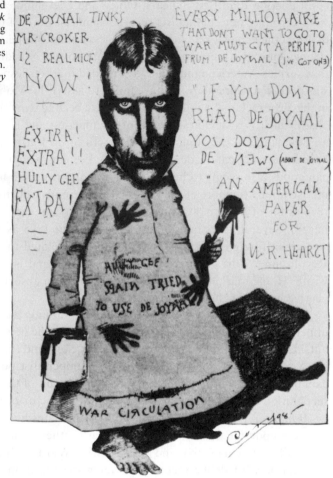

William Randolph Hearst and his sensational *New York Journal* are depicted as catering to the lowest taste in journalism and advocating a United States declaration of war on Spain. *The New York Public Library*

that involves guerrilla fighting, as Americans would learn in the Philippines in 1899–1901 and in Vietnam sixty years later, is sensational; it is cruel, treacherous, and frustrating when compared with conventional warfare, in which there are at least some rules and visible lines of combat. But the inherent sensationalism of the Cuban war was exploited by the New York press; a furious rivalry for circulation between William R. Hearst's *Journal* and Joseph Pulitzer's *World* set a standard for "yellow journalism" that is still unmatched. The extremism of the New York press, however, only added fuel to a fire already burning brightly.

Yellow journalism is not as important in explaining the popular outrage over the Cuban war as the new technology of the Communications Revolution. The American people, with their heritage of colonial rebellion, needed no urging to sympathize with the rebels; they only needed to learn of the Cubans' struggle for freedom. The Communications Revolution informed them and, indeed, did more. With pictures and sensational personal accounts by on-the-spot reporters, the news was relayed more quickly to a wider audience than ever before, making the war an experience as well as an event for millions of Americans. Democrats and Republicans, farmers and workers alike saw in the Cuban war an American and a Christian imperative to help an oppressed and valiant people. "The United States needs a war, and Spain needs a thrashing," wrote one Civil War veterans' journal in the summer of 1897. "Both wants can be supplied in Cuba. Order out the ships." In early 1898 one Bostonian wrote that he had not met a man of the upper class "who considers that we have any justifiable cause for war. Below that crust," he went on, ". . . the wish for war is *almost* universal."

The great popular interest in helping the Cubans, however, was not shared by the United States government. Neither the Cleveland nor the McKinley administrations wanted war over Cuba, though both recognized that the conflict there hurt Americans economically and endangered the peace with Spain. In this pacific attitude, both Presidents enjoyed the support of the business community, which only occasionally expressed a bellicose attitude toward Spain. But Congress and the press marched with the people. In early 1898 only one New York newspaper still opposed war.

Aggravation of the Cuban Issue. Several incidents provided opportunities for keeping up the popular pressure for war. One was the discovery and publication, in early February 1898, of an indiscreet letter from the Spanish minister in Washington, Depuy de Lôme, which described President McKinley as "weak and a bidder for the admiration of the crowd." De Lôme resigned when his words became known, and the Spanish government apologized. But popular American resentment against Spain rose, and with the departure of De Lôme, the Spanish government lost an excellent counterforce to the propaganda of the rebel junta in New York.

A more important incident was the mysterious explosion on (or next to) the United States battleship *Maine*. Late in January 1898 the ship had been dispatched to Havana harbor at the request of the American consul to protect the property of United States citizens. On February 15 a tremendous explosion sank the ship as it lay in the harbor, killing or drowning some 250 American sailors. The immediate assumption in the United States, given the general hostility toward Spain, was that the Spanish were responsible. A report issued on March 28 by a United States investigating commission, which concluded that the explosion was external, did nothing to scotch this belief, though no responsibility for the blast was assigned then or later. The press continued to refer to "Spanish treachery" and to preach sympathy for the Cuban rebels.

Nevertheless, as late as the end of March 1898, diplomatic conversations between the United States and Spain seemed to offer substantial hope that the war might be ended to the satisfaction of the United States. In early April, in fact, the Spanish government abandoned the objectionable *reconcentrado* policy throughout Cuba and a few days later agreed to suspend hostilities against the rebels for six months. By this time, unfortunately, American demands had jumped higher. Responding to pressure from Congress, the press, and public opinion, McKinley then asked for nothing less than complete independence for Cuba, something that

The sinking of the U.S. battleship *Maine* in Havana harbor, 1898, intensified American hostility toward Spain and led up to the Spanish-American War.

no Spanish government dared agree to, though autonomy within the empire was offered. The Spanish concessions of early April, it now appears, were futile, because some time during March the McKinley administration had decided that independence was indispensable. With that decision, war became inevitable.

Unwilling himself to make the ultimate decision to go to war, McKinley on April 11 turned the matter over to Congress. In a joint declaration on April 19, 1898, Congress declared Cuba to be free and independent and authorized the President to use the armed forces of the United States, if necessary, to compel Spain to relinquish the island. At the same time, in what came to be called the Teller Amendment, Congress declared by a unanimous vote that the United States "hereby disclaims any disposition or intention to exercise sovereignty, jurisdiction, or control over (Cuba). . . ." As a result of the joint Congressional declaration, Spain broke diplomatic relations with the United States on April 21, and three days later declared war; the following day, the 25th, Congress voted that a state of war existed between the two countries. Soon after war began, the conservative Republican, Senator John Spooner of Wisconsin, wrote to a friend, "I think . . . possibly the President could have worked the business without a war, but the current was too strong, the demagogues too numerous, and the fall elections too near."

"A Splendid Little War"

The First Encounter. Although the United States entered the war with enthusiasm, no substantial preparations for it had been made. Even so, the powers of

Europe, which had generally sympathized with Spain, foresaw victory for the powerful republic of the New World. They were taken aback, however, by the rapidity with which 200,000 men were mobilized and by the display of unity in the socially heterogeneous nation. Former Confederate officers tendered their services as eagerly as former Union men, and new immigrants and southern blacks flocked to the colors in response to McKinley's call for 125,000 volunteers.

Even Americans were surprised to learn that the first encounter came not in Cuba but in the western Pacific, some ten thousand miles away from the source of the conflict. As early as February, Assistant Secretary of the Navy Theodore Roosevelt had begun to make some plans. He alerted Admiral George Dewey, commander of the American far eastern squadron, then at Hong Kong, to be prepared to attack the Spanish fleet at Manila in the Philippine Islands. Although this action of Roosevelt's is often cited to show how a small group of expansionists managed to transform the Cuban war into an imperialist one, the fact is that in time of war all centers of Spanish power became legitimate and necessary objects of attack. Six days after the declaration of war Dewey completely annihilated the decrepit Spanish fleet in Manila Bay, at a human cost to the American forces of only eight slightly wounded. In June, Dewey, who had by then become a national hero, was joined by units of the Army. With the assistance of Filipino rebels led by General Emilio Aguinaldo, the combined forces proceeded to occupy the island of Luzon against only slight resistance from the Spanish.

Strolling into Cuba. The conquest of Cuba took longer. Incredible mismanagement and inefficiency in the United States were largely responsible for the

SPANISH-AMERICAN WAR, PHILIPPINE CAMPAIGN, 1898

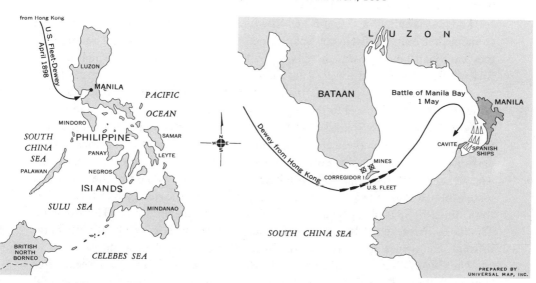

Spain's antiquated ships were no match for America's modern "steel navy," which swept into Manila Bay from Hong Kong and in one battle virtually ended the war with Spain in the Philippines. A show of force by the U.S. Army and Philippine rebels completed victory there.

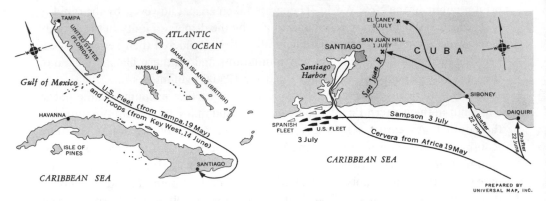

PREPARED BY
UNIVERSAL MAP, INC.

Unlike most wars, the Spanish-American War was very limited in nature. Even with the Philippine campaign, only a few battles, involving fairly small land and sea forces, were necessary to end it. Nor was it necessary to occupy all of Cuba in order to obtain victory.

delay, as was revealed later by investigations of the War Department. Troops did not even leave the staging area in Tampa, Florida, until mid-June. As Richard Harding Davis, one of the principal war correspondents, reported on the expedition to Cuba under General William Shafter, "It was a most happy-go-lucky expedition, run with real American optimism and readiness to take big chances, and with the spirit of a people who recklessly trust that it will come out all right in the end, and that the barely possible may not happen. . . . As one of the generals on board said, 'This is God Almighty's war, and we are only His agents.'"

The first landings at Daiquiri and Siboney on the southern shore of Cuba were so inept that only a more inept Spanish defense prevented disaster. The target of the American landings was the city of Santiago, in the harbor of which lay the Spanish fleet under Admiral Pascual Cervera. After some bloody and costly fighting at El Caney and a dramatic rush up San Juan Hill outside of Santiago, the American Army laid siege to the city. From beyond its harbor, the United States Navy watched for the Spanish fleet to make its inevitable break for the open sea. On July 3 Admiral Cervera elected to make his run through the tortuous harbor entrance in broad daylight, only to be overwhelmed by the waiting Americans. The Spanish suffered some 450 casualties, including over 300 dead; the American losses totaled two: one killed and one wounded. It was a victory like this, rather than the stiff Spanish opposition at El Caney, that inspired John Hay to write Theodore Roosevelt, "It has been a splendid little war, carried on with magnificent intelligence and spirit, favored by that Fortune which loves the brave."

The End of One Colonial Empire, the Beginning of Another. Two weeks after the destruction of the Spanish fleet, the city of Santiago surrendered to General Shafter, just as yellow fever was ominously spreading among his men. On August 12 Spain signed a preliminary agreement ending the war. The agreement granted

Cuba its freedom, ceded to the United States the island of Puerto Rico, which had been quickly overrun by General Nelson Miles' troops, and permitted the United States to occupy the Philippines, pending a final peace treaty.

The most obvious result of the war was the humiliation of Spain. "When I gave the order to fire," remembered Captain Concas of Cervera's flagship, "it was the signal that the history of four centuries of grandeur was at an end and that Spain was becoming a nation of the fourth class." The oldest and most successful colonial empire since the days of Rome was no more. For the United States, victory was not so much a sign of new power; Europeans had been well aware, long before the war began, that America was preeminent among the industrial nations of the world. It was the empire which came as a result of the war that was new.

The prospect of overseas colonies occasioned a great debate in the country, but in retrospect the efforts of the anti-imperialists seem to have been doomed from the beginning. Even before the end of the war with Spain, President McKinley signed a joint Congressional resolution on July 7 incorporating Hawaii into the territories of the United States, thus completing the effort aborted by Cleveland five years earlier. Extending the boundaries of the United States two thousand miles into the Pacific Ocean, however, was to the imperialists only the beginning.

They wanted the Philippines, too. During much of the last half of 1898 a furious debate raged in Congress and in the press over the issue. All the hoary arguments for expansion were trotted out: the need for markets, the need for prestige in a world of colonial empires, the virtue to be gained by Christianizing heathens (even though Catholic Spain had ruled the islands for four hundred years), and the necessity of helping an "immature" people, who otherwise would fall under the dominion of allegedly less qualified rulers like Germany or Japan. Businessmen, many of whom had opposed the entrance of the United States into war with Spain, now found the possibilities of an Asian market very tempting. Mark Hanna, President McKinley's close friend and campaign manager in 1896, declared that possession of the Philippines would enable the United States "to take a large slice of the commerce of Asia. That is what we want. We are bound to share in the commerce of the Far East, and it is better to strike for it while the iron is hot."

The immediate decision to acquire the Philippines, however, was McKinley's. Although he later said that he had arrived at his decision after prolonged prayer, the record shows that the forces that shaped his action were more mundane. While the treaty was being negotiated in the fall of 1898, he carefully, and probably accurately, tested public opinion by a speaking tour. On October 26, soon after his "poll" revealed a clear popular interest in keeping the islands, he instructed the American commissioners in Madrid to insist upon the whole archipelago, not just Manila, or the island of Luzon. In the final treaty, the United States secured the Philippines, Puerto Rico, and the island of Guam in the central Pacific in return for a payment of $20 million.

The treaty brought the debate over imperialism to a climax. The opposition was impressive. Included among the anti-imperialists were important intellectuals like William James, William Dean Howells, and Mark Twain, labor leaders such as Samuel Gompers and Eugene V. Debs, as well as prominent Republicans like Charles Francis Adams and Carl Schurz. They were joined by Democrats on both sides of the silver fight, including William Jennings Bryan, Grover Cleveland, and John G. Carlisle. The most powerful anti-imperialist argument was that the Filipinos did not want American rule substituted for Spanish rule; they simply wanted to govern themselves. The strength of this argument was amply demonstrated by the rebellion that broke out in February 1899 under the leadership of the Filipino nationalist, Emilio Aguinaldo. Superior American military power quickly forced the small, ill-equipped rebel army into guerrilla tactics, but that merely made the war more brutal without shortening it. Suppressing the Filipino rebellion ultimately required four times as many American soldiers as were used in the invasion of Cuba and three years instead of the three and a half months it took to conquer the Caribbean island. The loss of American lives was triple that for the whole Spanish-American War, while the number of Filipinos killed in military action alone was over fourteen thousand in the first year of the rebellion.

Significantly, both imperialists and anti-imperialists reflected in their arguments the widespread racism then infecting European and American culture. Surveying the world of 1898, white Europeans could not help but feel that they ruled supreme. In fact, they did, as the carving up of Africa and the commercial partition of China made evident. Instead of seeing this undoubted supremacy as temporary, growing out of a head start in technology and industrialization, Europeans and Americans chose to view it as a consequence of their racial superiority. Thus the imperialists justified the taking of the Philippines as a duty owed "our little brown brother," who was not yet capable of self-government. The implications of the argument were not lost upon southern racists in Congress, many of whom were anti-imperialists and almost all of whom were then taking steps to deny the ballot to southern blacks. Was this not the very argument, they slyly inquired, that southern whites had used in protesting Negro enfranchisement during Reconstruction, only to have it rejected by these same Republicans?

Nor were northern anti-imperialists free of racism in their objections to colonies. As Carl Schurz pointed out, if the Philippine Islands were acquired, they might well become states on an equal footing with others. "The prospect of the consequences which would follow the admission of the Spanish creoles and the negroes of the West India islands and of the Malays and Tagals of the Philippines to participation in the conduct of our government is so alarming that you instinctively pause before taking the step." Many of the anti-imperialists doubted that American institutions could exist in such a different climate and culture. As David Starr Jordan, the president of Stanford University, observed, "Civilization is, as it were, suffocated in the tropics."

The issue of empire was settled on February 6, 1899, when the treaty was accepted in the Senate by a vote of 57 to 27—only a single vote more than the necessary two thirds. Popular opposition to empire was probably even stronger, but William Jennings Bryan, as a leader of the anti-imperialists, dissipated its influence on the Senate when he advised acceptance of the treaty so that the issue of imperialism might be fought out in the election of 1900. As might have been anticipated, although Bryan and McKinley were the presidential candidates in 1900, imperialism was no longer a current topic, despite Bryan's valiant efforts. Once again Bryan was beaten by the issue of free silver, which the Republicans artfully made central to the 1900 campaign.

The entrance of the United States into Asia brought none of the bright consequences that expansionists had predicted and businessmen had anticipated. The Asian market proved to be an impoverished one, and the acquisition of the Philippines did nothing to develop it, though the United States proved to be a conscientious and humane, if slightly self-righteous, colonial ruler. As early as 1907, Theodore Roosevelt, now President, was complaining that the Philippines possessed no strategic value and, in fact, constituted the "Achilles heel" of American security. In 1916 the United States Congress, in the Jones Act, made its first promise of eventual Filipino independence, though consummation would wait another thirty years.

The Spanish war brought the United States not only into Asia but into the Caribbean as well. It was there, during the new century, that American imperialism would experience thorough testing and dismal failure.

Domestic Scene. The story of domestic affairs is a Republican tale. The Dingley Tariff of 1897 raised the rates above even those in the notorious McKinley Act of 1890. The party took somewhat longer to redeem its pledges on the money question. With the Gold Standard Act of 1900 the nation declared that gold was to be the only metallic base of the money supply. The act also authorized the President to float short-term loans for gold so that the Treasury would never again be caught in the vicious cycle of redemptions that had bedeviled the Cleveland administration in 1894–1895. The Republicans were also credited for the new boom in the economy, enjoyed by farmers as well as businessmen. The century closed, in short, with the United States as a new world power and, for the first time in many years, riding the crest of prosperity.

SUGGESTED READING

The decade of the nineties has been surveyed fully but in a rather pedestrian manner in Harold U. Faulkner, *Politics, Reform, and Expansion, 1890–1900* (1959). The two principal strikes of the decade have now been treated in detail by Almont Lindsey, *The Pullman Strike* (1942), and by Leon Wolff, *Lockout: The Story of the Homestead Strike of 1892* (1965). More favorably disposed than Wolff toward the strikers is Henry David, "Upheaval at Homestead," in *America in Crisis,* ed. Daniel Aaron (1952). See also Stanley Buder, *Pullman: An Experiment in Industrial Order and Community Planning, 1880–1930* (1967). No monograph treats the depression adequately; the best study of it is Charles Hoffman, "The Depression of the Nineties," *Journal of Economic History,* XVI (1956), 137–164. A helpful supplement to this is Samuel Rezneck, "Unemployment, Unrest, and Relief in the United States During the Depression of 1893–1897," *Journal of Political*

*Available in paperback edition.

Economy, LXI (1953), 324–345. The depression as an aspect of the money question is dealt with at some length in the technical but important study by Milton Friedman and Anna Schwartz, *A Monetary History of the United States, 1867–1960* (1963).

The standard study on the election that opens the decade is George Harmon Knoles, *The Presidential Campaign and Election of 1892* (1942). Among the political biographies that should be added to those mentioned earlier are James A. Barnes, *John G. Carlisle* (1931); Harry Barnard, **Eagle Forgotten, the Life of John Peter Altgeld* (1938), a splendid job; and Paxton Hibben, *The Peerless Leader* (1929), an overly caustic but very readable biography of Bryan. Since then Paul W. Glad, *The Trumpet Soundeth: William Jennings Bryan and His Democracy, 1896–1912* (1960), has thoughtfully and clearly placed Bryan in the intellectual context of his time. Paolo E. Coletta, *William Jennings Bryan, 1860–1908,* I (1964), is a full and friendly biography. Margaret Leech, *In the Days of McKinley* (1959), makes McKinley as important as he can be and is an excellent study of the man; a fuller analysis of his presidency is Howard Wayne Morgan, *William McKinley and His America* (1963).

The politics of the 1890s and the presidential election of 1896 have spawned a substantial body of literature. Thorough on political detail but rather weak on the social roots of politics is Stanley L. Jones, *The Presidential Election of 1896* (1964); complementary because it does probe into social politics is J. Rogers Hollingsworth, *The Whirligig of Politics: The Democracy of Cleveland and Bryan* (1963). The Republican party's triumph in the 1890s is dissected with skill in the important Richard Jensen, *The Winning of the Midwest: Social and Political Conflict, 1888–1896* (1971). Paul Kleppner, *The Cross of Culture* (1970), applies a similar social interpretation to the politics of the period. Samuel McSeveney, *The Politics of Depression* (1972), shows the importance of the depression in shaping the political revolution of the 1890s. Robert F. Durden, **The Climax of Populism* (1965), concentrates on the South and tends to take the Populists at their own value. Sheldon Hackney, *Populism to Progressivism in Alabama* (1969), is more critical. Walter T. K. Nugent, *The Tolerant Populists* (1963), absolves the Populists of charges of anti-Semitism and nativism. An important pioneering article on the urban component in the election of 1896 is William Diamond, "Urban and Rural Voting in 1896," *American Historical Review,* XLVI (1941).

The disenfranchisement of blacks is told in the two path-breaking books by C. Vann Woodward, **The Strange Career of Jim Crow* (2nd ed., 1966), and *Origins of the New South* (1951). J. Morgan Kousser, *The Shaping of Southern Politics* (1974), is an important quantified, revisionist analysis that stresses the political and class motivation behind disenfranchisement. Louis R. Harlan, *Booker T. Washington* (1972), which carries the story to the end of the 1890s, is a masterful job. On the intellectual life of blacks see the important study by August Meier, *Negro Thought in America, 1880–1915* (1963).

The most provocative study on the foreign policy of the decade is Walter LaFeber, *The New Empire* (1963), even though it sometimes overstresses economic explanations. Thomas McCormick, *China Market* (1967), also emphasizes the quest for markets in foreign policy. William Appleman Williams, *The Roots of the Modern American Empire* (1969), finds the farmers as much interested as businessmen in foreign markets. The whole debate over the role of markets in sparking the interest in Asia is put into balanced perspective in Marilyn Blatt Young, "American Expansion, 1870–1900," in B. J. Bernstein, ed.. *Towards a New Past* (1968). See also John A. S. Grenville and George B. Young, *Politics, Strategy, and American Diplomacy* (1966) and David Healy, *U.S. Expansionism: The Imperalist Urge in the 1890s* (1970). The broadest study of American involvement with Spain in 1898 is Ernest R. May, *Imperial Democracy* (1961); a more recent and briefer examination is Howard Wayne Morgan. *America's Road to Empire* (1965). Walter Millis, **The Martial Spirit* (1931), sets the satiric tone usually taken in regard to the Spanish-American War; the appropriateness of that attitude has been questioned successfully by Frank Freidel, **The Splendid Little War* (1958), which is drawn largely from contemporary accounts. Ernest R. May, *American Imperialism: A Speculative Essay* (1968), sees the foray into imperialism as a temporary distraction.

Two important aspects of the anti-imperalist movement are treated in the popular and sound Leon Wolff, *Little Brown Brothers* (1961), an account of the Filipino insurrection against the Americans, and in Christopher Lasch, "The Anti-Imperialists, the Philippines, and the Inequality of Man," *Journal of Southern History*, XXIV (1958), which exposes the racism among the anti-imperialists. For a readable discussion of the anti-imperialists see Robert L. Beisner, *Twelve Against Empire* (1968). Broader in scope is E. Berkeley Tompkins. *Anti-Imperialism in the United States: The Great Debate, 1890 – 1920* (1970).

CHAPTER SIX

THE SECULARIZATION OF AMERICAN SOCIETY AND THOUGHT

URING EVEN THE most religious or other-worldly times, people have had to deal with the mundane realities of life such as earning a living, rearing children, confronting disappointments, illness, and death. But some eras have been more religious than others, noticeably more than today. Part of the reason for a greater emphasis on religion in earlier times is that throughout most of history, life has been hard. In the absence of power-driven machines, most men and women had to work hard physically. Disease before the nineteenth century was barely controlled, and poverty was the lot of the vast majority. Under such circumstances men and women have often found religion a precious comfort as well as an explanation of God's purpose.

By the late nineteenth century, however, the triumph of democracy, science, and the Economic Revolution suggested to many people that life could be easier and better not only for the few but for the many as well. In a democracy, all people are equal before the law and entitled to seek a decent life; with universal suffrage, they have an opportunity to insist upon it. In an age that was scientific and technological as well as democratic, the means for improving the lot of the average person were also at hand. The biblical admonition that "ye have the poor always with you" no longer could be effective in smothering the hopes of the poor or assuaging the guilt of the rich. The science and technology of the Economic Revolution now made evident for the first time in history that human beings possessed the means to eliminate poverty. Indeed, it was precisely this vision that inspired reformers like Henry George and Edward Bellamy. With such prospects before them, Americans turned eagerly to remold the world, which at last seemed responsive to their desires. America's newfound power and ingenuity challenged the social order to make life on earth, not only the hereafter, a paradise.

Most Americans, of course, did not abandon their religious beliefs; they simply relegated them to a more remote part of their minds while they busied themselves with the material world. One sign of the new secular interest was the decline in the influence of the Protestant ministry. Prior to the Civil War, ministers had been the recognized leaders of the intellectual community; most college presidents were ministers, for example. By the close of the century those persons trained in worldly affairs were clearly the intellectual leaders, and the clergyman-president of the college or university was passing from the scene. Perhaps the most striking example of the secularization of society during the last decades of the nineteenth century was provided by the churches themselves, as they redefined their missions to fit the new world of cities and factories.

The Secularization of Protestantism

The Economic Revolution was probably the greatest secularizing force in the late nineteenth century. By 1900 it had shaped the modern patterns of American religion. In his stimulating book, *Protestant, Catholic, Jew* (1955), Will Herberg

"Be good and you will be lonesome" was Mark Twain's humorous comment on this picture of himself.
Harper Brothers, Mark Twain Memorial

points out that Americans, despite the great number of religious denominations to which they belong, generally place themselves in one of three major religious categories. This recognition of Catholicism and Judaism on a par with Protestantism is very recent. For most of the nineteenth century, the American people and their culture were overwhelmingly Protestant. Only with the influx of immigrants in the second half of the century did Catholicism and Judaism begin to change the pattern, taking their places beside Protestantism as significant religions of Americans. And while all three religious groups were remolded by the forces generated in the city and the factory, none was altered more than Protestantism.

In the 1870s as in previous years American Protestantism was a mélange of sects, with new ones emerging every decade. Most of the new sects were not destined to rise above the level of influence of local congregations, but from time to time one would assume the stature of a world religion, as in the case of the Mormons before the Civil War and the Christian Scientists in the postwar years. The overwhelming majority of native-born Americans, however, belonged to one of the large denominations, such as the Methodists, who comprised a third of all Protestants, or the Baptists, or the Presbyterians. The Lutheran Church, strong in the upper Mississippi Valley, was the fourth largest Protestant denomination in the country in the 1870s, its members largely of German and Scandinavian immigrant stock. All told, there were about 10-million Protestant church members in 1880; by 1900 the number would rise to almost 18 million.

Urban Life: New Challenges to the Churches. The new ways of life in the cities presented a severe challenge to Protestantism, involving it increasingly with worldly matters. Many Protestant ministers and leaders, alarmed by the crime, immorality, and disease that the cities seemed to foster, began to recognize that the urban areas were also the homes of the churchless. "The American Protestant Church, as a whole," said one minister in the 1880s, "has failed to win to itself the working class of the towns." It was true, too, that the churches did little to attract and much to alienate workingmen. Too often urban churches charged pew rent and affected an elegant decor that made working people feel uncomfortable and unwelcome. By seeming to prefer the attendance of employers, merchants, and professional men, the churches demonstrated their upper-class orientation. Samuel Gompers, the head of the American Federation of Labor, testified to this feeling in 1896 when he said that the workers "have come to look upon the church and the ministry as the apologists and defenders of the wrongs committed against the interests of the people by employers and men of wealth." Moreover, the churches often neglected or ignored the urban workers. As working-class districts filled up, the churches moved out and none came to replace them. In one area of Chicago containing 60,000 people, there was not a single Protestant church.

Social Gospel. Faced with a loss of influence and genuinely concerned about the poor working and living conditions of the urban masses, some Protestant clergymen in the 1870s and 1880s began to argue that the churches had a special responsibility to interest themselves in the problems of the world. These clergymen contended that the teachings of Jesus must be applied to the conditions of the slums and the low wages of industrial workers. The Reverend Charles Loring Brace, an established leader in philanthropic work in New York, was profoundly affected by the great railroad strike of 1877. He recognized that strikes of such magnitude and violence were new in America: "They ought not to occur here. The great problem of the future is the equal distribution of wealth out of the profits of labor. . . . I believe myself that, in general, the laboring classes do not receive their fair share. Strikes are one of their means of getting more. . . ." Washington Gladden, an Ohio clergyman prominent in the working-class movement, pointed out that if the church hoped to regain its influence, it must become interested in economic and social issues. The old, narrow theology of the seminaries was no longer sufficient. The new and different world of the city demanded a fresh and broader religion.

One of the first forms this new "Social Gospel" assumed was the organization of charitable services for the urban poor and the dispossessed. Women of the churches brought food, clothing, and spiritual assistance to workingmen's families. Churches provided recreational facilities for young people where none had existed. Kindergartens, church schools, and youth organizations were formed in response to the secular needs of people in the industrial cities.

The most striking example of the direct response of Protestantism to the demands of the urban world was the Salvation Army. Conceived in the slums of London, this army of Christians came to the United States in the late 1870s to minister to the lowest slum dwellers, who often were beyond the interest or the assistance of the established churches. At first the Salvation Army was roundly condemned by the conventional churches for its members' flamboyant practice of playing cornets, beating drums, and singing hymns on street corners. But the dedication and helpfulness of the men and women of the Salvation Army soon won the respect of the poor and the conventionally religious alike. They set up their havens in the center of the worst slums and offered soup, bread, and a bed to all who entered, even before religious commitment was demanded. By ministering to the urban poor, these Christians showed that they had adapted themselves extremely well to the new conditions created by the city and the factory. Their belief that a hungry person had to be fed before he or she could be expected to pray was a realistic recognition that the spirit cannot be reached when the flesh is ignored.

Along with the adjustment of church practice to urban circumstances, there occurred a transformation of Christian teaching and doctrine. By stressing the responsibility of society for its less fortunate members, Protestant Christianity was both socialized and secularized. In the seminaries and from the pulpits, ministers taught and preached the need for understanding social problems, for working on behalf of the poor and the laboring class. In 1892 seven seminaries instituted lectureships in social ethics; two years later three others had added similar courses to their curricula. In 1893 the students of the Union Theological Seminary in New York organized a society for the discussion of "the nature and method of sociological study and the minister's relation to the problems of the day."

The most articulate and best-known advocate of the Social Gospel was Walter Rauschenbusch, a scion of a long line of ministers. Soon after graduation from the Rochester Theological Seminary, Rauschenbusch became the pastor of a Baptist church in New York City's impoverished Hell's Kitchen, where, during the depression of 1893, he recalled later, "one could hear human virtues cracking and crumbling all around." He found that the religious principles he had learned in the seminary were becoming increasingly irrelevant in the social context of his slum parish. In 1897 he returned to the Rochester Seminary to teach, and in 1907 he published his first book, *Christianity and the Social Crisis*. "The ministry," Rauschenbusch wrote, "must apply the teaching function of the pulpit to the pressing questions of public morality," such as the problems of poverty, unemployment, low wages, poor housing, and unregulated business monopoly. Secular answers would have to be sought for these secular problems; the old-time religious answers to human problems were no longer adequate. Indeed, Rauschenbusch's concern ultimately made him a socialist in political philosophy. Only a small minority of the Social Gospel leaders followed him that far.

The Social Gospel reached a peak among Protestants with the formation of the Federal Council of Churches of Christ in America in 1908. Composed of thirty-three different Protestant denominations, the Council pledged in its state-

An artist's depiction of the Salvation Army on the steps of the City Hall in Brooklyn. *The Bettmann Archive, Inc.*

NEW YORK.—PRAISE AND EXHORTATION SERVICE OF THE SALVATION ARMY ON THE STEPS OF THE CITY HALL, BROOKLYN. FROM A SKETCH BY A STAFF ARTIST.—SEE PAGE 111.

ment of social principles to work for, among other things, the abolition of child labor, "a living wage in every industry, . . . the highest wage that each industry can afford," and the recognition of "the Golden Rule . . . as the supreme law of society and the sure remedy for all social ills." Now called the National Council of Churches, the organization remains a living symbol of Protestantism's shift in emphasis from individual salvation to recognition of a responsibility for the secular as well as the religious condition of society.

Although the Social Gospel had a dramatic impact upon some Protestant denominations, others escaped the initial shock almost entirely. Churches drawing predominantly upon a rural constituency, for instance, usually felt little need to change their ways. Hence whole denominations such as the Lutherans and the Presbyterians were conspicuously slow in responding to the new social Christianity. Even today the Lutheran Church, especially those synods made up largely of immigrant stock, is much less concerned with social issues than the Episcopal, Baptist, or Methodist churches, which were prominent in the nineteenth-century Social Gospel movement. Insofar as churches failed to move in a secular direction, they lost influence in a society that was becoming increasingly secular in outlook.

Urban Revivalism: A Rural Influence. It would be erroneous to imply that even all urban Protestants adopted the Social Gospel. Many of these Protestants, after all, had only recently come from farms and rural towns. With them they brought their belief in God, their Bibles, and their prayers. Yet they were alienated by the urban congregations, whose fashionable churches and intellectualized religion offered scant welcome and less comfort. What they really sought, they found in the urban revival meeting—that is, a religion and church like the one they had left in the country.

Historically, the revival was a rural phenomenon, tracing its origins back to the Great Awakening of the middle years of the eighteenth century. Intellectually, the revival was a democratic repudiation of an elitist view of salvation, for unlike the Calvinist doctrine of the elect, the central principle of the revival taught that salvation, open to everyone, was achievable through the individual's choice and effort. In the cities of the 1870s the revival meeting continued to appeal to the poor as well as to the middle class and to speak in a socially democratic idiom.

The most successful of the urban revivalists of these years was Massachusetts-born Dwight L. Moody, who began his preaching, significantly enough, in bustling, booming Chicago. In 1875–1876, after a sensationally successful revival tour of England, Moody and his gospel singer, Ira Sankey, brought the revival to the principal cities of the United States. The crowds that filled the meeting halls numbered in the thousands and the enthusiastic converts in the hundreds.

Moody's amazing success as a preacher was the result of both his personal magnetism and his democratic, down-to-earth approach to religion. Such an approach appealed strongly to the ordinary American, who often misunderstood or resented the formal language of the trained, traditional clergy. Moody's massive body (he weighed 280 pounds) and full beard gave him the appearance of an outsized biblical prophet. His speech, however, was colloquial rather than grandiloquent. His homely moral lessons and his recital of stories from the Bible were couched in everyday language and images, based on the experiences of ordinary people. The story of the prodigal son thus became the tale of a boy from the country lost in the strange and threatening environment of the city. This was a boy who had been ensnared by "the billiard hall and the drinking saloons." The Christian doctrine Moody preached was simple, direct, and comforting. Scorning the entire concept of an elect, he declared salvation open to all. God, he asserted, was all-merciful; He did not restrict salvation to a special few. Jesus asked simply that all believe in Him and all would be saved. "The way to be saved," Moody exclaimed, "is not to delay, but to come and take, t-a-k-e, TAKE."

Moody was no exponent of the Social Gospel, for his emphasis was upon the individual soul. Nevertheless, he was clearly the product of a society of equals, in which each individual had the same chance to get to heaven. This triumph of democratic idealism, embodied in the revival, shows how even the more primitive kind of Christianity was being influenced by the world. Yet Moody's refusal to interest himself in broad social problems of the time helped account for the limited impact of his movement. During the 1830s and 1840s revivalism had played a central role in the reform movement, particularly in the antislavery crusade. But Moody's shunning of the Social Gospel movement isolated his form of revivalism from increasingly popular issues. In short, the limited success of Moody's revivalism was also a sign of the growing secularism of the times.

Christian Science: Urban Product of a Scientific Age. Measured solely against the yardstick of the Social Gospel, Christian Science, like Moody's revivalism, appears to be indifferent to worldly affairs. Its doctrine firmly rejected any kind of social reform or concern. For instance, the founder of the religion, Mary Baker Eddy, prohibited her followers from introducing the innocuous strawberry festivals or Ladies Aid Societies, so familiar in most other Protestant churches. But in other ways Christian Science reflected the growing secularization of thought at the end of the nineteenth century.

Christian Science is the lengthened shadow of one woman, Mary Baker Eddy, a thrice-married New England farm girl. After overcoming a nervous condition with the help of a faith healer, Phineas Quimby, Eddy began instructing others in the art of mental healing. Since most of her first pupils were working people in the industrial cities of Lynn and Boston, it might be said that Christian Science began as a product of the city and the factory.

In 1875, with the financial assistance of some of her disciples, Eddy published her interpretation of Christianity in a book called *Science and Health.* She claimed no originality. Her definition of Christianity, she said, was simply the rediscovery of the true doctrine, lost since the apostolic age. In her book she taught the total unreality of evil in the world. God, she asserted, was all-good, and the world He created was without evil and therefore without disease or sickness. Matter did not exist; the sole reality was Spirit or Mind or Idea. Illness thus became a figment of human minds impressed with the false doctrine of the reality of material things. Christian Science was a form of philosophical idealism.

During the early years of the twentieth century Christian Science spread to most of the large cities of the United States and to many European countries, thereby becoming the second of the world's religions (the first being Mormonism) to originate in America, as well as one of the few to be founded by a woman. This remarkable growth was achieved in spite of bitter public hostility toward a religion whose members rejected modern medical science.

Even though Christian Science never participated in the Social Gospel movement, it reflected the interests and concerns of the late nineteenth century in at least three ways. The first and most obvious is inherent in its name: The Church of Christ, Scientist. Such a title could be acceptable only in a secular and scientific age in which a scientist's ability to probe the true nature of things was well recognized. In the second place, Christian Science mirrored the dominant cultural and intellectual attitudes of the time in that it was founded in a city during a period of great urban growth. Indeed, it has remained the most urban-based of any Protestant church in the United States. Christian Science was at once a product of, and a contribution to, the city.

The third way in which it was typical of its age is evidenced in its pragmatism. As we shall see a little later in this chapter, the last quarter of the nineteenth century witnessed the development of philosophical pragmatism—the doctrine that truth is to be tested through works. Of all religions, Christian Science is undoubtedly the most pragmatic. Its literature and history are filled with the testimonies of those who have been healed through belief in its tenets. The fundamental appeal to potential converts is the simple assertion that Christian Science can cure the sick. "If Christian Science lacked the proof of its goodness and utility," Eddy wrote, "it would destroy itself, for it rests alone on demonstration." Not even William James, the principal exponent of the philosophy of pragmatism, could subject religion to a more pragmatic test. In natural science, too, the supreme test of truth is practice or experiment.

The Growth of Catholicism

During the years when many of the Protestant churches were passing through the transforming fires of the Social Gospel, the Roman Catholic Church in the United States was only coming of age. Although Catholic parishes had existed in this country from the early part of the seventeenth century, the American Church had always been a tiny island in a Protestant sea. Then with the influx of Irish and German Catholics after 1830 membership leaped up only to expose Catholics to nativist fears and bigotry during the Know-Nothing agitation of the 1850s.

At the time of the Civil War, Catholics were still establishing their place in American society. It was not clear then that Roman Catholicism was to be a predominantly urban-based religion. Thousands of German Catholics and even some Irish Catholics took up land in the West, almost counterbalancing the tendency of Irish Catholics to settle in eastern cities, such as New York, Boston, and Baltimore. In the 1880s and after, however, hundreds of thousands of Polish, Italian, and Irish-Catholic immigrants settled in the expanding cities, causing a remarkably rapid growth in American Catholicism and placing an unmistakably urban stamp upon the Church. In 1850 the Catholics in the United States numbered approximately 1.5 million; by 1880 the figure was over 6 million; at the end of the century it had reached almost 12 million.

Though the Church grew rapidly, it still remained outside the mainstream of American life. Protestants monopolized the political, intellectual, and social leadership of the country. Catholics, if they were thought about at all by the Protestant establishment, were regarded as unassimilated immigrants, and therefore justly without social influence. Like most immigrants, Catholics were generally poor; a Catholic middle class hardly existed. Moreover, Catholic traditions were derived mainly from the peasant cultures of Europe and did not include the Protestant middle-class ethic of hard work, frugality, and abstemiousness which, given the heretofore Protestant character of the United States, had become synonymous with America. Their local churches were controlled by the clergy, not by the congregation, a difference that many Protestants thought inconsistent with American democracy. The Catholics' commitment to a carefully defined religious dogma and theology also stood in sharp contrast to Protestantism's latitudinarian conception of doctrine and its increasing tendency to confine theology to an occasional sermon and to the seminaries. Even the hierarchy of the Church, though better educated than the laity, was largely European born and European trained. Thus, both as immigrants and as non-Protestants, the Catholic minority was set apart from the native American majority. For their part, many Catholics, in the face of a hostile Protestant culture, drew even closer together, increasing their alienation from American society and offering justification for Protestant charges of "clannishness."

New World Proponents. By the decade of the 1880s forces of accommodation were at work. The mere increase in the number of Catholics as well as their acquisition of wealth and position over the years eased their adjustment. Furthermore, about this time a new group of church leaders came forward, dedicated to narrowing the gulf between the Church and American culture. The most prominent of such men were Cardinal James Gibbons of Baltimore, Archbishop John Ireland of St. Paul, Minnesota, Bishop John Keane of Catholic University, and Bishop John Spalding of Peoria, Illinois. In speeches and in actions, these leaders stressed the American character of the Church and its loyalty to the historic principles of the nation. Their purpose was to help Catholics feel at home in America and to encourage other Americans to accept Catholics as fellow citizens. Both Gibbons and Ireland repeatedly called attention to the essentially favorable social climate in the United States for the growth of the Church. Ireland contrasted this to the tumultuous, often anticlerical, contemporary experience of the Church in traditionally Catholic countries such as Italy and France and in Germany under Chancellor Otto von Bismarck. Gibbons and Ireland, in fact, were so well-disposed toward American society that they were often blind to its flaws. Archbishop Ireland, for example, fulsomely praised capitalists like Andrew Carnegie and extolled the virtues of unregulated competition at the very time when reformers and even some Protestant ministers were finding good reasons for lashing out at the inequities of an industrial society.

Gibbons and Ireland also acted as mediators between a Protestant America and the Holy See in Rome. In 1887 Gibbons successfully prevented the Vatican's public condemnation of Henry George's *Progress and Poverty* and of the Knights of Labor, to which many Catholics as well as Protestant Americans belonged. Recognizing the conflict between the American belief in secular public schools and the Catholic commitment to religious education. Archbishop Ireland worked to find an accommodation. In speeches to Catholics, he defended the secular schools as indispensable in a socially and religiously diverse nation like the United States. Before Protestant groups, he praised the public schools and suggested that, if religious instruction could be included in some way, the Church would have no objection to Catholics attending state-supported schools. A few communities actually practiced a form of Ireland's educational ideas, notably Poughkeepsie, New York, and Faribault, Minnesota, but neither the majority of Protestants nor most Catholics accepted his compromise on the school question.

Ireland made no secret of his belief that Catholics, even including members of the clergy, should participate in all phases of American life. He was outspoken in support of the Republican party, temperance, and American democracy. Ireland was well known in Europe for his advocacy of American Catholicism as a model for liberal Catholics, particularly in the light of the Church's remarkable success in the United States.

The Gradual Achievement of Acceptance. By the close of the century Catholic educational, philanthropic, and social organizations testified to the improved position of Catholics and their church in American society. Another measure of accommodation was the success with which the Church withstood the attacks of the American Protective Association in the 1890s. The APA was a violently nativist organization that singled out Catholics for vicious attacks, sometimes winning political success among Protestants. But the important point is that the APA captured no support among respected Americans as the Know-Nothings had easily done in the 1850s. Both major parties repudiated the APA's support in the election of 1896, and leading Protestants like Theodore Roosevelt and Washington Gladden publicly and vigorously defended the loyalty of American Catholics.

Slow Response to Social Needs. Catholic response to the social influence of city and factory came more slowly than Protestant adjustment, and when it did come it was less dramatic, if only because the Catholic Church in late-nineteenth-century America was a poor people's church. Indeed, one Protestant minister in 1887 said, "The Catholic Church is emphatically the workingman's church. She rears her edifices in the midst of the densest population, provides them with many seats, and has the seats well filled." This close connection between working class and church can be attributed partly to the immigrant nature of the Church; as a familiar rock in a strange and sometimes hostile world, it retained the immigrants' loyalty even in the city. Furthermore, the Church has historically concerned itself with ministering to the poor and handling problems which Protestant churches were only beginning to confront in the cities of America. In short, the Roman Catholic Church was already meeting at least part of the needs of the city folk—certainly to a greater extent than the Protestant churches of the 1880s.

The first indication that the Catholic Church, too, was responding to the new demands of an industrial society came from Europe. In 1891 Pope Leo XIII issued his important social encyclical, *Rerum Novarum*, which announced the Church's position on the problems of industrial labor, trade unions, monopoly, and class warfare. Pope Leo urged employers to recognize the "dignity of labor" and to honor their "moral obligation to pay fair wages." Despite the encyclical, the twentieth century was well advanced before the American branch of the Church acted in any obvious way to adjust its practices and outlook to the changed conditions of an urban and secularized America. In 1917 Father John A. Ryan received permission to establish the *Catholic Charities Review*, a journal of social service. Then, immediately after the First World War, the four bishops constituting the leadership of the National Catholic War Council issued a Program of Social Reconstruction, signaling a new turn in Catholic concern for social issues. Since then the Roman Catholic Church officially and to an ever increasing degree has addressed itself to the problems of society. In the 1950s and 1960s Catholic clergymen were unprecedentedly prominent in protests against racial discrimination in both the North and the South.

New World Judaism

The First Wave. Like the Roman Catholics, the Jews of the United States became a significant minority only with the influx of immigrants in the nineteenth century. Some Jews, like some Catholics, had come to the colonies as early as the middle of the seventeenth century, but these Spanish and Portuguese Jewish communities were tiny in both size and influence. The great Jewish immigration of the nineteenth century came in two quite different waves. The first came principally from Germany between 1830 and 1860, while the second, which began in the 1880s and continued down to the First World War, was Russian, Romanian, Lithuanian, and Polish.

Before 1880, then, American Jews were largely German in background and constituted only a small proportion of the total population. In 1860, for example, there were no more than a quarter of a million Jews in the country. Moreover, unlike the Jews of a later America, those of the years before 1880 were not concentrated in the great cities but were rather widely, if thinly, scattered around the country. One informed estimate is that as late as 1880 Jews constituted a larger proportion of the population in the West than they did in the Northeast. By that date many German Jews were already prosperous and rising in social status as businessmen, professionals, and white-collar workers. The generally high economic position of the German Jews was suggested by a government survey in 1890, which reported that almost 40 percent of them maintained at least one domestic servant.

Innovation and Renewal: Reform, Orthodox, and Conservative Judaism. In the history of Judaism in America, the great contribution of this first wave of German Jews was the introduction of Reform Judaism, destined to become one of the two distinctively American forms of Judaism. Reform Judaism is both a product of the Enlightenment of the eighteenth century and a reaction against Orthodox Judaism. During the Middle Ages and into modern times, traditional or Orthodox Judaism had been relegated to the intellectual backwaters and cultural ghettoes of Europe by Christian prejudice. Thus forced back upon itself for centuries, Orthodoxy had become a mass of ancient, frequently outmoded ritual, and minutely detailed religious law; interpretation was left to the iron authority of the rabbi or scholar.

Judaism emerged as a modern religion only in the last years of the eighteenth century, when the French Revolution, wielding the battering ram of the Enlightenment, broke down the physical and intellectual ghettoes in western Europe that for so long had isolated Jews from the mainstream of European civilization. In the wake of this liberation, many Jews, who later came to be called Reformers, sought to reshape their tradition-encrusted religion along the lines of the religions they saw about them, particularly Christianity; that is, in the age of the Enlightenment, they wished Judaism to be rational and respectable in the eyes of the gentile community. They removed rituals whose significance was long forgotten, delivered sermons in the vernacular language so that they would be intelligible to those who knew no Hebrew, and simplified the service and the law. Because this Reform group hoped to make its religion acceptable to Jews and non-Jews alike, it also abandoned doctrines that carried significance only for Jewish people, such as the belief in the coming of the Messiah and the expectation of a return to the homeland in Palestine. Reformers hoped thereby to destroy the old Christian stereotype of the "wandering Jew" by showing that the Jew as a full citizen was as much attached to the land of his birth as any Christian.

Despite its European origins, Reform Judaism became identified with America; in no other country has this variety of Judaism flourished as it has in the United States. The beginnings go back to the middle of the nineteenth century when a number of German Reform rabbis migrated to America, among whom were Isaac M. Wise, David Einhorn, and Max Lilienthal. Undoubtedly the most influential was Isaac Wise, who established Cincinnati as the center of Reform Judaism. Among many accomplishments, Rabbi Wise created an American ritual for the Reform synagogues and published *The Israelite*, a newspaper of Reform Judaism.

As Reform Judaism had been the special religious contribution of the German immigration of the 1850s and 1860s, so a resurgence of Orthodoxy was the contribution of the Jews from eastern Europe. Between 1880 and 1900 about 500,000 Russian, Polish, Lithuanian, and Romanian Jews migrated to America, more than tripling the Jewish population of 1860. An even greater number arrived during the first fifteen years of the twentieth century. This influx from the eastern European ghettoes transformed American Judaism, not only religiously but socially as well. Like the Catholic immigrants who were arriving at the same time, these eastern European Jews settled in the expanding industrial centers, particularly in the Northeast and Middle West, for there on the new urban "frontier" opportunities to make a living were to be found. Judaism, like Catholicism, became a religion of the big cities.

The tension between the Reform and Orthodox approaches to Judaism soon produced a third variety—Conservative Judaism—a sort of compromise between them. Many American Jews, while unwilling to adhere to the extremely differentiating customs and rituals of the Orthodox Jews, still could not bring themselves to follow the Reformers in abandoning so many of the traditional forms. Styling themselves Conservatives to emphasize their connection with the Orthodox past, this third branch of Judaism pragmatically abandoned some but not all of the eastern European manifestations of Judaism. In 1901 the Conservatives established a firm doctrinal base with the reactivation of the Jewish Theological Seminary in New York City.

Despite the name of this third branch of American Judaism, its willingness to reshape its theology to fit the American environment was, like Reform Judaism itself, an admission that in an increasingly worldly society religion had to adjust. Even more than Reform, Conservative Judaism is distinctly an American movement. One historian of Judaism even refers to it, after Mormonism and Christian Science, as the third American religion of the nineteenth century.

By the end of the second decade of the twentieth century, the Jews, like the Catholics, had assumed a place of some prominence in American religious and social life. As with the Catholics, this improvement brought upon the Jews increasing social discrimination. In the early nineteenth century, when the Jewish community was tiny, there was little overt anti-Semitism. But by the 1870s, as their numbers increased and some Jews with newly acquired wealth sought to move into the upper-social strata, they encountered social barriers. In 1877, for instance, a prominent Jewish banking family was denied accommodations at Saratoga Springs, then a fashionable summer resort. During the 1880s, the stereotype of the Jew as an unscrupulous moneylender or an international banker appeared in some popular literature and in the private writings of a few patricians, like historian Henry Adams. But there was little organized anti-Semitism and certainly nothing comparable to the American Protective Association's organized attacks and political campaigns against Roman Catholics. Important milestones on the road to acceptance for Jews in America were the appointment in 1906 of Oscar Straus as Secretary of Commerce and Labor, the first Jewish Cabinet member, and in 1916 of Louis D. Brandeis as the first Jewish judge to sit on the Supreme Court of the United States.

A New Position for Women

If the expansion of the city and the growth of the factory enriched the American religious experience, the effect of the city upon the family and the home was quite the reverse. In a city house or flat, the work of the wife and mother differed

AMERICAN EDUCATION 1870-1900

ILLITERACY (Percentage of the population over 10 years old)

		1870	1880	1890	1900
	Native	– –	8.7	6.2	4.6
WHITE	*Foreign born*	– –	12.0	13.1	12.9
	Total	11.5	9.4	7.7	6.2
NON-WHITE		79.9	70.0	56.8	44.5
	*TOTAL	20.0	17.0	13.3	10.7

SCHOOL ENROLLMENT (Percentage of the population between 5 and 19 years old)

		1870	1880	1890	1900
	White	56.0	63.5	58.5	53.4
MALE	*Non-White*	9.6	34.1	31.8	29.4
	Total	49.8	59.2	54.7	50.1
	White	52.7	60.5	57.2	53.9
FEMALE	*Non-White*	10.0	33.5	33.9	32.8
	Total	46.9	56.5	53.8	50.9
	White	54.4	62.0	57.9	53.6
MALE and	*Non-White*	9.9	33.8	32.9	31.1
FEMALE	*Total*	48.4	57.8	54.3	50.5

HIGH-SCHOOL GRADUATES (Percentage of the population over 17 years old)

1870	1880	1890	1900
2.0	2.5	3.5	6.4

INSTITUTIONS OF HIGHER EDUCATION, NUMBER AND ENROLLMENT

		1870	1880	1890	1900
NUMBER	*Institutions*	563	811	998	977
	Pupils	52,000	116,000	157,000	238,000
ENROLLMENT	*% of pop. between 18–21*	1.68	2.72	3.04	4.01

INSTITUTIONS OF HIGHER EDUCATION, DEGREES CONFERRED

		1870	1880	1890	1900
B.A. or FIRST	*Male*	7,993	10,411	12,857	22,173
PROFESSIONAL	*Female*	1,378	2,485	2,682	5,237
	Total	9,371	12,896	15,539	27,410
M.A. or SECOND PROFESSIONAL		– –	879	1,015	1,583
PH.D. or EQUIVALENT		1	54	149	382
TOTAL of ALL DEGREES		9,372	13,829	16,703	29,375

Percentage of total population

considerably from what it had been on the farm. The size of the family and the physical dimensions of the home became smaller in the city. Both these changes made women's work lighter. Moreover, certain tasks that were entirely the responsibility of women on the farm—like raising chickens and selling eggs, making clothes, churning butter, baking bread, and canning vegetables—now were often done outside the home in factories or shops. By 1850 cheap, ready-made clothing was commonplace in the bigger cities, and by the 1870s commercial laundries and city bakeries were available to middle-class urban householders.

Out of the Home, into the Factory and Shop. The reduction in home tasks made it possible for women to work outside the home; increasing industrialization provided opportunities for them to do so. All over the world, wherever the factory has taken root, female labor has been indispensable to its growth. From the beginnings of the factory system in the United States in the 1830s, women had worked outside the home. The Civil War, by draining off male labor, stimulated the employment of women—usually unmarried—in arsenals, factories, schools, and in the new bureaucracy spawned by the war. Once the fighting was over, many women, finding it difficult to go back to the home-centered life of old, stayed on in mills, schoolrooms, offices, and shops. In the 1880s and 1890s whole new fields of women's employment opened up due to the rise of big business and the widespread use of inventions like the typewriter and the telephone.

Work outside the home also changed women's image. The Victorian stereotype of them as fragile, innocent, and weak could not survive the sight of thousands of working women trudging through crowded streets in the early light of dawn, working ten hours a day, six days a week, and effectively countering the sexual advances of aggressive foremen.

New opportunities for higher education broadened women's horizons in the years after the Civil War. During the first half of the century, women could gain admission to only a few colleges, like coeducational Oberlin College in Ohio or Elmira College for women, founded in New York State in 1855. The great change came in the 1860s and 1870s, with the opening of Vassar, Smith, Wellesley, and other women's colleges. The time was more than ripe, as shown by the large number of applications Vassar received when it opened in 1865 with 350 young women students. Smith College, started in 1875, was the first American college endowed by a woman, and Wellesley, founded the same year, was the first with an all-woman faculty headed by a woman president. At the same time, as more and more state universities opened their doors to qualified women (Iowa accepted women at its opening in 1856) and as the number of private, coeducational colleges increased, it became clear that the long resistance to women's pursuit of higher education was over. At the century's end more young women were graduated from high school than young men.

As the new social forces drew more and more women out of the home, women's organizations of all kinds sprang into being. Some, like the Women's Christian Temperance Union (WCTU), were composed largely of urban, married women interested in applying their newfound leisure to some constructive purpose.

Under the leadership of Frances Willard in the 1880s and 1890s, the WCTU attained a membership of five hundred thousand and made its influence felt far beyond the liquor question. It supported women's suffrage, argued for better laws for working women, and agitated for kindergartens in the public schools. The growing importance of women's organizations was recognized by the United States Congress in 1901, when it issued a national charter to the General Federation of Women's Clubs. The local women's club in many towns was often the sole civic agency working for better parks, recreation centers, and improvement of the public schools.

Working women also organized. As early as the 1870s, women weavers in Fall River, Massachusetts, organized a strike without male assistance. Women delegates attended the General Assembly of the Knights of Labor held in Richmond in 1886. By 1908 almost sixty-five thousand working women had joined over five hundred trade unions. Some of the unions were overwhelmingly female in membership, as in the garment industry, tobacco manufacturing, and laundries.

When Lord Bryce published his *American Commonwealth* in 1888, he remarked upon the wider opportunities for employment that women in the United

In 1895 these working women of Lynn, Massachusetts, file out of the shoe factory where they worked 10–15 hours a day, and earned six dollars per week. Note the shirtwaist and skirts above the ground, the outfit of working women by the end of the century. *Library of Congress*

States enjoyed as compared with European women. Yet as late as 1900 women offered little real competition to men in the job market. Women workers filled only a narrow range of occupations; almost 40 percent of working women in 1900, for example, were in domestic service. Yet even that figure suggests a broadening and rising place for women when one recognizes that in 1870 almost 60 percent of working women were household servants.

Although the number of working women rose steadily in the last decades of the nineteenth century, virtually all such women were unmarried. The typical working woman was single, widowed, or divorced; the usual pattern was for young women to work before they married and then to leave the work force to rear their children. Only the very poor deviated out of necessity from this pattern in the late nineteenth century; they were chiefly immigrants and blacks.

Before the century was out, however, women's narrow role in society after marriage was challenged in several ways. Kate O'Flaherty Chopin (1851–1904) examined the question in a compelling novel, *The Awakening* (1899), in which the heroine, a respectable wife and mother, discovered that the conventional marriage of the time met neither her need for independence and self-fulfillment as a person nor her need for sexual expression as a woman. Chopin's writing is distinguished by its subtlety, evocativeness (the novel is laid in Louisiana), and its perception of women's place in society. The subject of women's role was approached more bluntly in Charlotte Perkins Gilman's *Women and Economics* (1898), a powerful tract which argued that economic independence was essential if women were to live as autonomous, fully realized persons. Gilman raised the question of combining marriage with work outside the home long before society was prepared to take this step in the emancipation of women. *Women and Economics* became a leading book in the women's movement in the United States and Europe in the early twentieth century, and Charlotte Gilman (1860–1935), a leading intellectual of the women's cause.

In Search of Equality. The changing economic position of women lent a new impetus to the feminist movement, which had been agitating for women's equality ever since the 1840s. Although women had secured some gains in the 1850s and 1860s, particularly in legal rights respecting the property of married women and in divorce laws, as late as 1898 some states continued to discriminate against women. In all but seven states, for example, the father possessed primary authority over children, and six states still designated the father as head of the family, with the wife subordinate to him. In three states the double standard was law: Adultery was a ground for divorce only when the wife was the offender.

Almost nowhere in the United States in 1865 could a woman legally vote for any office or on any issue. The enfranchisement of blacks in 1870 brought new interest to the movement for women's suffrage; but all through the nineteenth century progress was discouragingly slow, despite the incentive provided in 1869 by the Wyoming Territory, which granted complete female suffrage. During the next forty years, after dozens of exhausting campaigns in states throughout the Union, only the three western states of Idaho, Utah, and Colorado followed Wyoming's example. A parallel movement to obtain suffrage through an amendment to the federal Constitution also failed. It would take the shock of a world war to reduce the barriers to women's participation in the political life of the nation.

Secularizing Force of Darwinism

Charles Darwin's *On the Origin of Species by Means of Natural Selection,* published in 1859 in London, was a strictly scientific work, but its influence extended far beyond biology. Before the century was out, *The Origin of Species* would shake traditional religion to its foundations, bolster the ideas of laissez faire, and add a new, secular dimension to thought.

Natural Selection. Although Darwin is associated with the word "evolution," his book never mentioned it. In fact, the theory of evolution––the view that ideas and institutions change through time—was not new at all; it can be traced to the ancient Greeks. Darwin's achievement was to explain how the large number of varieties or species of animals and plants had come about. Orthodox religions explained them as acts of creation by God, but by the middle of the nineteenth century much scientific evidence suggested that the thousands of species had evolved from a much smaller number over eons of time. Though other investigators before Darwin had tried their hand at an explanation, none was really satisfactory.

The theory of natural selection, Darwin's answer to the problem, declared that the different species had developed out of the competition of organisms to gain favorable conditions of life—access to food and water, immunity from enemies, adjustment to weather, and so forth. In his biological investigations Darwin had noticed that every organism exhibited slight physical differences from its parents and other members of the species. Aware of the intense struggle for survival in nature, Darwin concluded that any plant or animal that developed differences (for whatever reason) which would serve it better in the struggle for survival would thereby secure an advantage over its competitors. These advantages would be passed on genetically to its offspring; and gradually, over many generations, the accumulated differences would constitute a new species. Thus he spoke of the origin of a species as coming about through "natural selection."

Although some biologists found weaknesses in his explanation, many more were attracted to his theory by its remarkable simplicity on the one hand and by its breadth of scope on the other. The enormous range of animal and plant species was now explicable by the single principle of natural selection. Nothing had so effectively dramatized the power of science since Isaac Newton's similar achievement in the seventeenth century, when he demonstrated that the same force that drew a falling apple to the earth held the planets in their vast, sweeping orbits around the sun.

Scientific and Religious Resistance and Acceptance. In many respects, the world was ready for Darwin's theory, since developments in geology and biology had already prepared the way; indeed, discussion of the mechanisms of biological evolution had been carried on for a generation. Certainly, many scientists in England, on the European continent, and in America accepted natural selection almost immediately. Yet not all scientists would be persuaded then or later. Harvard's renowned zoologist, Louis Agassiz, rejected natural selection down to his death in 1873.

The most outspoken opponents, however, were church leaders. Their opposition was to be expected, for by placing human beings in the continuum of nature, shaped by the same forces that ruled the rest of the animal kingdom, Darwinism had challenged deeply held theological convictions. What, for example, became of the religious belief that a human being was superior to the brute and cast in the image of God, possessed of a soul, and destined for immortality? The doctrine of natural selection even questioned the old religious argument that the complexities of living organisms and the multiplicity of species, by their very profusion and elaborate detail, were proof of the existence of God and His awesome creative powers. Now all was said to be explained simply by the process of natural selection.

The threat that Darwinism posed to traditional religious beliefs caused many Protestant clergymen to attack it vehemently. Some, like the leaders of the fundamentalist sects, continue to oppose it today. The Roman Catholic Church also objected to the application of natural selection to man, arguing that man was a special creation, blessed with a soul and therefore not a part of the evolutionary process. Yet after varying (but short) periods of alarm or doubt, most Protestant denominations and Jewish congregations accepted the tenets of Darwinism. As early as 1882 Henry Ward Beecher, minister of Plymouth Church in Brooklyn, openly defended his acceptance of Darwinism with the remark, "I would just as lief have descended from a monkey as from anything if I had descended far enough." An important sign of the rapid acceptance of Darwinism in America was a series of lectures in 1893 on evolution, given by a Scottish Darwinist at the conservative and very religious Lake Chautauqua summer school.

The spectacular achievements of science in the last half of the century caused some Americans to reject conventional religion completely. Perhaps the best known among such agnostics or freethinkers was Colonel Robert G. Ingersoll, a prominent lawyer and Old Guard Republican. In the 1870s Ingersoll lectured widely to enthusiastic crowds on such topics as "Why I Am Not a Christian." Referring to God, he commented, "I do not deny, I do not know, but I do not believe." In place of traditional religion, he urged his listeners to accept science as their "religion" and to forsake the supernatural entirely. Secularism could receive no stronger support.

Judaism's counterpart to Protestantism's Ingersoll was Dr. Felix Adler, who founded the Society for Ethical Culture in 1876. Like Ingersoll, Adler had had a very religious upbringing. Yet he was deeply disturbed by the wide gap between the scientific knowledge of his time and the teachings of conventional religion about the world. Unlike Ingersoll, Adler did not seek to elevate science to a religion; instead, he retained the ethics of the Judeo-Christian tradition while abandoning its supernatural framework. His essentially secular religion appealed largely to Jewish and Protestant intellectuals who had lost their religious faith in an age of science.

Influence of Darwinism on Social Thought and Philosophy

Throughout the history of western civilization, governments have interfered in economic activity in one fashion or another. This generalization is as true for the Middle Ages as for the Age of Mercantilism that followed. It was even true of the United States in the first half of the nineteenth century, when both state and federal governments aided in the building of canals and railroads and encouraged infant industries through the protective tariff.

The opposite and historically recent view that government should keep its hands off the economy as much as possible—the doctrine of laissez faire—first gained widespread support only in the 1870s and 1880s. The explanation for the change is too complex to be discussed here. Certainly one cause was the realization that the burgeoning American economy no longer needed the kinds of aids and encouragement that an earlier and less developed society demanded from government, though the protective tariff continued to be accepted. With industry booming and production high, laissez faire could be practiced as well as preached. And preached it was, from pulpit, classroom lectern, and editorial desk.

Social Darwinism. A misreading of Darwinism provided one of the popular justifications for laissez faire. Perhaps the foremost exponent of what later came to be called "social Darwinism" was Herbert Spencer, a widely known English advocate of evolution. In fact, as an evolutionist prior to the publication of *The Origin of Species,* Spencer had helped create the favorable climate of opinion that accounts for the rapid acceptance of Darwin's ideas. Unlike Darwin, Spencer did not confine his evolutionary ideas to biology but extended them to encompass all phenomena, including thought itself. It was Spencer who coined the phrase "the survival of the fittest," which crops up so often in the writings of social Darwinists and which Darwin himself accepted as an apt summary of the theory of natural selection. Simply put, Spencer's social Darwinism justified the industrial millionaires and other social leaders of the time as products of natural selection. To criticize them or seek to limit them would contradict a law of nature, a position that was almost sinful after the acceptance of Darwin's argument. Needless to say, social Darwinism was not part of Charles Darwin's original theory of natural selection, which was intended to apply only to the field of biological evolution.

In the United States the foremost exponent of social Darwinism was a Yale professor of sociology and economics, William Graham Sumner. Like Spencer, Sumner appealed to Darwinian biological theory to justify his belief in laissez faire, which, he repeatedly said, would permit the best to prosper and let the incompetent fall by the wayside. As an uncompromising individualist, Sumner opposed all the reform measures of his day, from free silver to the Interstate Com-

SELECTED TRAVEL TIME AND COST 1870

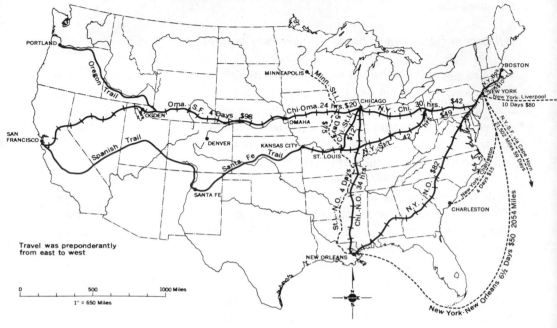

PORTLAND

Oregon Trail

MINNEAPOLIS

Minn.-St.L.

BOSTON

N.Y.-Bos.

NEW YORK
New York-Liverpool
10 Days $80

OGDEN

Oma.-S.F. 4 Days $98

Chi-Oma. 24 hrs. $20

CHICAGO

N.Y.-Chi. 30 hrs. $42

N.Y.-Chi. 42 hrs. $49

SAN FRANCISCO

Spanish Trail

OMAHA

Chi.-St.L. 15 Days $75

St.L.-Chi. 12 hrs.

N.Y.-St.L.

N.Y.-S.F. via Cape Horn 21,592 Miles 99 Days

DENVER

KANSAS CITY

Santa Fe Trail

ST. LOUIS

New York-Charleston 4 Days $15

SANTA FE

St.L.-N.O. 4 Days

Chi.-N.O. 34 hrs.

N.Y.-N.O. $82

CHARLESTON

N.Y.-S.F. via Panama 6½ Days $50 2054 Miles

Travel was preponderantly
from east to west

NEW ORLEANS

0   500   1000 Miles

1" = 650 Miles

N
W   E
S

New York-New Orleans 6½ Days $50 2054 Miles

SELECTED TRAVEL TIME AND COST 1900

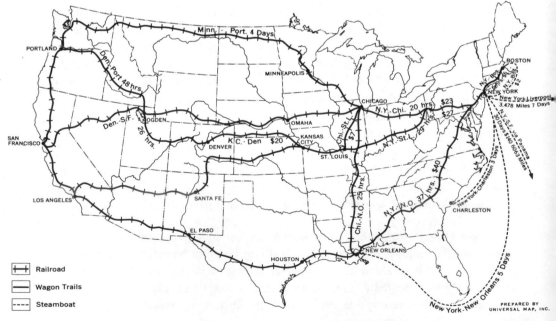

Minn.-Port. 4 Days

PORTLAND

Den.-Port. 48 hrs.

MINNEAPOLIS

BOSTON

N.Y.-Bos.

NEW YORK
New York-Liverpool
3,478 Miles 7 Days

Den.-S.F. 26 hrs.

OGDEN

OMAHA

CHICAGO

N.Y.-Chi. 20 hrs. $23

N.Y.-Chi. 29 hrs. $27

SAN FRANCISCO

K.C.-Den. $20

DENVER

KANSAS CITY

Chi.-St.L. $7

N.Y.-St.L. 29 hrs.

N.Y.-S.F. via Panama 30 Days $40 6063 Miles

LOS ANGELES

SANTA FE

ST. LOUIS

New York-Charleston 3 Days

EL PASO

Chi.-N.O. 25 hrs.

N.Y.-N.O. 37 hrs. $40

CHARLESTON

HOUSTON

NEW ORLEANS

PREPARED BY
UNIVERSAL MAP, INC.

┼┼┼	Railroad
───	Wagon Trails
----	Steamboat

New York-New Orleans 5 Days

merce Act. He defended the leaders of big business as the natural result of a beneficent social evolution and therefore privileged to be unfettered by any government or social control. "The men who are competent to organize great enterprises and to handle great amounts of capital," he wrote, "must be found by natural selection, not by political election. . . ."   .

Although Sumner used social Darwinism to protect the status quo from change by the reformers, he was also tough minded and consistent enough to assail those businessmen who demanded government favors for themselves while denying them to the poor. He opposed the protective tariff as vehemently as the income tax. Moreover, unlike more smug proponents of social Darwinism, Sumner did not ignore the poverty, want, and misery that industrialism seemed to leave in its train. Such evils, he admitted, constituted the price modern society paid for its gains; forthrightly, if cold-bloodedly, he acknowledged that he, for one, was willing to pay the price.

Although probably very few businessmen read Darwin or Spencer, they sometimes defended their practices in the language of both. For instance, when a member of a Congressional investigating committee asked a businessman what might be done to raise wages above 75 cents a day, the witness answered: "I don't think anything could be done. . . . The law of the 'survival of the fittest' governs that." Andrew Carnegie, the steel magnate who had risen to eminence despite his early poverty and foreign birth, also justified the status quo in the language of social Darwinism. Although the law of unrestrained competition, he admitted, "may be sometimes hard on the individual, it is best for the race, because it ensures the survival of the fittest in every department."

But William Graham Sumner's remorseless application to society of the principle of social Darwinism found few supporters even within the business community. The principal reason was that in a democratic society where ordinary citizens could influence the government through their votes, unconditional appeals to the self-reliant doctrine of social Darwinism were not sufficient. Andrew Carnegie, for one, recognized that something more was needed if government interference in the economy were to be avoided and large fortunes were to be protected from an income tax. Thus, in his essay "Wealth" (or as it came to be called, the "Gospel of Wealth"), published in 1889, he moved away from a strict application of social Darwinism, suggesting instead that the great fortunes accumulated by individuals were actually being held in trust for society. The impartial law of competition may have put such aggregations of wealth in the hands of a few highly competent men, he conceded, but ultimately such accumulations of money would be expended for the benefit of those not so talented or fortunate. Carnegie, along with other new millionaires of the Economic Revolution, spent millions of dollars on a variety of philanthropic enterprises, all of which, by their very assistance to the allegedly unfit, repudiated in practice the tenets of social Darwinism while serving to refurbish in part the tarnished image of the renowned robber barons.

Reform Darwinism. Some social reformers made a use of Darwinism that was quite the opposite of the social Darwinism of Spencer and Sumner. Prince Peter

Kropotkin of Russia, for instance, in a series of articles in the 1880s, later published as *Mutual Aid,* brought together a wealth of zoological evidence to show that even in nature, ruthless competition was not the sole law. The cooperative behavior of the social insects and herd animals proved, he contended, that cooperation among human beings in society was at least as "natural" as competition. In the United States, Lester Frank Ward, often called the founder of American sociology, asserted in a number of books and popular articles that competition may be the rule in nature but that cultivation, careful breeding, and "unnatural" surroundings produce much finer quality than uncontrolled competition. Hence government intervention in the economy was desirable and justified. Ward's writings received very little attention in the 1880s and 1890s, but in the twentieth century his influence on sociology was great.

Pragmatism: A Darwinian Philosophy. Darwinism, along with science in general, profoundly affected philosophical speculation in the United States. By demonstrating that apparently stable and fixed units like the natural species were actually mutable and that the world itself was continuously changing, Darwinism overturned a basic human supposition about the nature of the universe. Whereas before, stability had been considered the ideal state of things, now change was taken as typical of nature and hence equated with the good. Indeed, by showing that change was the order of the universe, Darwinism offered a new and powerful support for social reform. But if everything in the world was in a state of flux, the old search for final truth became fruitless. How could there be final truth in an evolutionary world?

When Darwinism is analyzed in this way, it is evident that the social Darwinists were not philosophical Darwinists at all. True, they talked incessantly of survival of the fittest and of the virtues of competition, but these conceptions were not peculiar to Darwinism; in fact, they were the time-worn shibboleths of classical economics and laissez faire. Moreover, insofar as the social Darwinists were defenders of the social status quo, they could hardly qualify as Darwinians, who accepted the philosophical doctrine of incessant change. Their use of Darwinist slogans merely reflected the impact of Darwin's ideas, not a real understanding or acceptance of them. At the end of the nineteenth century it was fashionable to use Darwinian phraseology even when the thrust of Darwinian ideas was completely ignored.

Some thinkers did recognize the philosophical implications of evolutionary thought, and their development of the philosophy of pragmatism proved to be the most important American contribution to formal philosophy. Pragmatism is both a measure of the great success of contemporary science and a sign of the rejection of a theistic basis for life. In method it followed the natural sciences, emphasizing precision, clarity of thought, and reliance on the senses. It is no accident that the two men to whom pragmatism owes its formulation and popularity, Charles S. Peirce and William James, were both practicing scientists. The secularism of pragmatism was equally obvious. Pragmatists paid little or no attention to the traditional concerns of religion or even of metaphysics; God, revelation, and the nature of being were beyond the senses and therefore beyond their interest. Pragmatism was the philosophy of those who believed in results, tangible objects, and this world.

Philosophically, what is pragmatism? The best-known popularizer of it, William James, defined it as "first a method; and second, a genetic theory of what is meant by truth." It was as a method that pragmatism was first presented in 1878 by Charles Peirce in a now celebrated essay, "How to Make Our Ideas Clear." Peirce was brought to formulate his new philosophy by his impatience with the vagueness, inconclusiveness, and unverifiability of such traditional philosophical abstractions as God, Truth, Beauty, and Good. Impressed by the great successes of the natural sciences, which tested truth by experimentation and measurement, he sought to apply similar tests to ideas.

The meaning of an idea, Peirce argued, was ascertainable only from its effects. "Our idea of anything," he wrote, "is our idea of its sensible effects; and if we fancy that we have any other we deceive ourselves, and mistake a mere sensation accompanying the thought for a part of the thought itself." Thus, if the same consequences follow from two ideas, then there are no differences between the ideas, regardless of how different they may appear. Furthermore, as William James pointed out, if any abstract concept, no matter how remote from everyday life, "can be shown to have consequences for our life, it has meaning." Thus if a belief in God has practical consequences—if people go about their daily tasks taking that belief into consideration—then God is a meaningful concept for them, though not necessarily for others. In general, however, pragmatism was secular in its outlook; it gave scant support to religion, God, or the intricacies of theology.

Truth for the pragmatists lay in an idea's usefulness, in its ability to work when tested. "Pragmatism," said Peirce, is "only an application of the sole principle of logic recommended by Jesus: 'Ye may know them by their fruits.'" If an idea "works, it will have some truth that ought to be held to," James advised. "True ideas are those that we can assimilate, validate, corroborate, and verify. False ideas are those that we cannot." This distinction, of course, is the same as that made in the natural sciences. Pragmatists, as these remarks make clear, conceived of truth as relative, not absolute. As James phrased it, "Truth is *made,* much as health, wealth, and strength are made, in the course of experience." For the pragmatists there was no such concept as Truth; there were only truths.

As the son of a famous theologian and the brother of a great novelist, William James may appear to have had little in common with the new, often ruthless, and in some cases unlearned business leaders who gave the Gilded Age its name. Yet his life and thought were quite closely attuned to the robust era of the Economic Revolution. A vigorous personality who viewed the universe as unfinished and growing, James thrived on challenge and risk; he gloried in the knowledge that pragmatism demanded "toughness of mind." He was speaking for pragmatism as a philosophy as well as for himself when he said that in life "I am willing that there should be real losses and real losers, and no total preservations for all that is." An anxious quest for security and a love of quiet contemplation were no more among

James' attributes than among John D. Rockefeller's or Jay Gould's. James heaped scorn upon Asian philosophies that preached the contemplative life. "The hindoo and buddhist, for this is essentially their attitude, are simply afraid—afraid of more experience, afraid of life," he contended. In another context James would refer to the "bitch goddess Success," but in pragmatism he advocated a philosophy eminently at home in the earthy, secular age of the "Great Barbecue" (as historian Vernon Parrington described the post–Civil War boom years), when what worked was often judged to be thereby good and true.

The Secularization of Culture: Realism in Literature, Art, and Architecture

In an age of Darwinism, democracy, and pragmatism, one would expect literature and art to be increasingly concerned with reality, with seeing life honestly. Probably the most profound single impact upon the contemporary literature came from Darwin's demonstration that hitherto hidden forces were the truly operative ones. Indeed, the whole history of science since the seventeenth century was studded with crucial experiments that had shown appearances to be untrustworthy when not actually false. Darwin's inclusion of human beings in the spectrum of nature and his ingenious accounting for the origin of species were only the most recent examples. This success of Darwin in uncovering the true and constant sources of change in nature encouraged some writers to seek a similar realism in their various artistic portrayals of men, women, and society.

Realism had not always been the office of literature in America. For the popular writer the purpose had been to entertain the reader, while for the serious writer it had usually meant idealizing the past and extracting from experience lessons for the present. The principal test of cultivated writing during most of the previous century had been the ability to express in pleasing language and elevated tone the beauties of nature and the pleasures of society. Before 1870 the romance was the typical form of the novel; by the end of the century the novel had been transformed into a mirror of the world and an instrument of social protest. The general causes of the metamorphosis were rooted in the triumphs of science and the Economic Revolution; the specific cause was a remarkable group of writers. Out of the interaction of the two issued modern American literature.

William Dean Howells: Democracy of Facts. William Dean Howells was not the first writer to champion realism in literature, but in the last half of the nineteenth century he was undoubtedly the most influential. As editor of the highly esteemed *Atlantic Monthly* between 1871 and 1881 and *Harper's Monthly* in the 1890s, Howells was in a strategic position to encourage those young writers who brought a new realism into their work. A critic's test of a novel, Howells once wrote, was to ask if it "was true to the motives, the impulses, the principles that shape the life of actual men and women." At another time, he articulated a central tenet of realism, the importance of detail and accuracy. The realistic writer, he said, "feels in every nerve the equality of things and the unity of men." To him nothing was "insignificant," and "nothing that God has made is contempt-ible." In such statements can be read the influence of the great contemporary European realists, Honoré de Balzac, Émile Zola, and Ivan Turgenev, from whom Howells and other American realists drew their principles. The democ-racy of facts that Howells advocated also neatly reflected science's own rever-ence for the relevant fact, no matter how humble or minute.

It would be a mistake, however, to take Howells' definition of realism literally. His own novels, for example, hardly seem realistic in our post-Freudian age; his counsel of realism did not extend to the bedroom or the bathroom. Yet the gate he pushed ajar would eventually swing wide. In 1920, the year Howells died, Sinclair Lewis' realistic novel, *Main Street,* was to head the best-seller list. This coinci-dence marked a fitting close to the life of the man who, more than any other, had prepared the way for the popular acceptance of Lewis' novel.

Howells' most successful novel, as well as his best, is *The Rise of Silas Lapham* (1885). More than any other novel of the age, it illustrates the thought and outlook of its time. Unlike Edward Bellamy's *Looking Backward, or 2000—1887,* it is first-rate literature, and unlike *The Adventures of Huckleberry Finn,* it deals with contemporary society in an urban setting. *The Rise of Silas Lapham* is truly a so-cial novel in that it depicts the life of á newly rich and uneducated manufacturer who is trying to make his way up the social ladder. Yet the book does not resort to muckraking, for Silas Lapham is a likable and, in some ways, even an admirable person. He is honest, if uncultivated, and in Howells' mind, it is clear, the hard work that brought Lapham his millions is preferable to the dilettantish indolence of the aristocratic Corey family, which represents the "old order" that Lapham and his kind were displacing.

The Minister's Charge (1887) and *A Hazard of New Fortunes* (1890) similarly exhibit Howells' social realism. Both novels portray the poor accurately and sym-pathetically, without being sentimental. In emphasizing the responsibility of the individual for the welfare and future of society, *The Minister's Charge* fore-shadowed Howells' later, more explicit call for reform in *A Traveler from Altruria* (1894). In that utopian novel, Howells sharply contrasted the individualistic, capi-talistic society of his own America with the rational, tranquil, cooperative society of the mythical land of Altruria.

By the time Howells wrote *A Hazard of New Fortunes* and *A Traveler from Altruria,* he had been strongly influenced by his reading of Laurence Gronlund's *Cooperative Commonwealth,* a popular exposition of socialism published in 1884. From then on, Howells' thought turned permanently in the direction of non-Marx-ian socialism. He was never a radical nor even a social reformer in any active sense; yet his commitment to literary realism would not let him overlook the vis-ible paradox of progress and poverty. Despite his own considerable stake in the status quo, for example, he vigorously condemned the unfair treatment of the eight anarchists charged with the Haymarket bombing.

Henry James: Portrayer of the Sensitive Protagonist. Howells was only one of three giants of American letters in these years; the other two were Mark Twain

(Samuel Langhorne Clemens), and Henry James, the brother of William James, the philosopher of pragmatism. All three authors are properly described as realists, but aside from their literary commitment they had little in common. As men and as writers they were far apart. For instance, by the 1890s both Howells and Twain had lost much of their earlier enthusiasm for American society, but their disenchantment never caused them to abandon their native soil. James, on the other hand, found his most congenial abode in England, where he lived almost continuously after 1876. Yet the impress of his American origins remained on his work, providing one of his principal literary themes. His novels *The American* (1877) and *The Portrait of a Lady* (1881) contrast the innocence of young America with the sophistication of old Europe. Though James clothed his realism in the form of a novel of manners, his interest clearly lay in uncovering the inner emotions and drives of his sensitive characters as they found society changing about them. Unlike Howells, he had no wish to depict social change or the lot of the poor.

Only two of James' numerous novels can be taken as an expression of his realization of social problems. *The Bostonians* (1886) was James' pronouncement on the women's movement, though he concentrated on the individuals involved, not on the reform, in which he had little interest and for which he displayed scant sympathy. Yet his realism can be seen here, too, though it is hedged, as always, with circumlocutions and indirect statement. The relationship between the two principal women characters is fraught with homosexual implications, which vaguely disturbed his conventional readers, temporarily clouding his popularity. The other novel in which he seriously touched upon a social issue was *Princess Casamassima* (1886). The social theme in the book is anarchism, then a sensational form of radical social protest in both Europe and the United States. Once again, however, James was neither sympathetic to the movement nor interested in it as such. His purpose was to probe the feelings and attitudes of his characters.

Mark Twain: Against the Genteel Tradition. Probably the greatest of the three American realists of the age was Samuel Clemens, or Mark Twain, as he has become universally known. Unlike Howells and James, Twain fits the popular stereotype of a realistic writer. He came from a rough-and-tumble background in rural Missouri and the mining camps of the Far West. Moreover, his successes had come as a humorous writer who deflated literary pomposities and poked fun at gentility. The greatness of Twain, however, does not lie in his western or frontier humor, but in his perceptive portrayal of human conflict and morality in *The Adventures of Huckleberry Finn* (1884), which is one of the leading works of world literature. Ostensibly the story of a boy's adventurous trip on a raft floating down the Mississippi, the book is actually a probing examination of the morality of slavery, the relation of the individual to society, and the nature and obligations of platonic love.

For our purposes, however, the importance of *Huckleberry Finn* rests in its realism, in its sharp break with the genteel tradition that had smothered both popular and serious writing in sticky conventions and ideality. The language as well as the substance of Twain's novel is realistic. Profound moral issues are clothed in everyday circumstances and settings, while the words and syntax are the uncultured but often poetic talk of the poorly educated Huck and his slave companion, Jim. One of Twain's stock devices in his humorous writings was to mock the pompous, idealized language of the literary world of his time. Huck Finn is admirably suited to carry on this quest for reality through the ridicule of artificiality. In Huck, as Henry Nash Smith has pointed out, Twain created a figure who is far freer from convention and tradition than his earlier Tom Sawyer. For despite Tom's reputation for mischief, he in fact accepts the conventions of his society as Huck does not. He stays home, he goes to school, and in the end he does mind Aunt Polly. With Huck, who deeply rebels against pomposity and hypocrisy, Twain fashioned a sharper instrument for exposing moral weakness and dishonesty. Its keen edge is apparent in Twain's satirizing of the social mores of the river towns Huck and Jim visit as they drift down the Mississippi on their raft.

Besides illustrating the realism of an age of science, *Huckleberry Finn* also exhibits the influence of democracy. The deepest of moral issues is argued in the humble tongue of a runaway schoolboy and an escaped slave. Twain quite frankly admitted that he wrote for the common people, and not for the "cultivated classes." And it was the ordinary citizen who provided an audience for his humor. Proud of his own modest origins, Twain believed fervently in the virtue and potential of the common American.

Although the influence of American democratic ideals upon Twain reveals itself in his greatest work, it is even more evident in *A Connecticut Yankee in King Arthur's Court* (1889). In fact, the book was intended to show how the improvements of technology, which much impressed Twain, had encouraged the moral improvement of man. Its plot ingeniously depicts the adventures and successes of a self-taught American miraculously transported back to early medieval England. Once there, the main character, Hank Morgan, demonstrates the superiority of American democracy and industrial society over feudalism, superstition, and an established church. The book was a paean to the practical, common-sense approach to life that Twain thought he discerned in the ordinary American. Unaffected, simple men were his ideal; he scorned the manners and affectations of the intellect as heartily as did Commodore Vanderbilt. When Howells read *A Connecticut Yankee,* he called it "an object lesson in democracy" and drew a parallel between the barons of medieval England, who overworked their serfs, and the industrial "capitalist of Mr. Harrison's day who grows rich on the labor of his underpaid wage men." Radical and reform groups also seized upon Twain's novel as a support for their opposition to big business.

Although Twain had been born and raised in a slave state, his quest for reality and honesty twice led him to a critical examination of racism. The first time was in *Huckleberry Finn;* the second was in the novel *Pudd'nhead Wilson* (1894). His second effort was less powerful and profound than the first. In *Pudd'nhead Wilson,* for example, he resorted to the time-worn literary contrivance of mistaken identity, in which two babies from different families arc switched at birth. Even so, he effectively exposed the inadequacies in the racist assertion of black inferiority. The novel is not only an example of realistic writing, particularly in its portrayal of the black woman, Roxy, but also of Darwinian environmentalism. Against the racists' assertion that heredity was the principal determinant of personality, Twain argued that social environment was primary.

George Washington Cable: Mirror to the South. The realism of Twain, Howells, and James can also be seen in the work of a lesser figure, George Washington Cable of Louisiana. Like Twain, Cable exhibited his realism on the double levels of language and content. His painstaking, faithful reproduction of the speech of blacks and French Creoles in New Orleans in *Old Creole Days* (1879) and *The Grandissimes* (1884) anticipated Twain's use of ordinary rural speech in *Huckleberry Finn.* His realistic content deals with the complicated, biracial society of New Orleans. In *The Grandissimes,* his finest novel, Cable frankly portrayed the enmity between the new American rulers of recently acquired Louisiana and the proud French Creoles of New Orleans. He probed the moral issues of slavery and miscegenation which had helped shape Creole society and values. In fact, Cable's realism cut so deeply that New Orleans society soon snubbed him, despite the fact that this was the first time the fascinating life of Louisiana's Creoles had been brought to the attention of the nation.

His honesty and passion for social justice took Cable, a Southerner, into territory no other realistic writer of his time had entered. In his two collections of essays of social criticism, *The Silent South* (1885) and *The Negro Question* (1890), Cable patiently, thoroughly, and devastatingly exposed the injustice of racial segregation in the South, pleading with his fellow white Southerners to grant the Negro full equality before the law. (He never advocated social equality, though he practiced it.) His text was the national creed of equality and his goal the regeneration of the South. Despite the undeniable cogency of his arguments, his influence in the South shrank with the publication of each essay. Indeed, because of his frigid reception in the South, he moved to Massachusetts in 1885.

Stephen Crane: Beyond Realism to Naturalism. For all Cable's courage in daring to probe the race question, his literary realism was of the Howells variety—applied only within the conventional boundaries. The first to cross these limits was Stephen Crane. Indeed, literary historians speak of him more often as a naturalistic (rather than realistic) writer precisely because he went beyond realism. Realists like Howells, Twain, and Cable believed in accurate, honest reporting of the world, but only of an acceptable world; for them, certain aspects of life were simply outside a writer's legitimate concern and unsuited to appear in a book. The naturalistic writers, however, placed no such limitations on their conception of the writer's world; for them it included everything—vice as well as virtue, misery as well as happiness, poverty as well as affluence. The connection between the naturalistic writers and Darwinism is apparent. Both saw nature or the environment as amoral, and the human being a product of its forces; both shared a deterministic concept of the universe, in which they included men and women. In the world of nature there was no free will. Inexorable forces seemed to shape all individuals (and things), whether they were mountains, giant redwood trees, or people. Naturalistic writers viewed society along with nature as the powerful forces that determined the fate of individuals.

Stephen Crane's novella, *Maggie, a Girl of the Streets* (1893), focuses on the then forbidden subject of prostitution, not in the usual moralistic fashion of individual responsibility and personal failure but in the new and shocking language of social responsibility. Maggie's fall from virtue to prostitution and her tragic suicide are clearly the consequences of forces beyond her control. Since without control there is no responsibility, she could not be the author of her degradation, as many moralists insisted. When first published, *Maggie* was buried in shocked silence, only to be widely reprinted in 1896 after the success of Crane's second novel. At that date, one literary historian remarked, "modern American fiction was born." Significantly, by the end of the nineties the environmentalist view of prostitution that Crane's *Maggie* advanced was the accepted assumption in the several municipal investigations of "The Social Evil."

Crane's second novel, *The Red Badge of Courage* (1895), is not as sensational as *Maggie,* but it is equally realistic, while its prose is more economical and direct. Like *Maggie, The Red Badge of Courage* concerns a young person confronted by fear. In this case a young Civil War soldier is faced for the first time with the threat of death in battle. There is no sentimental glorification of war, only a stripped, taut depiction of its pressures and the anatomy of the human fear that paralyzes reason and controls the will. By its frank assertion of the inadequacy of individual will in the face of overwhelming circumstances and environment, the novel travels far beyond Howells' realism. Later, in the twentieth century, naturalism would come to dominate American fiction in the work of Frank Norris, Theodore Dreiser, Jack London, and Upton Sinclair.

New Architecture: Skyscrapers Evolve. The drive to represent life without illusions or obscuring decoration, seen in the philosophy of pragmatism and in the literature of Howells, Twain, and Crane, also had a counterpart in architecture. Developments in architecture responded to the new social and technological changes of the late 1880s and 1890s.

The tall building provides an excellent example of how an emerging, realistic philosophy of design and social and technological innovations combined to produce a new architecture. In the crowded cities of the 1880s, where urban land was increasingly precious, the tall building offered a solution. It would cut costs by using less land, yet provide additional housing and office space. Two technological innovations, the elevator and the structural steel frame, made a building of more than five or six stories practical for the first time. The elevator alone was not sufficient. By introducing an elevator, architect Richard Morris Hunt was able to construct the ten-story New York Tribune Building in 1874, but such height required massive walls, which consumed precious space. In 1891, construction of Chicago's sixteen-story Monadnock Building—the tallest masonry building ever erected—required walls that were six feet thick at the base to sustain the weight of the floors. It was only after 1884, when William LeBaron Jenney boldly introduced a steel frame into the construction of the Home Insurance Building in Chicago, that structures of ten or more stories became practical. Thereafter, architects were able to erect tall buildings with walls as thin as their aesthetics demanded and with much consequent saving of interior space.

The man who fashioned a distinct style of architecture out of the new technology and the needs of urban life was Louis H. Sullivan of Chicago. By using the steel-frame construction to great advantage in the Wainwright Building in St. Louis in 1891, Sullivan set the style for skyscrapers in the United States for the next half century or more. Although the Wainwright Building is only ten stories high, its design embodies Sullivan's forthrightness and artistic integrity. The practice had been to interrupt or obscure the long, upward-flowing lines of the tall building with embellishments or different window designs on successive floors. Sullivan broke decisively with this convention, asserting that the building's height was to be emphasized rather than disguised. Since it was in fact tall, why try to make it appear to be anything else? Here and in his other architectural designs, Sullivan's governing principle was that the form of a building ought to be an honest statement of its use. Form should not obscure or mislead. With Sullivan, sham, sentimentality, and romanticizing came under attack in architecture just as it was in philosophy and literature.

Louis Sullivan's Wainwright Building, St. Louis, 1891, used steel-frame construction and decoration to emphasize the height of the structure. *Chicago Architectural Photographing Company*

Sullivan's passionate commitment to the wedding of form and purpose and to honesty of statement was carried on in the work of his student and disciple, Frank Lloyd Wright, perhaps the best-known American architect of the early 1900s. The realism and candor which Sullivan insisted upon became a central principle of architectural design in the twentieth century.

The Art of Homer and Eakins. Painting, even more than architecture, lent itself to realism. In America, Winslow Homer and Thomas Eakins were the leading exponents of a contemporary European movement that rejected the sentimentalizing and idealizing then dominant in art. Long before he became known as a painter of seascapes, Homer scorned traditional art and its falsification of feeling. "If a man wants to be an artist," he once remarked, "he should never look at pictures." The only model was the real world of nature. As an illustrator for popular magazines during the Civil War, Homer sketched army life with a fidelity that was not equaled in literature until Stephen Crane's *Red Badge of Courage.* Homer's best-known works are those canvases which catch the moods of the sea. Men are often included in his pictures, but even if they fill half the canvas they are subordinated to a powerful and overwhelming sea, much as the characters in the novels of naturalistic writers are dominated by social and natural forces. Probably no artist in America or Europe has equaled Homer's skill in capturing the ocean, especially in its darker moods. Unlike the contemporary European impressionist painters, who were fascinated by bright sunlight playing on water or clouds or flesh, Homer chose to fill his pictures with somber clouds, threatening skies, and dark water, as evidenced in such well-known oils as "Fog Warning" (1885), "Winter Coast" (1890), and "The Gulf Stream" (1899).

Like the philosopher-pragmatists Charles Peirce and William James, Thomas Eakins maintained a healthy disdain for tradition. He painted what seemed real and meaningful in his own time and place. Eakins, one art historian has written, "was the first American artist—as distinct from craftsman or folk-artist—to make his painting out of what was there instead of relying on tradition." Much in the manner of Mark Twain, Eakins was offended by the devices and conventions of contemporary art. He considered the artists of his time false and dishonest. His vehemence in denouncing them reminds one of Twain at his most explosive. In a letter to a friend, Eakins offered his frank opinion of the work of the seventeenth-century Dutch artist, Peter Paul Rubens, and at the same time expressed a clear statement of his own commitment to honesty of expression and fidelity to fact: "[Rubens'] modelling is always crooked and dropsical," he wrote, "and no marking is ever in the right place or anything like what he sees in nature . . . everything must be making a big noise and tumbling about, there must be monsters, too, for his men are not monstrous enough for him. His pictures put me in mind of chamber pots and I would not be sorry if they were all burnt." Even to the closing vulgarity, he sounds like the earthy Twain.

For his part, Eakins meticulously recorded on canvas only what he saw. His many years of anatomical study at the Jefferson Medical School in Philadelphia help account for his several paintings of medical clinics in operation. As a result of

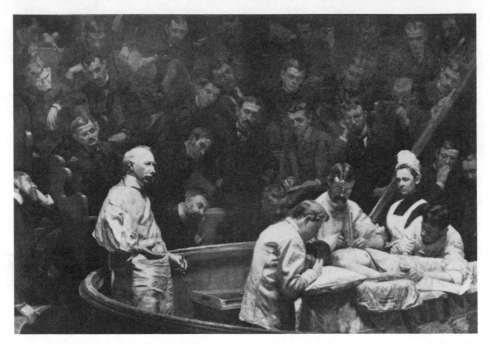

In this realistic painting by Thomas Eakins, a doctor performs surgery on a patient whose flesh is seen being pierced by the scalpel. *University of Pennsylvania*

his studies, he commanded a knowledge of the structure and mechanics of the human body that few artists of his time could equal. Demanding from his students the same detailed knowledge, he urged them to "get to the character of things." The unflinching realism of his portraits and the long sittings he required of his subjects sometimes cost him clients who wanted prettier pictures and easier sittings. Even the physicians in his paintings of clinics complained of his realism, which required that they be portrayed with blood on their hands. Eakins' relentless pursuit of reality was carried through with fanatic zeal, sometimes in the face of a less committed society. In 1886 he lost his teaching post at the Philadelphia Academy of Art because of the public outcry at his stripping the loincloth from a male model to better illustrate musculature to his class of women students.

Although there is no idealization in his work, Eakins was never a slavish copier, either of other artists' work or of nature's. As he said, the capstone of any work is the intuition and sensitivity that transforms a meticulously detailed reproduction of life into a work of art. His portraits, for which he was well known in his own time, reveal not only his attention to realistic detail but also his ability to catch the emotion and inimitable character of the subject. "The Gross Clinic" (1875) was a masterpiece of unconventionality, showing the famous Dr. Samuel Gross in his clinic, hands bloody from an operation upon a man, whose buttocks are exposed to the viewer. Shocking at the time to critics,

"The Gross Clinic" has been compared with Melville's novel *Moby Dick* as a nineteenth-century masterpiece unappreciated in its time. When Eakins in 1889 painted another clinical study, "The Agnew Clinic," in which a woman patient's breast was uncovered, the work was denied exhibition by the Pennsylvania Academy of Art. Eakins always attempted to capture the essence of things, to penetrate appearances, just as Twain and Howells, Peirce and William James, and Bellamy and George tried to do.

Although Eakins recognized that even the most carefully detailed painting was different from a photograph, he found the new techniques of photography of great importance in his studies of motion in humans and animals. Indeed, some of his technical innovations in photographing moving objects in the middle 1880s anticipated the later motion-picture camera. Eakins brought to his art a precision, a dedication to accurate detail, and an impersonality that clearly reflected the scientific bias of the age in which he worked. He even advocated the use of mathematics in art because of its precision and accuracy. His use of new technical advances to enrich his art, such as his experiments with photography, is reminiscent of Jenney and Sullivan, who also incorporated the new technology into their path-breaking architectural design for the tall building.

Perhaps more than any other artist, with the possible exception of Mark Twain, Thomas Eakins summed up the spirit of the age in his work, his habits, and his outlook. Like Twain he was fascinated by tools, contrivances, and scientific machinery. He worshiped the here and now, the practical, and the forthright; he could only ridicule idealities. His art was tough and earthy, much the same as William James' philosophy. Not many of the rising businessmen and tycoons of the age liked his frank paintings, but in their own practices in business and in their outlooks on life, they were as frank, outspoken, and brutal as he. They simply were not used to seeing their own values mirrored in art. An Eakins, a Twain, or a William James was really not far removed from a Carnegie or a Rockefeller in fundamental values. The realism of science, the materialism of an industrial society, and the social democracy of a mobile society influenced them all. By the end of the century, then, ministers and artists, tycoons and reformers were all primarily concerned with the world, either as it was or as it should be. But in either case the outlook was secular and materialistic.

SUGGESTED READING

A general work that seeks to relate industrial development, social order, and intellectual changes is Robert Wiebe, *The Search for Order, 1877–1920* (1967). Paul F. Boller, Jr., *American Thought in Transition: The Impact of Evolutionary Naturalism, 1865–1900* (1969), is a good introduction to intellectual developments.

A suitable starting point for religion during these years is Sydney A. Ahlstrom, *Religious History of the American People* (1972); Part VII treats the closing decades of the

*Available in paperback edition.

nineteenth century. A more detailed and informed examination is Paul A. Carter, *The Spiritual Crisis of the Gilded Age* (1971). The two standard works on the Social Gospel are Charles H. Hopkins, *Rise of the Social Gospel in American Protestantism, 1865–1915* (1940), and the broader, more readable treatment by Henry F. May, *Protestant Churches and Industrial America* (1949). Herbert A. Wisbey, *Soldiers Without Swords* (1955), interestingly and authoritatively treats the Salvation Army. The story of revivalism is told with verve in Bernard A. Weisberger, *They Gathered at the River* (1958), and in the more scholarly William McLoughlin, *Modern Revivalism* (1959). Critical of the founder of Christian Science is Edwin F. Dakin, *Mrs. Eddy: The Biography of a Virginal Mind* (1929). More sympathetic and informed is Robert Peel, *Mary Baker Eddy: Years of Discovery* (1966), and *Years of Trial* (1971). Peel has also written a sympathetic, philosophical interpretation of his religion in *Christian Science: Its Encounter with American Culture* (1958). Probably the best overall study is the recent Stephen Gottschalk, *The Emergence of Christian Science in American Religious Life* (1973).

No excellent general history of Catholicism in the United States has yet been written, though John Tracy Ellis, *American Catholicism* (1956), is adequate. A first-rate historical study is the important Thomas T. McAvoy, *The Great Crisis in American Catholic History, 1895–1900* (1957). See, too, McAvoy's general study, *The Formation of the American Catholic Minority* (1967). More popularly written is Andrew M. Greeley, *The Catholic Experience* (1967). Robert D. Cross, *The Emergency of Liberal Catholicism in America* (1958), does justice to the variety of views within the Church.

The best introduction to Judaism is Nathan Glazer, *American Judaism* (1957). Marshall Sklare, *Conservative Judaism: An American Religious Movement* (1955), is informative. On Reform Judaism in the United States the easiest introduction is Israel Knox, *Rabbi in America: The Story of Isaac M. Wise* (1957). David Philipson, *The Reform Movement of Judaism* (1907), places the movement in its European background. Concerning hostility to Jews, an important article is John Higham, "Anti-Semitism in the Gilded Age: A Reinterpretation," *Mississippi Valley Historical Review,* XLIII (1957), 559–578.

The best general study of the women's movement is Eleanor Flexner, *Century of Struggle: The Women's Rights Movement in the United States* (1959). William O'Neill, *Everyone Was Brave: The Rise and Fall of Feminism in America* (1969), is provocative and important. Helpful on the occupational side of the movement is Robert W. Smuts, *Women and Work in America* (1959). A valuable source on the same topic is Dorothy Richardson, *The Long Day: The True Story of a New York Working Girl, as Told by Herself* (1906).

The standard work on the defense of industrial society is Richard Hofstadter, *Social Darwinism in American Thought, 1860–1915* (1948); it needs to be qualified now by Irwin G. Wyllie, "Social Darwinism and the Businessman," *Proceedings of the American Philosophical Society,* CIII (1959), 629–635. The argument over the role of government in the economy is further elaborated in Sidney Fine, *Laissez Faire and the General-Welfare State* (1956). The best study on the author of pragmatism is Ralph Barton Perry, *The Thought and Character of William James,* 2 vols. (1935).

Books on the writers of the period are numerous. Covering all the writers in authoritative and concise fashion is *Literary History of the United States,* ed. Robert Spiller et al. (1963). It also contains a voluminous bibliography. Among the works on individual authors only a few selected ones can be mentioned. One of the best is Henry Nash Smith, *Mark Twain: The Development of a Writer* (1962). The most recent and perhaps the finest biography of Twain is Justin Kaplan, *Mr. Clemens and Mark Twain* (1966). The eminent critic Maxwell Geismar has written *Twain: An American Prophet* (1970). Thomas Beer, *Stephen Crane* (1923), is the most thought provoking of Crane studies, but it contains errors of fact; more reliable but not as well written is John Berryman, **Stephen Crane* (1950). Two complementary works on Howells are Everett Carter, *Howells and the Age of Realism* (1954), and Van Wyck Brooks, *Howells: His Life and World* (1959). Kenneth S. Lynn, *William Dean Howells, an American Life* (1971), is first rate. The nature of realism and naturalism is explored in Warner Berthoff, *The Ferment of Realism* (1965). The definitive life of Henry James is Leon Edel, **Henry James,* 5 vols. (1953–1972). A good single-volume work is F. W. Dupee, **Henry James* (1951). Arlin Turner, *George W. Cable: A Biography* (1956), is the best book on that writer. Interpretive and informative is Hugh Morrison, **Louis Sullivan: A Prophet of Modern Architecture* (1935). Also very good on architecture is Carl W. Condit, *The Rise of the Skyscraper* (1952). The most rewarding analyses of the relevant painters are two by Lloyd Goodrich, *Winslow Homer* (1959), and *Thomas Eakins, His Life and Work* (1933); and one by Fairfield Porter, *Thomas Eakins* (1959). Gordon Hendricks, *The Life and Work of Thomas Eakins* (1974), is a magnificent tribute and appreciation, lavishly illustrated. Barbara Novak, *American Painting of the Nineteenth Century* (1967), puts Eakins and Homer into an artistic perspective, but ignores the social meaning of their art.

INDEX

A

Adams, Charles Francis, 151
Adams, Henry, 115, 122, 168
Addams, Jane, 12
Addystone Pipe and Steel Company v. *United States*, 42−43
Adler, Felix, 174−75
Adventures of Huckleberry Finn, The (Twain), 181, 182−83, 184
Africa, 152
Agassiz, Louis, 174
Age of Reform, The (Hofstadter), 119
"Agnew Clinic, The" (Eakins), 189
Agricultural Wheel, 71
Agriculture, and exports, 65, 68; revolution in, 17, 64−68, 73. *See also* Farmers.
Aguinaldo, Emilio, 152
Alger, Horatio, 78
Altgeld, John Peter, 10, 115, 120, 126
American, The (James), 182
American Commonwealth, The (Bryce), 111, 171
American Federation of Labor, 11, 81, 84−85, 120, 121, 158
American Protective Association, 165
American Railway Union, 125
American Sugar Refining Company, 36
American Tobacco Company, 38
Anaconda Copper Company, 38, 56
Anaconda silver mine, 56
Anarchism, and anarchists, 115, 181. *See also* Haymarket riot.
Ancient Order of Hibernians, 80
Anti-Monopoly party, 71
Anti-Semitism, 119, 168
Antitrust movement, 40−43. *See also* Sherman Antitrust Act.
APA. *See* American Protective Association.
Architecture, 185−87
Armour and Company, 36
Armour, Philip D., 38
Arthur, Chester A., 89, 90, 91, 96, 97, 106
ARU. *See* American Railway Union.
Atlantic Monthly, 141, 180
Awakening, The (Chopin), 172

B

Baker, Ray Stannard, 124
Baltimore and Ohio Railroad, 21, 23
Balzac, Honoré de, 181
Banking. *See* Investment banking.
Banking Act of 1863, 30
Banking Act of 1864, 30

Beard, Charles, 34
Beard, Mary, 34
Beecher, Henry Ward, 174
Bell, Alexander Graham, 1, 32
Bellamy, Edward, 12−14, 142, 157, 181, 189
Bell Telephone Company, 32
Belmont, August, 127
Bemis, Samuel Flagg, 140, 141
Bethlehem Steel Company, 34
Big business, 36−40, 70, 104, 175, 177
Bimetallism, 127
Bismarck, Otto von, 104, 164
Blacks. *See* Negroes.
Blaine, James G., 89, 90−92, 103, 106, 143
Blair Education Bill (1880s), 96, 99
Blair, Henry, 96
Bland-Allison Act (1878), 101
Bland, Richard, 129
Borden, Gail, 34
Bostonians, The (James), 182
Bourbons (southern conservative Democrats), 96
Brace, Loring, 159
Brandeis, Louis B., 168
Brazil, 145
British Guiana, 144
Brown, William Wells, 140
Bryan, William Jennings, 120, 131, 133−35, 137, 151
Bryce, James, 111, 171
Buchanan, Joseph, 82
Burlington Lines, 65
Butler, Marion, 133

C

Cable, George Washington, 184
Calvinism, 161
Campaigns, political. *See* Political campaigns.
Canada, and Indians, 63−64; and violence, 63−64
Carlisle, John G., 126, 143, 151
Carnegie, Andrew, 34, 35, 164, 177, 189
Carnegie Steel Company, 38
Catholic Charities Review, 166
Catholicism and Catholics, 91, 163−66, 168, 174; and racism, 166
Cattle raising, 59−61
Central Pacific Railroad, 23
Century of Dishonor, A (Jackson), 4
Cervera, Pascual, 150
Charles River Bridge case, 30
Chestnutt, Charles W., 140
Chicago Exposition (1893), 115
Child labor, 13, 74, 77

China, commercial partition of, 152; Open Door policy in, 141
Chinese Exclusion Act (1882), 8. *See also* Immigrants, Chinese.
Chopin, Kate O'Flaherty, 172
Christianity and the Social Crisis (Rauschenbusch), 160
Christian Science, 158, 162–63, 168
Cigar Makers Union, 83
Civil Service, 91, 105–7
Clapham, John, 18
Clemens, Samuel Langhorne. *See* Twain, Mark.
Cleveland, Grover, 89, 90, 91, 92, 93, 99, 102, 106, 119–20, 127–28, 130, 143, 144, 151; and Congress, 110; and gold standard, 122, 127, 129, 143; and Mugwumps, 106, 129; and presidential prerogatives, 108, 109, 110, 111; and tariff, 109–10, 129
Coeur d'Alene strike, 117
Coinage Act (1878), 100
Coin's Financial School (Harvey), 132
Coit, Stanton, 12
Commercial and Financial Chronicle, 121
Commons, John R., 75
Communications, revolution in, 17–18, 28, 67, 69, 146. *See also* Railroad.
Compromise of 1877, 95
Comstock, Henry, 55
Concas, Captain, 150
Congressional dominance, 107–10
Congressional elections. *See* Elections, Congressional.
Congressional reorganization, 106
Conkling, Roscoe, 90–91, 92, 108
Connecticut Yankee in King Arthur's Court, A (Twain), 183
Contract Labor Law (1864), 30, 81
Cooperative Commonwealth (Gronlund), 181
Corporate financing and organization, 39–40
Coxey, Jacob S., 123–24
Crane, Stephen, 184–85
Crédit Mobilier, 20
Crime and lawlessness, 62. *See also* Haymarket riot; Strike.
"Crime of '73," 100, 119
Crocker, Charles, 23
Croker, Richard, 98
Cuba, 141, 142, 145–50, 152
Cullom Committee (1885), 40
Currency and currency reform, 100–102. *See also* Free Silver; Gold Standard; Greenbackers.
Curtis, George W., 91
Custer, George A., 4

D

Daly, Marcus, 56
Darrow, Clarence, 14
Dartmouth College case, 30
Darwin, Charles, and Darwinism, 173–74, 175–79, 180; and naturalistic writers, 184. *See also* Social Darwinism.

Davis, Richard Harding, 149
Dawes Act (1887), 4–5, 107
Debs, Eugene V., 117, 125, 126, 151
Democratic party, 93, 102, 129. *See also* Political campaigns; Elections.
Depression, of 1873, 80, 100; of 1893, 115, 121–22, 126–27, 129, 135, 143. *See also* Great Depression.
Desert Land Act (1877), 66
Dewey, George, 149
Dingley Tariff (1897), 153
Dreiser, Theodore, 185
Drew, Daniel, 22
DuBois, W. E. B., 140
Dunbar, Paul Laurence, 140

E

Eads, James B., 19
Eakins, Thomas, 187–89
Eastman, George, 18
Eddy, Mary Baker, 162
Edison, Thomas A., 32–33
Eight-hour day, 81, 83
Einhorn, David, 167
Elections, Congressional: (1874), 93; (1892), 93; (1894), 129, 136; frauds in, 92; national, (1876), 89, 90, 93; (1880), 90, 93; (1884), 90, 91, 93, 96, 97; (1888), 92, 93; (1892), 120–21; (1896), 129, 133–35, 136
Entrepreneurs, 34–36. *See also* under specific name.
"Equal but separate," 139–40
Erie Railroad, 22
Expansionism, 140–45
Expansionists of 1898 (Pratt), 141

F

Farmers and farming, 1; commercial, 68–73; organization, 69–70; plains, 61; and political action, 72; protest, 69–73, 117; surplus labor, 73; tenant, 69. *See also* Agriculture; Populism.
Federal Communications Commission, 27
Federal Council of Churches of Christ in America, 160
Federal Reserve System, 132
Federal Trade Commission, 27
Field, James G., 118
Field, Stephen J., 115
Fifteenth Amendment, 138
Fisk, "Jim," 22
Fletcher v. *Peck*, 30
"Fog Warning" (Homer), 187
"Force Bill" (1890), 98
Ford Motor Company, 40
Fortune, T. Thomas, 140
Free silver, 100, 117, 120, 128, 130–31, 133–35, 177; and election of 1896, 133–35
Frick, Henry Clay, 115, 117, 120
"Full dinner pail," 135

G

Garfield, James A., 89–92, 96, 99, 105, 106, 108; and Congress, 107, 110
General Allotment Act. *See* Dawes Act.
General Federation of Women's Clubs, 171
George, Henry, 12–14, 108, 120, 157, 165
Gibbons, James, 164–65
Gilman, Charlotte Perkins, 172
Gladden, Washington, 159, 165
Godkin, E. L., 105, 129
Gold mining, 54–56, 62, 137
Gold standard, 123, 127–28, 129, 130, 131–32, 134, 153
Gold Standard Act (1900), 153
Gompers, Samuel, 80, 83, 84, 120, 121, 151, 158
Gorman, A. P., 128. *See also* Wilson-Gorman Tariff.
"Gospel of Wealth, The" (Carnegie), 177
Gould, Jay, 82, 180
Grand Army of the Republic, 109
Grandissimes, The (Cable), 184
Grange and Granger laws, 26, 70–71
Grant, Ulysses S., 2, 107, 108, 110
"Great Aberration, The," 140
"Great Barbecue," 180
Great Depression (1930s), 130
Great Northern Railroad, 20, 24
Greenbackers and Greenback party, 71, 99, 100, 118
Gronlund, Laurence, 181
"Gross Clinic, The" (Eakins), 188–89
Guam, 151
"Gulf Stream, The" (Homer), 187

H

Hancock, Winfield Scott, 90
Hanna, Marcus, 133, 134, 135, 151
Harlan, John Marshall, 139
Harper's Monthly, 180
Harper's Weekly, 106, 129, 134
Harriman, Edward, 34
Harrison, Benjamin, 89, 91, 92, 93, 106, 120, 121; and protectionism, 102; and the South, 97; and the trusts, 41; and Whig attitude toward presidency, 110
Harvey, William ("Coin"), 132–33, 142
Hawaii, 144, 151
Hay, John, 105, 141, 150
Hayes, Rutherford B., 9, 89, 90, 95, 108; and Congress, 107–8, 110; and free silver, 101; and the South, 95, 137
Haymarket riot, 9–11, 81, 83, 115, 120, 181
Hazard of New Fortunes, A (Howells), 181
Hearst, William R., 145
Herberg, Will, 157–58
Hicks, John, 129
Hill, James J., 20, 24, 125
Hofstadter, Richard, 119
Homer, Winslow, 187

Homestead Act (1862), 59, 65
Homestead strike, 116, 121, 123
Hopkins, Mark, 23
Howells, William Dean, 151, 180–81, 182, 183, 184, 185
How the Other Half Lives (Riis), 46
"How to Make Our Ideas Clear" (Peirce), 179
Hull House, 12
Hunt, Richard Morris, 185
Huntington, Collis P., 23

I

Immigrants and immigration, 7–8, 44, 78, 93–94, 136, 158, 161; and Catholic Church, 163–64, 165; Chinese, 8, 23, 74; and Jews, 166, 167–68; and labor, 73–75, 81, 84; and Populism, 119; restriction of, 8, 118; and Spanish-American War, 148; and urbanism, 98–99; and voting, 98–99
Income tax, 128, 177; unconstitutionality of, 115, 117, 128
Independents (southern), 96
Indians, 3–5, 23, 63–64
"Industrial armies," 123–24
Industrial Commission (1901), 73
Industrial labor, 73–78
Industrial Workers of the World, 85
Influence of Sea Power Upon History, The (Mahan), 141
Ingersoll, Robert G., 174, 175
International Harvester, 36
Interstate Commerce Act (1887), 27, 31, 41, 107, 177
Interstate Commerce Commission, 7, 27
Investment banking, 39–40
Ireland, John, 164–65
Iron Molders Union, 81
Israelite, The (Wise), 167

J

Jackson, Andrew, 91, 105, 107, 110, 119
Jackson, Helen Hunt, 4
James, Henry, 181–82, 184
James, William, 151, 189; and pragmatism, 163, 178–80, 187, 189
Jefferson, Thomas, 119
Jenney, William LeBaron, 186
Jensen, Richard, 136
Jewish Theological Seminary (NYC), 168
Jews. *See* Judaism.
Johnson, Andrew, 107, 108, 110
Johnson, Lyndon B., 107
Johnson, Tom, 14
Jones Act (1916), 153
Jordan, David Starr, 152
Josephson, Matthew, 35
Journal (NYC), 145
Judaism, 166–68, 174; Conservative, 167, 168; Orthodox, 167, 168; Reform, 167–68

K

Keane, John, 164
Kearney, Denis, 8
Kelley, Oliver H., 70
Kelly, "Honest John," 98
Kelly, William, 32
Key, David M., 95
Kleppner, Paul, 136
Knights of Labor, 11, 79, 81–84, 117, 165, 171
Know-Nothings, 7, 163, 165
Kousser, Morgan, 138
Kropotkin, Peter, 178

L

Labor, conditions of, 76–78
Labor unions, 11, 78–85. *See also* Industrial labor; Trade unions.
Labor unrest, 116–17, 123–24. *See also* Strikes.
LaFollette, Robert M., 2, 136
Laissez faire, 13, 100, 122, 173, 175
Lathrop, Julia, 12
Latin America, 90, 103, 143, 145. *See also* Brazil; Venezuela.
Lease, Mary Elizabeth, 119
Leo XIII, 166
Lewis, Sinclair, 181
Lilienthal, Max, 167
Lincoln, Abraham, 2, 6, 71, 91, 110, 128
Lloyd, Henry D., 133
Lodge Bill, (1890), 98
Lodge, Henry Cabot, 97, 141
Lôme, Depuy de, 147
London, Jack, 185
Looking Backward (Bellamy), 12, 14, 181. *See also* Bellamy, Edward.

M

McCormick reaper, 66
McCoy, Joseph, 58
McKinley Tariff and Tariff Act (1890), 6, 98, 102–3, 110, 119, 128, 143, 151
McKinley, William, 103, 135, 136, 141, 142, 147, 152; and Gold standard, 133; and Spanish-American War, 148–51
Macune, Charles W., 72
Maggie, a Girl of the Streets (Crane), 185
Mahan, Alfred T., 141, 143
Mahone, William, 96
Maine, 147
Main Street (Lewis), 181
Marxism. *See* Socialism.
Maximum Freight Rate case (1896), 27–28
Meat-packing industry, 38
Mechanization, 31–34, 53
Mergenthaler, Ottmar, 18
Miles, Nelson, 150
Military pensions, 108–9
Mills Tariff Bill (1888), 103

Minister's Charge, The (Howells), 181
Molly Maguires, 80
Monroe Doctrine, 144
Moody, Dwight L., 161–62
Morgan, J. P., 34, 39, 40, 127, 134
Mormonism and Mormons, 53, 54, 158, 163, 168
Mugwumps, 105–6, 129
Munn v. *Illinois*, 26, 71
Mutual Aid (Kropotkin), 178

N

National Alliance. *See* Northern Alliance.
National Association of Manufacturers, 143
National Banking Act (1864), 131
National Banking System, 71–72
National Biscuit Company, 38
National Catholic War Council, 166
National Colored Farmers' Alliance, 71
National Farmers' Alliance, 71
"Nationalism," 142
Nationalist, The, 14
National Labor Union, 81
Nation, The, 105, 115
Nativism, 165
Naturalism, 184–85
Natural resources, 28–29
Natural selection, 173–74, 175
Negro and Negroes, 1, 6, 71, 108, 184; disenfranchisement of, 137–38, 152; and Populism, 118–19; and Spanish-American War, 148; and unions, 84; and voting, 6, 95, 97–98, 172
Negro Business League, 140
Negro Question, The (Cable), 184
New Deal, The, 70, 99, 105
Newton, Isaac, 173
New York Central Railroad, 22, 26
New York Evening Post, 129
New York Herald, 115
New York Times, 9, 106
Nickel Plate Line, 25
NLU. *See* National Labor Union.
Norris, Frank, 185
Norris-LaGuardia Act (1932), 126
Northern Alliance, 71, 72
Northern Pacific Railroad, 24, 65
Nugent, W. T. K., 119

O

Old Creole Days (Cable), 184
Olney, Richard, 42, 125, 126, 144–45
On the Origin of Species by Means of Natural Selection (Darwin), 173, 175
Open Door policy, 141

P

Pacific Railway Acts (1862), (1864), 19, 23
Page, Walter Hines, 141

Panic of 1837, 79
Panic of 1857, 79
Parrington, Vernon, 180
"Patriots of America," 142
Peirce, Charles S., 178, 179, 187, 189
Pendleton Act (1883), 106, 107
Pennsylvania Railroad, 21, 23
Pension Bureau, 108
People's party, 72, 117 – 18. *See also* Populism.
Perlman, Selig, 84
Philadelphia and Reading Railroad, 121
Philadelphia Gas Ring, 98
Philadelphia Exposition (1876), 1
Philippines, 140, 144, 145, 149, 151, 153
Pillsbury, John S., 34
Pinkertons, 116 – 17
Plessy v. *Ferguson,* 139
Political campaigns (1884), 91; (1892), 118 – 20.
  See also Elections, Congressional; Elections,
  national.
Polk, James K., 107, 110
Pollack, Norman, 119
Populism and Populists, 61, 72, 105, 115 – 20,
  122, 129, 130, 132, 133 – 34, 135, 137, 138,
  142
Populist Response to Industrial America, The
  (Pollack), 119
Portrait of a Lady, The (James), 182
Powderly, Terence V., 83, 117
Power, revolution in, 17. *See also* Mechaniza-
  tion.
Pragmatism, 178 – 80, 187; and Christian
  Science, 163. *See also* James, William.
Pratt, Julius, 141, 143
Presidential weakness, 89 – 91, 107 – 8, 110 – 11,
  119 – 20, 128
Princess Casamassima (James), 182
Progress and Poverty (George), 12, 14, 108,
  165. *See also* George, Henry.
Progressives (twentieth-century), 14, 99, 105,
  136
Protectionism, 102 – 3, 175, 177
Protestant, Catholic, Jew (Herberg), 157
Protestantism and Protestants, 35, 163, 164,
  165, 166, 174; secularization of, 157 – 63
Pudd'nhead Wilson (Twain), 183
Puerto Rico, 151
Pulitzer, Joseph, 145
Pullman, George, 124, 135
Pullman Palace Company, 124
Pullman strike (1894), 124 – 25

Q

Quimby, Phineas, 162

R

Racism, 152, 184
Radicalism (southern), 95; and Catholic clergy,
  166

Railroad and railroads, 18 – 28; Brotherhoods,
  81, 85; construction, 18 – 20, 122; and gov-
  ernment, 19 – 20, 24 – 28, 100, 117; monopoly,
  6 – 7, 24 – 27; rate wars, 24 – 27. *See also* under
  name; Strike of 1877; Strike of 1894.
Rauschenbusch, Walter, 159 – 60
Readjuster party, 96 – 97
Reagan, John H., 26
Realism, 180 – 89
Reconcentrado policy, 145, 147
Red Badge of Courage, The (Crane), 185, 187
Reed, Thomas B., 107
Republican party, 93, 99, 101 – 2, 136 – 37,
  152, 153; and the economy, 99; and the
  South, 95 – 96, 97 – 98; victories, 129 – 30,
  136 – 37. *See also* Campaigns; Elections.
Rerum Novarum, 166
Resumption of Specie Act (1875), 100, 131
Review of Reviews, 141
Rhodes, James Ford, 9
Riis, Jacob, 46
Rise of Silas Lapham, The (Howells), 181
Rochester Theological Seminary, 160
Rockefeller, John D., 34, 35, 39, 180, 189
Roosevelt, Franklin, 107
Roosevelt, Theodore, 2, 14, 59, 107, 115, 149,
  150, 165; and expansionism, 136, 141, 143
Rubens, Peter Paul, 187
"Rum, Romanism, and rebellion," 91
Ryan, John A., 166

S

Sackville-West, 92
Salvation Army, 159
Sankey, Ira, 161
Santa Fe Railroad, 24
Santo Domingo, 141
Schurz, Carl, 103, 105, 151, 152
Science, 157, 174 – 75, 178 – 79
Science and Health (Eddy), 162
Securities and Exchange Commission, 27
Shafter, William, 149, 150
Shaw, Albert, 141
Sheep raising, 61
Sherman Antitrust Act (1890), 7, 41 – 43, 99, 104,
  107, 111
Sherman, John, 41
Sherman Silver Purchase Act (1890), 101, 110,
  122
Ship Carpenters' union, 81
Silent South, The (Cable), 184
Sinclair, Upton, 185
Single Tax, 12. *See also* George, Henry.
Slavery, 1, 69, 182 – 84. *See also* Negroes.
Smith, Henry Nash, 183
Social Darwinism, 175, 177 – 78
Social Gospel, 158 – 61
Socialism and socialists, 12 – 13, 14, 99, 126,
  142, 181
Social mobility, 78

Society for Ethical Culture, 174
Southern Alliance, 71, 72, 117
Southern Pacific Railroad, 24, 26
South Improvement Company, 35
Spalding, John, 164
Spanish-American War, 141, 145, 148−52
Spencer, Herbert, 175, 178
Spoils system. *See* Civil Service.
Spooner, John, 148
Sprague, Frank J., 33
Springer v. *Illinois,* 128
Standard Oil Company, 35, 39, 92, 134
Stanford, Leland, 23
Starr, Ellen G., 12
Star Route frauds, 91
Stephens, Uriah, 81−82
Strasser, Adolph, 83
Straus, Oscar, 168
Strike and strikes, 78, 82, 115, 116−17, 124−25, 142; of 1877, 9, 10, 108, 159; of 1894, 115, 124−25; women's, 171
Sugar Trust, 42
Sullivan, Louis H., 186, 187
Sumner, Charles, 105
Sumner, William Graham, 99, 175, 177, 178
Survival of the fittest, 175, 176
Sutter, Johann, 54
Swift, Gustavus, 34, 38
Sylvis, William, 81

T

Tammany Hall, 98
Tariff and tariffs, 100−3, 111; Commission, 102; in 1892 campaign, 120. *See also* Dingley Tariff; McKinley Tariff; Wilson-Gorman Tariff.
Taylor, Frederick W., 34
Teller Amendment (1898), 148
Tenure of Office Act (1887), 108
Tesla, Nicholas, 33
Texas and Pacific Railroad, 95
Thernstrom, Stephen, 78
Thomas, Norman, 14
Thomson, J. Edgar, 23
Tillman, Benjamin, 120
Timber and Stone Act (1878), 66
Timber Culture Act (1873), 65
Trade unions, 79; and women, 171. *See also* Industrial labor; Labor unions.
Traveler from Altruria, A (Howells), 181
Trevellick, Richard A., 81
Turgenev, Ivan, 181
Turner, Frederick Jackson, 115
Twain, Mark, 151, 182−84, 187, 189
Tweed, William M., 98

U

Unemployment, 47, 78, 99, 121, 123
Unionism and unions, bread and butter, 82, 83; industrial, 81−82, 126; Utopian, 81−83. *See also* Labor unions; Trade unions.

Union Pacific Railroad Company, 19, 20, 23, 24, 26, 82
Union Theological Seminary, 159
United Fruit Company, 38
United States Industrial Commission (1901), 66, 73, 77, 78
United States Steel Corporation, 34, 36
United States v. *Debs,* 126
United States v. *E. C. Knight Company,* 42, 43
United States v. *Trans-Missouri Freight Association,* 42
Urbanism, 1, 2−4, 43−49, 126, 137, 158−62, 185−86; and bossism, 98−99; and crime, 46−48; and education, 49; and election of 1896, 134, 135; and fire and health hazards, 44−46, 47; and housing, 46

V

Vanderbilt, Cornelius, 22, 35, 183
Vanderbilt, William, 25
Veblen, Thorstein, 14
Venezuela, 144
Violence, 10, 62−63, 80−81, 115, 116−17

W

Wabash, St. Louis and Pacific Railroad v. *Illinois,* 26
Waite, Morrison, 26
Ward, Lester Frank, 178
Washington, Booker T., 140
Watson, Thomas E., 119, 133
WCTU. *See* Women's Christian Temperance Union.
"Wealth" (Carnegie), 177
Weaver, James B., 118
Wells, David A., 18
Westinghouse, George, 33, 34
Weyler, Valeriano, 145
Whig party and Whigs, 95, 96, 110; and presidency, 107−11
White, J. Maunsel, 34
White, Leonard, 106
Willard, Frances, 171
Wilson-Gorman Tariff, 128
Wilson, William L., 128, 129, 143
Wilson, Woodrow, 102, 107, 110, 136
"Winter Coast" (Homer), 187
Wise, Isaac M., 167
Women, 168−73, 182; and feminist movement, 172; higher education of, 170; and suffrage, 172−73; and trade unions, 171
Women and Economics (Gilman), 172
Women's Christian Temperance Union, 170−71
Woodward, C. Vann, 119
World (NYC), 145
Wright, Frank Lloyd, 187

XYZ

Zola, Émile, 181